A GUIDE TO
Christian
SPIRITUAL
Formation

A GUIDE TO
Christian
SPIRITUAL
Formation

· · · · · · · · · ·

How Scripture, Spirit,
Community, and Mission
Shape Our Souls

EVAN B. HOWARD

Baker Academic

a division of Baker Publishing Group
Grand Rapids, Michigan

Published by Baker Academic
a division of Baker Publishing Group
PO Box 6287, Grand Rapids, MI 49516-6287
www.bakeracademic.com

Printed in the United States of America

Library of Congress Cataloging-in-Publication Data

Names: Howard, Evan B., 1955– author.
Title: A guide to Christian spiritual formation : how scripture, spirit, community, and mission shape our souls / Evan B. Howard.
Description: Grand Rapids : Baker Academic, 2018. | Includes bibliographical references and index.
Identifiers: LCCN 2017042697 | ISBN 9780801097805 (pbk. : alk. paper)
Subjects: LCSH: Spiritual formation.
Classification: LCC BV4511 .H69 2018 | DDC 248.4—dc23
LC record available at https://lccn.loc.gov/2017042697

18 19 20 21 22 23 24   7 6 5 4 3 2 1

Contents

PART FOUR The Ministry

Preface

Why write *A Guide to Christian Spiritual Formation*? Well, the story goes something like this. About fifteen years ago, I was inspired to write an introductory textbook on Christian spirituality. I wanted to cover the field, so to speak, from beginning to end. I wanted to lay out the basic theological and historical background against which people have understood Christian spirituality for the past few decades. But I also wanted to teach readers that knowing how people actually live out their relationship with God can be useful as we nurture their growing relationship with God. And I wanted the book to have lots of charts, cartoons, and helps of every kind.

And so I wrote what was published as *The Brazos Introduction to Christian Spirituality*.[1] Many of the people who endorsed the book described it as "comprehensive." And comprehensive it was. Unfortunately, however, at nearly five hundred pages of small print, it was not really the most accessible book. So ultimately I was invited to rewrite the book—to make it shorter and more practical.

But the more I thought about this rewriting project, the more I knew it had to be a completely new book. First, in order to be more practical, it could not be a book about Christian spirituality—that is, a simple empirical, historical, or anthropological summary of how people actually live out their relationship with God. I needed to write a book on Christian spiritual formation, one that would equip Christians to help others mature or grow in their relationship with God. It needed to be something of a guide.

Not only this, but things had changed over the past decade. When I wrote about Christian spirituality, I was summarizing a field of study that originated in contemplative Catholic culture. The worlds of John of the Cross, Julian

of Norwich, and François Fénelon were somewhat different from the world
of my evangelical upbringing, but I knew that each world had something
to offer the other. I published my thoughts on evangelicalism's contribution
to the field of Christian spirituality in my essay "Evangelical Spirituality,"
which was included in *Four Views on Christian Spirituality*.[2] But during all
this time I was seeing my own framework challenged—and rightly so. Was
community or congregation just an aside to the central aspect of personal
devotional life? And what was the place of mission in all this talk about
Christian spirituality? Is Christian spirituality just some privatized, religious
self-improvement scheme? Consequently, I knew that if I was going to rewrite
my book, I had to present Christian spiritual formation with community
and mission at its center.

And then someone at church asked me to teach a simple Sunday school class
on the Bible. (Thanks, Kathy Parish.) I taught a survey of the entire Bible in
ten weeks, and this class solidified my sense of what I thought of as the Big
Story (see chap. 2). From there my dream for this book took shape. Spirit,
Scripture, community, mission, and more—all had their place and could be
combined to develop a practical guide to the task of spiritual formation: the
work of nurturing communities and individuals in an ever-growing relationship with God spanning every area of life.

Such was the birth of *A Guide to Christian Spiritual Formation*.

As I wrote this book, I had in mind an audience similar to the one for
whom I'd written the *Brazos Introduction*, though I aimed to make this text
even more accessible. The readers I imagine are Christians who have begun to
experiment and grow spiritually (people who have started to practice spiritual
disciplines, read devotional classics, or the like) and now want to know more.
Some of these readers will want to understand how the world of spiritual
formation squares with primary Christian doctrines and with a relevant,
life-giving understanding of the human person, Christian community, and
the mission of God. Some may have had valuable experiences of the part but
are interested in seeing a vision of the whole. Thus, an introductory guide to
Christian spiritual formation is what I have written.

Rather than aiming for this book to be comprehensive, I have tried to
make it clear. Rather than providing a spectrum of viewpoints, I have summarized my own impression of the biblical sense of things. I only provide
representative bibliography when I cite works. And, as always, I quote people
that you (or I) may disagree with; just because I cite sources does not mean
I agree with them. I cite people in order to illustrate a point, and I hope the
quotations (fewer in this work than in the *Brazos Introduction*) will indeed
help make matters clearer.

I also want this book to be practical. While it is a textbook, covering the main topics that ought to be treated in an introduction to Christian spiritual formation, I also want it to be a helpful guide, serving to equip pastors and spiritual directors and friends to become ministers of Christian spiritual formation among individuals and communities around them. To this end, I have used a number of imaginary case studies to get us thinking about various aspects of both the elements and the work of Christian spiritual formation. Because I imagine the ministry of Christian spiritual formation as being exercised by different types of people, I have varied the chief figure of these case studies: they are businessmen, young converts, spiritual directors, pastors, and so on. I have also intentionally set them in different locations and cultures, because the church comprises people from different locations and cultures. So you may find that you relate to some of the case studies more easily than others. I encourage you to discuss these scenarios in conversation with other readers as you seek together their application.

My conviction is that once we see the features and task of formation in practice, we will be better able to understand how it works in our own lives.

One thing I have learned during my years of writing is that I enjoy both the process and the product better when others are involved. So, when I knew that I would be writing this book, I asked a team of friends to help me with ideas, resources, and reactions to the first draft of my chapters. Some went so far as to comment on the entire manuscript. This book owes a great deal to the partnership of Howard Baker, Paul Bramer, Mark Fields, Michael Flowers, Philip Harrold, Donna Hawk-Reinhard, Elaine Heath, Marti Isler, Klaus Issler, Michael Palandro, Greg Peters, Steve Porter, Kyle Strobel, Steve Summerell, Alex Tang, Jim Wilhoit, and Diane Zemke.

At times I needed to confirm that my stories and case studies were on-target. Ineda Adesanya, Charles Bello, David Nixon, Gina Kim, and John Shorack offered their knowledge and perspective in this regard. Others, including Marc Cortez, Joanne Jung, Linda Bond, Michael Glerup, Diane Chandler, and Vicki Walker, pointed me to valuable resources.

The material in this book emerged in part from dialogue with my students in a variety of institutions and training programs: the Center for Early African Christianity, CenterQuest, the Diploma in the Art of Spiritual Direction at Fuller Theological Seminary, Trinity School for Ministry, and Tyndale College and Seminary. I owe chapter 2 to Kathy Parish's request that I offer an adult education class on "the whole Bible" at All Saints Anglican church.

The team at Baker Academic has been wonderful to work with from start to finish. Bob Hosack stimulated me to dream of a book that was a fresh contribution to the understanding and practice of Christian spiritual formation. A number of marketing staff helped guide this project toward readers: Steve Ayers, Kara Day, Christina Jasko, Shelly MacNaughton, Louis McBride, Mason Slater, and Jeremy Wells. Jade Doyel and Alex Nieuwsma assisted with rights and permissions. Brandy Scritchfield, Paula Gibson, and Jane Klein have all contributed to the fine design of this volume. Finally, Tim West and Jennifer Seidel have simply worked magic: improving my communication, attending to the details I neglected, and making this text a much more coherent, readable book.

As always, my thinking and writing is informed by my interactions with two key individuals. Coky Hartman, my spiritual friend of nearly twenty years, has kept me faithful to the tasks of prayer and study all along. Without his wise oversight, I would be lost, greasing squeaky wheels. And Cheri, my wife, lives all of this with me from day to day. Christian spiritual formation has been the subject of endless meal conversations and family experiments. I am formed deeper and deeper into Christ and the gospel through her love, much richer at forty years of marriage than at five.

Finally, the idea for this book was born in conversations at an Association of Vineyard Churches mission leaders meeting a few years ago. I sat with Bob Logan and Mark Fields, and we brainstormed about the need to link formation, community, Spirit, and mission together. There was a good deal of energy around this idea, and at the end of our conversations I felt like I had a sense of where to go. Mark has supported this book at every stage of the process: reading drafts, clarifying stories, suggesting resources, sharing ideas, and more. Really, this is your book, Mark, and I hereby dedicate it to you and to the mission of God you catalyze.

Visit www.bakeracademic.com/professors
to access study aids
and instructor materials for this textbook.

PART ONE
THE BASICS

1

....

Christian Spiritual Formation

Overview

In this chapter, we will make our first acquaintance with the notion of Christian spiritual formation. After hearing a few stories about increasing interest in this practice, we will examine the general concept of spiritual formation: where it came from, what it has meant over the centuries, and what it is becoming. We will see that, particularly today, the ideas of *formation*, *community*, and *mission* are intertwined, making a tidy definition of Christian spiritual formation difficult to establish. We will then examine the key terms *formation*, *spiritual*, and *Christian* in order to bring us one step closer to a definition of Christian spiritual formation. We will compare a few common definitions, which vary in how they address key elements of Christian spiritual formation. Then we will venture to create our own definition, which will guide our basic understanding of the topic through the course of this book. Finally, with this definition in mind, we will preview the upcoming chapters.

Spiritual Formation Matters

Christians of all stripes agree: the practice of spiritual formation matters. Without it—we are beginning to learn—church, and even the Christian faith, simply does not work.

Take Willow Creek Community Church. The assumption was that increased participation in church activities—small groups, weekend worship services, and volunteering—increases a person's love of God and others. "That's what we believed at Willow Creek," recounts researcher Greg Hawkins. Willow Creek, one of the largest churches in the United States and a leader among megachurches, had invested much in this assumption. Dozens of people administrated the parking lots each Sunday morning. Superb music was performed at gatherings. No expense was spared in making Willow Creek activities both attractive and relevant. Hawkins and the research team were hoping to discover, through their 2003 self-study, which activities produced the most spiritual growth.

What they discovered through their interviews, however, was surprising. Merely increasing participation in church activities barely moved people to love God and others. This naturally led them to explore the further question, How do people grow spiritually? Their findings regarding the needs for ongoing spiritual growth (published in *Move: What 1,000 Churches Reveal about Spiritual Growth*) led the Willow Creek Association of churches to reshape their entire approach to ministry—no small task for a religious association involving tens of thousands of people.[1]

Spiritual formation matters.

A flame of interest in spiritual formation is spreading globally through the Vineyard, an association of charismatic evangelical churches that grew in size and popularity in the 1980s with increased interest in spiritual gifts such as healing.[2] As many pastors and leaders in this movement will testify, it is one thing to experience showers of God's blessing. It is another to dig deep wells of spirituality that can quench our thirst in downpour or in drought. In the 1990s, some key leaders discovered fresh means of walking in the Spirit. By 2002, Judy Davids, a pastor and counselor, had pioneered Pastors' Sabbath Retreats, a vehicle that provided rest and taught balanced living to many Vineyard leaders. Pastor David Nixon had founded Sustainable Faith, an organization that promotes spiritual direction training throughout the Vineyard. In 2008, pastor Steve Summerell presented some of the insights from his doctoral thesis, "Overcoming Obstacles to Spiritual Formation in the Lives of Vineyard Pastors," to a regional conference of Vineyard leaders.[3] Mark Fields, director of the Vineyard's Missions Task Force, attended that presentation and invited Summerell to lunch. Fields shared his own story of burnout and ultimately invited Summerell to join him on a trip to Nepal and present some of his material to leaders there. Thus was born the Vineyard's global effort known as Caring for Leaders. Leaders from Russia, Indonesia, Chile, Brazil, and the Philippines, among other countries, all eagerly welcomed training in spiritual formation and were refreshed.

By then, however, Todd Hunter, once president of Vineyard USA, had become an Anglican. In his memoir, *The Accidental Anglican*, Hunter recounts how in 1979, at age twenty-three, he moved to West Virginia to start a Calvary Chapel church that later became a Vineyard congregation.[4] By 1995, Hunter had helped plant several Vineyard churches and was acting as national coordinator for the organization. By 2005, he had moved on from that position to foster creative church planting through a group called Allelon and through the Alpha Course. It was in this season of reimagining that Hunter first thought, "Someday I would be saying daily prayers with a group of Christians who were serious about the twin tracks of following Jesus: (1) spiritual formation into Christlikeness (2) for the sake of others."[5] Hunter was ultimately invited into the Anglican community. Under the influence of theologians such as J. I. Packer and John Stott, he found that his interests in evangelical faith and spiritual formation had a long history in the Anglican tradition and that Anglicanism was "a huge treasure chest of tools for contemporary evangelism and spiritual formation."[6] He was formally invited to help plant an Anglican congregation in California, ultimately confessing to a respected elder, "I think the Holy Spirit may be calling me to do this."[7] Ultimately, in rather quick succession, Hunter was ordained as a priest and later as a bishop. In a companion book to his memoir, *Giving Church Another Chance*, Hunter uses the framework of a typical Anglican worship service as a way of presenting "new meaning in [traditional] spiritual practices."[8] Hunter is one among a growing community of Christians exploring and reappropriating liturgical traditions.[9]

Again, my point is this: spiritual formation matters. I hear Christians discussing it in many different circles. As we will see below, evangelical churches and institutions of higher education are making spiritual formation a subject of study, even hiring pastors of formation and redesigning training programs. Spiritual formation is on our screen, so to speak, these days.

I will go further. I believe that Western culture in general is beginning to acknowledge the need for and importance of spiritual formation. Indeed, perhaps the recent evangelical interest in spiritual formation indicates not a fad but rather a crisis. Recent surveys of young "outsiders" (people who are not a part of the Christian community) and young "leavers" (people who no longer consider themselves part of the Christian community) point to the lack of formation among Christians as a key reason for their distancing themselves from the faith. Barna Research Group president David Kinnaman urges Christians that "to embrace the perception that we are focused only on converts, we have to embrace a more holistic idea of what it means to be a Christ follower. This requires us to focus our attention on spiritual transformation—or spiritual formation, as some describe it. In the last two years, we have completely re-engineered the Barna organization around this concept—that the church must become a catalyst and environment for genuine and sustainable transformation."[10]

Similarly, in response to findings regarding the wave of young adults leaving Christianity, Kinnaman concludes: "The dropout problem is, at its core, a faith-development problem; to use religious language, it's *a disciple-making problem*. . . . Like a Geiger counter under a mushroom cloud, the next generation is reacting to the radioactive intensity of social, technological, and religious changes. And for the most part, we are sending them into the world unprepared to withstand the fallout."[11]

Christian spiritual formation matters. It matters to those who are leaving the church. It is beginning to matter to those of us within the church. And it matters that it matters. If it didn't matter, we might really be in trouble.

What Is Spiritual Formation?

But just what is this spiritual formation that matters so much? Actually, this is not an easy question to answer. Each of these words—*spiritual* and *formation*—has been used in different ways at different times; as a result, the phrase *spiritual formation* means slightly different things to different people.

Christians' use of *formation* has origins in the writings of the New Testament. In Galatians 4:19, for example, Paul uses the imagery of childbirth to expresses his intense desire for the Galatian church's growth, stating that he is suffering "the pains of childbirth" until "Christ is formed in you." In Ephesians, Paul uses the imagery of a building to communicate the church's formation in Christ. He speaks of Christ as the cornerstone of this ongoing construction (and formation) project. "In him," Paul declares, "the whole building is joined together and rises to become a holy temple in the Lord. And in him you too are being built together to become a dwelling in which God lives by his Spirit" (Eph. 2:21–22). The author of the Epistle to the Hebrews describes Christian formation as a development of faith ("Let us draw near . . . with the full assurance that faith brings," 10:22), hope ("Let us hold . . . to the hope we profess," 10:23), and love ("Let us . . . spur one another on toward love and good deeds," 10:24). For the author of Hebrews, our ongoing formation—which entails securing our roots and strengthening our growing connection to Christ—is brought about when we exercise the fundamental virtues of our character: faith, hope, and love. And as we see in these passages, our formation is something that the Spirit works in us through the very life of the church (e.g., "spur one another"). Similarly, 1 Peter uses the metaphors of newborn development ("grow up in your salvation" through "spiritual milk," 2:2) and construction ("being built into a spiritual house," 2:5) to communicate this desire for formation into Christ.

The theme of formation, with all its rich imagery, was picked up and developed throughout the history of the Christian church. Thus Irenaeus in the second century speaks of the Creator forming us for the sake of growth.[12] We're formed for the sake of formation. Augustine speaks of our growth as a purification of our minds, so that we can increasingly appreciate our relationship with God. In his treatise *On Christian Doctrine*, he urges his readers to "consider this process of cleansing as a trek, or a voyage, to our homeland."[13]

The word *formation* acquired a particular meaning in reference to nurturing believers who made special commitments to God: the training of nuns, monks, and priests.[14] For example, one nun might be placed in charge of the formation of young trainees (often called *novices*) at a convent. The novice mistress's job was to guide novices into their new life as nuns. It involved education and character training. But most importantly, her work was to facilitate the development of young novices' living relationship to God. Without this living relationship, none of the other training made any sense. Here *spiritual formation* refers to consciously fostering a living relationship with God in the context of a religious community.

A similar process was developed for training parish priests. For example, regarding pastoral trainees in seminary, the "Decree on Priestly Formation" (*Optatam Totius*) from the Second Vatican Council (1965) urges,

> Spiritual formation should be closely linked with doctrinal and pastoral training. Especially with the help of the spiritual director, such formation should help seminarians learn to live in familiar and constant companionship with the Father, through Jesus Christ His Son, in the Holy Spirit. . . . They should be taught to look for Christ in many places: in faithful meditation on God's word, in active communion with the most holy mysteries of the Church, . . . especially the poor, the young, the sick, the sinful, and the unbelieving.[15]

Interest in spiritual formation spread from Roman Catholic institutions to Protestant circles in the 1960s and 1970s. In 1964, Asbury Seminary received a grant to found the first Department of Spiritual Formation.[16] Other schools followed suit. Wheaton College voted to form the Department of Formation and Ministry in 2003. Talbot School of Theology's Institute for Spiritual Formation has been offering advanced programs in spiritual formation for years. Dallas Theological Seminary now offers a doctorate of ministry degree with an emphasis in spiritual formation. Moody Bible Institute also advertises a certificate in spiritual formation. A wide range of Protestant groups began to experiment with academic programs and practical training centers in spiritual formation. And during this season, the meaning of spiritual formation itself was blurred. Often the term *formation* was not comprehended within an established faith culture like it had been in monastic or priestly circles; rather, it communicated a nexus of practices, relationships, events, and such initiated by a spiritual seeker. Similarly, the term *spiritual* at times indicated not, as described above, "companionship with the Father, through Jesus Christ His Son, in the Holy Spirit," but rather the development of the depths of the human soul—*our spirit*.

A landmark publication amid developing interest in spiritual formation was Richard Foster's *Celebration of Discipline*, released in 1978.[17] Within a decade, Foster, along with fellow author Dallas Willard and others, had founded Renovaré, an organization dedicated to the promotion of spiritual formation. By 1990, one could identify spiritual formation movements influencing a wide range of Christian circles. But by then spiritual formation meant whatever each religious circle wanted it to mean.

The Christian Scriptures use a rich array of metaphors to describe our developing relationship to God and the gospel—for example, growing plants (Matt. 13:31–32; 1 Cor. 3:6–8), athletic training (Acts 20:24; 1 Cor. 9:24; 1 Tim. 4:7; Heb. 12:1–2), stewardship (Matt. 25:21; Luke 19:11–27), and construction (Eph. 2:22; 1 Pet. 2:5). Paul speaks of increase, progress, growing, strengthening, and more. We could drop the phrase *spiritual formation* and start talking about the "Christian increase" movement, but I'm not sure it would catch on. *Spiritual formation* is already the established term, and it is best to live with it. So, then, how shall we define it?

What Is Spiritual Formation Becoming?

Defining the term is complicated, because recently, concepts of spiritual formation have been merging with various other interests and terms. As a result, defining spiritual formation is like shooting at a moving target.[18]

Once upon a time, there was "Christian education." The world of "Christian ed" involved learning about *learning*: social scientific studies, educational psychologist Benjamin Bloom's taxonomy, curriculum design, and the like, all packaged within a model of faith development and often focused on children. Similarly, Christian universities and seminaries saw themselves as providing a quality education for their students by assembling the smartest teachers with the widest, deepest intellectual backgrounds who would share their insights in a context of both reasoned evaluation and practical application.

But times have changed. We are asking different questions about education. Is education about *in-formation* or *formation*? What is the role of *practice* in our assimilation of the Christian faith? How do we teach the heart as well as the mind? Many Christian educators are suggesting that spiritual formation may help us navigate these kinds of questions. Spiritual formation affirms direct experience, fosters character development, and is nurtured within a context of personal and congregational practices. So now we find that many schools are offering degrees in Christian *formation* instead of Christian *education*. Congregations are hiring pastors of formation, whose responsibilities include not merely directing the Sunday school program but also ministering within many other aspects of congregational life. The Association of Theological Schools and the Association for Biblical Higher Education now mandate development in "personal and spiritual formation" as part of a legitimate curriculum.[19]

Once upon a time, there were "missions." The "missions people" and the "spirituality people" (typically) kept their distance from one another. Spirituality people learned about devotion, meditation, and prayer. Missions people learned about cross-cultural communication, ministry multiplication, and outreach strategy.

But times are changing. People are asking questions about missions. And people are asking questions about spirituality. Mission organizations, seeing many staff suffer from burnout, are beginning to think about spiritual direction, team rhythms, and other features of member care that look a lot like spiritual formation. Missiologists are exploring the lives of ancient monks and medieval friars, turning to stories that would normally be the fare of students of Christian spirituality. Similarly, students of Christian spirituality are asking, Is holiness simply a matter of private devotion? Perhaps union with God is not only a harmony with God's Spirit in prayer but also a conformity with God's vision for the restoration of this earth.[20] In this case, spiritual formation must be reinterpreted in light of such an aim. Consequently, the worlds of missions and formation begin to blend.[21]

Once upon a time, there was "church": an amalgamation of worship services, preaching, pastoral care, and so on. Of course there were always a few spiritual types in our churches, subjects of both respect and concern. There were those who started small groups in an effort to foster spiritual growth among those who desired "more." But for the most part, *church* was just what Christians did, and *spiritual formation* described the extracurricular practices and experiences of a select group of devoted individuals.

But times are changing. People are asking questions about church and about formation: What really goes on in church? Aren't congregations communities of mutual formation? If so, then how are we living this out? What does worship do to us? Are we formed through preaching, through the structure of the liturgy? How so? Every aspect of church life is currently being reexamined with an eye toward formation. Similarly, the notion of spiritual formation itself is being reexamined in light of a rich theology and the practice of church.[22]

Spiritual formation can no longer be neatly separated from community, liturgy, mission, or education. Our life with God is whole cloth, and the tidy containers the church has kept for fellowship, worship, mission, teaching, and spiritual life will simply have to be laid aside as we learn anew what it means to be the church, what it means to learn, what it means to be sent, and what it means to be devoted to Jesus.

But then the question now plagues us even more: How are we to define spiritual formation?

Christian Spiritual Formation

While it is clear that we are in no place to formulate a precise definition of Christian spiritual formation, I think we can make some progress by exploring each of the key terms: *Christian*, *spiritual*, and *formation*. We will explore them in reverse order.

Formation

What does it mean to be formed? I like the image of a potter working clay (Isa. 64:8; Jer. 18:1–6). A potter forms a lump of clay into a bowl, gently pushing it this way or pulling it that way as it spins on a wheel. The bowl is set aside to dry and then placed in a kiln and exposed to high heat. After the bowl cools from the firing, the potter adds a glaze to the bowl, which will further influence the character of the bowl. The bowl is placed into the kiln and fired a second time. Then the bowl is finally ready.

Or is it? Using the bowl continues to change it day after day. In time—perhaps in a long time—the bowl will break or decay. So when is it really the *bowl*? In one sense, the bowl was formed when the pushing and pulling was done. But in another sense, the bowl was being formed when the clay was maturing deep underground and continues to be formed even when it becomes old and cracked.

The fact of the matter is that everything is being formed all the time. Reality itself is in a continuous process of formation: coming to be, changing, ceasing to be.[23] A sunflower—seed, sprout, plant, young flower, new seeds drying and then falling, plant decaying—is being formed through each moment of the process. The sunflower is what it is in the very midst of that formation.

And so are we. We are what we are even in the midst of a constant process of formation: birth, growth, death, and beyond. Each reality has a unique *process* of formation, a process we will explore in the chapters ahead.

Formation involves the interaction of a complex of forces. It is not just a matter of a potter and some clay. Think of the bowl. The clay must be kneaded properly: no air pockets or else it will explode in the kiln. The moisture level of the clay must be just right—firm enough to hold a shape, yet not so stiff that it cannot be easily shaped. The heat of the kiln, the mixture of the glaze, the care of the potter as she places the bowl into the kiln—all play a part in its formation. Is the potter using a kick wheel or an electric wheel? Perhaps there is no wheel at all, and this is a pinch pot. Air, water, heat, potter, clay, technique, glaze, and more all influence the bowl as it's formed. And we humans are just the same. Culture, relationships, beliefs, and practices are some of the many factors that have a role in spiritual formation. I will, in this book, talk about the *contexts* and the *means* of formation. It is important to respect the contexts, because to neglect them is not to treat things as they really are; it is important to respect the means, because results differ when different means are employed.

Formation, furthermore, is always productive. It is always producing something (sunflowers, persons). Formation always has an aim by nature of the forces' interaction. As a result, in this book—a book on spiritual formation—it will be important for us to explore the *aims* of spiritual formation, to ask into what we are being formed.

Finally, particularly in human experience, formation is fostered through the influence of people. Teachers form young students. Drill sergeants form young recruits. The novice mistress forms the novices. So in this book, I will speak of the *agents* of formation. Other people, we ourselves, and especially God the Spirit act to shape us closer to Christ.

In sum, our understanding of the nature of formation itself leads us to pay attention to a few things. We notice the process of formation as it emerges in a person or group. We recognize the contexts within which formation is being encountered and the means used to facilitate it. We attend to the aims toward which it is heading. And, finally, we regard the agents of formation, including other people, ourselves, and the Spirit of God.

Spiritual

And this brings us to our second term, *spiritual*. The terms *spirit* and *spiritual* are notoriously difficult to define. What, then, is Christian *spiritual* formation?

In many cases, *spirit* refers to the core of our own human personality. In this sense, it is somewhat synonymous with *heart*. David, in Psalm 51:17, declares, "My sacrifice, O God, is a broken spirit; / a broken and contrite heart / you, God, will not despise." Paul, in 1 Corinthians 2:11, asks, "For who knows a person's thoughts except their own spirit within them?" To speak of our spirit is to speak of who we are in the depths of our being— who we really are. Thus a transformation of spirit is not merely a change of a few habits but a renovation of our character. We also use the word *soul* to indicate something similar (e.g., "That music touched me to my very soul"). To understand spiritual formation given this understanding of spirit, then, is to see it as a process of deep personal transformation. Renovaré ministry team member Richella Parham, in *A Spiritual Formation Primer*, writes that "in short, Christian spiritual formation is the process in which believers co-operate with God and one another so that their souls are nourished and their characters are transformed into Christlikeness."[24]

But *spirit* does not only identify the depths of the human; it also refers to the Third Person of the Trinity, the Holy Spirit. First Corinthians 2:11, cited above, continues, "In the same way no one knows the thoughts of God except the Spirit of God." And verse 12 declares, "What we have received is not the spirit of the world, but the Spirit who is from God." In these two verses, Paul moves us from considering the core of our person to considering the core of God's person; from there, he leads us to reflect on our own participation in relationship with God's own core through "the Spirit who is from God." When we read further we learn about the "unspiritual" person and the "spiritual" person (vv. 14–15). The spiritual person is clearly the one who evaluates their life in light of the teaching that comes through the Spirit of God (see, e.g., Gal. 6:1 [following 5:22–23]; Col. 1:9; 3:16). When we understand spiritual formation in relation to the person of the Holy Spirit, we begin to address theologian Gordon Fee's plea "that we more consciously allow the Spirit to have a much more major and focused role in our thinking about 'spirituality.'"[25]

Spirit also refers to the immaterial, the supernatural, that which has to do with the divine. We contrast feeding the body and feeding the spirit. Paul urges the Corinthians to purify "body and spirit" (2 Cor. 7:1), encompassing the whole of human experience—both outer and inner aspects. Likewise, Paul declares in Romans 8:10 that although our body is dead due to sin, our spirit is alive due to righteousness.[26] With this understanding of spirit, we come to see spiritual formation as the aspect of our growth and maturity that deals more specifically with our relationship with God. Such was the perspective of those who trained priests, nuns, or monks. Young trainees were required to have academic formation, practical formation, and character formation. But they were also subject to spiritual formation—namely, the intentional practices by which a trainee was likely to develop a meaningful relationship with God.

Yet how can we mature in relationship with God (and the Spirit) without it affecting not only our inner life but, indeed, every aspect of our human existence? On the one hand, spiritual formation works toward the transformation of a single, identifiable aspect of human life: the spiritual. But on the other hand, God cannot establish a transforming relationship with us without that influencing other parts of our life. Given that is the case, some are shy to use the term *spiritual* and simply use the term *Christian formation* to communicate the broad effects of growth in Christ.

So what are we to make of all these ways of approaching *spirit/Spirit* and spiritual formation?

As we will see in the course of this book, each of the perspectives through which we understand spirit is important.[27] I do not think we can adequately understand *spirit/Spirit* and *spiritual* unless all perspectives are welcomed into a singular and synthetic understanding of spiritual formation. Spiritual formation must address both the transformation of the human character and the depths or spiritual core of the human life, but it must also address our ongoing relationship with God through the person of the Holy Spirit. Spiritual formation, then, is about relationship with God, and—because of that very fact—it is about the transformation of every aspect of our lives, both as individuals and as communities.

Read the many passages that speak of *spirit* and *Spirit*. Read them, again and again, in the Old and New Testaments, in different translations. This alone may be the best introduction to Christian spiritual formation you will ever have. We will develop these themes surrounding *spirit/Spirit* and *spiritual* in the pages that follow.

Christian

Having explored the terms *formation* and *spiritual*, we now turn to a few reflections on *Christian*. It may seem scarcely necessary to mention what we mean by *Christian* spiritual formation: it is our formation within the Christian faith, in the context of relationship with God through Christ in the Holy Spirit. That's true, but there is still more to be said. For when we see what Christian spiritual formation actually is, we discover its magnificent potential.

First, Christian spiritual formation is being formed into the image of the Christian God. Christians are Christ-people. Christ is our context, our aim, our means, and (through the Spirit) our agent. We Christians set our minds on Christ. That is what I mean by Christ being our context. Our thoughts and feelings are continually shaped by the life, death, resurrection, and ascension of Jesus Christ. Christ is also our aim. The purpose of Christian spiritual formation is relationship and likeness to the person of Christ, the conformity of our life as communities and individuals to the wonderful life and message of Christ. The Christian God is a trinitarian God: Father, Son, and Holy Spirit. Our communities move toward the life of divine communion. The glorious excellency of our God is at the start and end of all our formation. Furthermore, we employ Christian means in our endeavor to be formed as Christians. People choose various means to be spiritually formed—for example, meditation, bodywork, or dream interpretation. Yet while these various means of formation might be helpful, spiritual formation that is specifically Christian will major on those means that are characteristic and distinctive of our faith: Scripture, prayer, church fellowship, sacraments, and the like. And, as was already mentioned above, Christ, through the Holy Spirit, is the primary agent of formation. Spiritual formation, in one important sense, simply is experiential formation in the Holy Spirit. Christian spiritual formation is formation into the Christian God.

Christian spiritual formation is also a formation within and into the Christian Story. I capitalize the word *Story* here because it is the source of all stories. Christians are the people of a Big Story. We call it the good news, the gospel, and it is good news. The Christian Story is a tale—and a history and an eschatology—of hope, of brokenness, and of amazing restoration. As you will see in chapter 2, I call it the "all things new" story. And, in fact, that is just what Christian spiritual formation is about: making "all things new." When we undertake to realign our relationship with Jesus Christ, everything is up for grabs. Or, looking at it another way, the re-formation of any area of life just might bring us face-to-face with a spiritual transformation.

Of course, this Christian Story is housed in Scripture; consequently, Christian spiritual formation is a biblical formation. Christians may disagree on matters of interpretation and have our share of unanswered questions, but we all esteem the Bible as the sacred text of our faith. And this commitment to Scripture influences the way we are formed. We use Scripture as a means of formation when we listen to sermons or when we slowly and prayerfully read the Bible. Scripture is an aim of formation when we seek to conform our practices to a teaching we have found in the Bible (e.g., when we discover God's heart for the poor in Scripture). "Respect for and submission to the Scriptures," asserts author Jonathan Morrow, "is a vital presupposition for spiritual formation."[28] Christian spiritual formation is formation into the Christian Story, a story found in Scripture.

Finally, *Christian* spiritual formation is formation into the Christian community. Christianity was not established when Jesus preached, or died, or even resurrected. Jesus's followers were floundering even after the resurrected Christ appeared to them. What galvanized believers into a common life and faith was the outpouring of the Spirit at Pentecost and the birth of the Christian church. Christianity is not merely a belief system, a code of ethics, or an experience of love. Christianity is membership in a people. It is partnership with traditions and questions and saints and sinners that are centuries old and global in breadth. Even committed Christian hermits live their life of prayerful hermitage as a ministry of the body of Christ. Thus the medieval Camaldolese recluse Peter Damian writes, "When I in my solitude utter the common words of the Church I show that I am one with her and that by the indwelling of the Holy Spirit I truly dwell in her."[29] Damian found encouragement in this thought, though others have been less encouraged about their association with the Christian church. Nevertheless, like it or not, we cannot escape our heritage. We believers are members of the Christian church, and we are formed *by* and *into* that church.

We are also formed in local gatherings. Indeed, the Greek word *ekklēsia* (church) is primarily an identification of a gathering. Christians are formed in the context of many different kinds of community. This diversity is especially significant when we consider global Christianity. Some gather in large buildings, whereas others gather in a living room or under a shade tree. Some pay careful attention to the precision of rituals. Other gatherings are very fluid, improvising their rituals as their common encounter develops. This diversity has been present from the earliest years of the earliest churches. And yet we are all baptized into one body. And yet we all drink of the same blood of Christ. As we will see in the chapters ahead, I will present Christian spiritual formation as characterized by both ritual diversity and sacramental unity. Christian spiritual formation is formation into Christian community.

Christian, spiritual, formation—this is what it is all about. We place our individual and corporate selves within the sphere of influence of the sovereign Christian God, the Christian Spirit, the Christian Story, the Christian community, and the Christian faith. In so doing, we are changed. We are changed in spirit, in the core of our personality. Our relationship with God and many other areas of our life are rearranged and formed into something new. Christian formation is the making of a new people, a new life, a new embodiment of the life of Christ in this world.

Toward a Definition of Christian Spiritual Formation

We are moving closer to a working definition of Christian spiritual formation and, with that, to a sense of what this book is all about. Here are definitions of Christian spiritual formation as crafted by several theologians and writers (including myself) over the last twenty-five years or so. Below, we will discuss the ways in which they agree and those in which they diverge.

- M. Robert Mulholland Jr.: "Spiritual formation is a process of being conformed to the image of Christ for the sake of others."[30]
- Dallas Willard: "*Spiritual formation for the Christian basically refers to the Spirit-driven* process *of forming the inner world of the human self in such a way that it becomes like the inner being of Christ himself.*"[31]
- Paul Pettit: "Spiritual formation, then, *is the ongoing process of the triune God transforming the believer's life and character toward the life and character of Jesus Christ—accomplished by the ministry of the Spirit in the context of biblical community.*"[32]
- Evan B. Howard: "The intentional and semi-intentional processes by which believers (individuals and communities) become more fully conformed and united to Christ, especially with regard to maturity of life and calling."[33]
- Jeffrey P. Greenman: "Spiritual formation is our continuing response to the reality of God's grace shaping us into the likeness of Jesus Christ, through the work of the Holy Spirit, in the community of faith, for the sake of the world."[34]
- James Bryan Smith: "Christian spiritual formation is the process of being transformed into the image of Christ, through a relationship of intimacy with God, by the power of the Spirit, in order to live a good and beautiful life of faith, hope, love, joy, and peace—a life that will be a blessing to oneself and to others and will glorify God now and for all eternity."[35]

Process of Change

A few comments on these definitions will bring us even closer to the definition we will be using in this text. First, one thing the definitions above have in common is a sense that the task of spiritual formation involves a *process of change. Process, formation, transformation*—these words characterize our sample definitions. *Growth in relationship with Christ, maturity of our spiritual life*—this is the language of change. Thus I will choose in this text to define *formation* by speaking of maturing, a process of change.[36]

Aim

Second, there is general agreement in these definitions that the aim of Christian spiritual formation is some kind of union with Christ. *Transformation toward*, *becomes like*, *into the likeness*, and such are the phrases used to communicate this idea. I want to affirm and yet expand this idea. To start, what is not explicitly mentioned in these definitions—but ought to be—is that this likeness implies the development of *relationship* with Christ. Spiritual formation is not simply a matter of character development but also, or perhaps even more deeply, the maturing of our relationship with God in Christ through the Spirit. The union of relationship, as we will see in chapter 7, may involve but is not limited to our awareness or connection to the presence of God. Our likeness to or union with Christ is a relational participation of all we are with the fullness of the revealed God. Furthermore, as we will see in chapter 2, I understand the Christian faith as aiming not only at conforming our life to the *character* of Christ but also at conforming our life to the *gospel and purpose* of Christ.

At the same time, I want to suggest that Christian spiritual formation might not always have as its main intention change for the sake of others. Worship is for the glory of God. Maturing in the practice of praying in tongues may at times have our own edification in mind (see 1 Cor. 14). There are seasons in life when it is wisest simply to focus on our own personal development of obedience and the virtues, leaving the issues of our influence on others to the mysterious work of the Spirit. I want to acknowledge with Smith ("a life that will be a blessing *to oneself* and *to others* and will *glorify God*," italics added) the breadth of the consequences of Christian spiritual formation.

Agents

Third, I want to affirm the comment made by many that the Holy Spirit is the primary agent of Christian spiritual formation. It is time to put the Spirit back in spirituality, and I will do just this in the chapters to follow. Yet, as I have mentioned above, I see the involvement of a number of human agents as being essential to the formation process: spiritual directors, small groups, even we ourselves.[37] I will, therefore, speak of Christian spiritual formation as being both Spirit- and human-led.

Object

Fourth, I want to expand our view of the agency involved in spiritual formation as well as our view of the object of Christian spiritual formation. In the definition I gave in my earlier book, I indicated this by the phrase *individuals and communities*. I believe that community is part of the context of formation, as mentioned by Pettit and Greenman; in addition, I believe that communities themselves are formed through a Spirit- and human-led process into an increasing depth of relationship with God and ever-greater likeness to the life and gospel of the Christian God. Therefore, I address the formation of groups (families, churches, networks, and so on) as well as the formation of individuals, using the term *communities* to refer to these groups more generally.

But what is really the particular object of Christian spiritual formation? Is it our alignment with the Holy Spirit? Is it our own spirit, the interior life of prayer? Is it our relationship with God? Perhaps it is best to drop the term *spiritual* altogether and simply speak of Christian formation as a way of affirming that formation in the gospel of Christ necessarily involves all of who we are. My choice here is simply to say an unqualified yes to all of the above, with the exception that I will not drop the term *spiritual*. In keeping with the centuries-old tradition of formation, I see a special need to take intentional steps toward nurturing our relationship with God—a relationship that addresses both the depths of the human spirit and attunement with the Spirit of Christ. Yet that very effort to nurture our relationship with God is bound to affect many areas of our lives. Spiritual formation will shape educational formation, liturgical formation, our approach to health, and so on. That being the case, this text will include Spirit, spirit, and the breadth of human experience—both corporate and individual—as we explore how to develop our particularly spiritual life.

Contexts and Means

Apart from mentioning community, none of the definitions included above addressed the *contexts* of Christian spiritual formation. And none included a statement about the *means* of formation. I think that this is because the contexts and means of formation vary so greatly from situation to situation that it is counterproductive to describe either in a definition of what is central and common to the phrase.

A Working Definition

I am now in a place where I can offer a definition of Christian spiritual formation that will serve as a guide for this text. I see Christian spiritual formation as *a Spirit- and human-led process by which individuals and communities mature in relationship with the Christian God (Father, Son, and Holy Spirit) and are changed into ever-greater likeness to the life and gospel of this God.* This way of looking at Christian spiritual formation shapes the way this text approaches Christian spiritual formation.

Figure 1.1
Elements of Christian Spiritual Formation

Object: Who/what is being formed (person, community . . .)

Aim: The goal or end toward which formation is directed

Context (and Charism): The environment within which (and the unique characteristics with which) an object is formed

Agents: Those who possess a degree of responsible influence for one's formation

Process: The way that formation develops and is realized in time

Task: The work of formation itself

Means: The various instruments through which the agents of formation (Spirit, self, others, etc.) accomplish the aim

Where Do We Go from Here?

In coming chapters, we will explore all of the dimensions of spiritual formation mentioned above and more. Chapters 2 and 3 provide the biblical and
theological backbone to our introduction to Christian spiritual formation.
Chapter 2 offers a survey of the Big Story of the Christian faith and the implications that this story brings to our understanding of Christian spiritual
formation. Chapter 3 then examines the fullness of formation and how that
fullness has consequences for the aims of Christian spiritual formation.

Chapter 4 introduces us to the contexts and agents of Christian spiritual
formation. Here we learn about families and friends, countries and cultures.
More particularly, we see how we ourselves, the Holy Spirit, and spiritual directors help us grow. Chapter 5 treats the cooperative tasks of transformation.
We examine not only how Savior and Spirit work in the lives of individuals
and communities but also how we experience and nurture that work. We also
consider stages of growth and how transformation influences one area and
then another. Chapter 6 treats the means of formation. We will learn how to
recognize God's Spirit, and I will address spiritual disciplines, community,
sacraments, and the trials of life.

Chapters 7 through 10 present Christian spiritual formation in the practice
of life: a life of prayer, a life together, a life of personal integrity, and a life of
mission. This section provides something of a guide to the actual wisdom of
spiritual formation as it is lived out in various areas of the life of the church.

The last two chapters of the book guide our discussion of formation
through two critical topics. Chapter 11 treats the issue of discernment, one
of the most commonly discussed issues in Christian spiritual formation and
a topic toward which previous chapters have been pointing. Finally, chapter
12 will sum up the entire book by looking at the possibilities of exercising
the ministry of Christian spiritual formation.

Going Deeper

1. Think back to a time in your life that you would say was spiritually
   formative. What happened? What was that like? Can you identify
   some of the elements of Christian spiritual formation in that event
   or season?

2. In this chapter, we glimpsed only a couple of biblical images for formation: construction and child development. Yet the Bible uses a wide
   range of vocabulary to communicate the theme of spiritual growth.

What are some of these other images, and what might they contribute to a full-orbed theology of Christian spiritual formation?

3. This is a book on *Christian* spiritual formation. As such, our examination of the aims, means, and so on of formation focuses on those that are distinctively Christian. But we live in a religiously plural world. Compare the Christian approach to spiritual formation to the approaches advocated by other religions or to the kinds of formation promoted by agnostics and atheists. What are the similarities and differences? What does a comparative perspective to spiritual formation tell us about the development of our own lives as Christian individuals and communities?

4. Why all the fuss with defining Christian spiritual formation? Does it really make a difference, for example, if we define *spiritual* with relationship to the human spirit or the Holy Spirit? What about some of the other issues mentioned in the discussion of the terms used? Explore various definitions of Christian spiritual formation, and imagine the significance of living out those definitions.

5. This chapter has introduced the subtle distinctions between spirit, spiritual, and Holy Spirit. One way of venturing more deeply into the topic of Christian spiritual formation is to learn to pay attention to the Holy Spirit, to your spirit, and to the spiritual part of your life. Here's one simple exercise to help train your attention to this: Ask yourself each evening, Where did I notice Spirit or spirit today? You need not be overly meticulous in your meditation. Just open yourself for a moment and see what comes to mind. Try this little exercise for a few weeks. Then try doing it at a different time of day. After a month or so, ask yourself what you have learned about spiritual formation.

2

The Story of Christian
Spiritual Formation

Overview

The nature of Christian spiritual formation is grounded in the Christian story. And how we tell that story shapes the way we look at (and practice) spiritual formation. Accordingly, in this chapter we will take a closer look at the Christian message. We will examine the purposes of God expressed in the very beginnings of Judeo-Christian history. Then we will delve into the end of the story and see how the beginning is reflected in the end. I will show that similar purposes are communicated at both the origin and the conclusion and that these purposes encompass a grand vision. Looking between the beginning and the end, we will discover the development of God's grand vision: one aspect highlighted here and another there. We will find that through a pattern of deliverance, covenant renewal, invitation, and provision for the covenant life, the Christian God opens a pathway for all things to be made new. This "all things new" gospel, furthermore, is a story of formation—a story that incorporates the elements of Christian spiritual formation into a beautiful and practical way of life, enabling us to mature in ever-increasing likeness to Jesus's life and the gospel message.

We often find ourselves within stories. A character reminds us of our own personality, and we take special notice of how that character navigates the challenges presented in the story. Or perhaps a cast of diverse characters offers a range of approaches to life's questions, and we find they are exploring our own questions in unexpected ways. Sometimes a plot resembles the trajectory of our own life, and we are set on edge, anticipating how this plot—and our own lives—might work out in the end. In fact, we often express or even discover the meaning of life through the language of stories.

In the previous chapter, we learned that Christian spiritual formation matters. We also learned something about what Christian spiritual formation *is*—namely, a Spirit- and human-led process by which individuals and communities mature in relationship with the Christian God and are changed into ever-greater likeness to the life and gospel of this God. In *Christian* spiritual formation, the Christian God (Father, Son, and Holy Spirit) and the Christian faith are critical components of both the context within which we are formed and the aim toward which we are formed. This book is about our formation as *Christians*. We cannot understand this formation apart from our knowledge of the Trinity, redemption, church, eschatology, and more. Christian doctrine and, even more so, the Christian life are vital to the soil from which the plant of our relationship with God grows. They indicate not only the ground of our formation but also the end. How can we speak of what we, as Christians, should be formed into without speaking of the Christian faith? The whole point of formation is that we are aiming toward conformity with the wonderful life and message of Christ.

This conclusion, then, is unavoidable: Christian spiritual formation is and must be a formation both *within* and *into* the Big Story. You see, the story of creation, fall, redemption, restoration, and glorification is not just a story like other stories. The gospel is *the* story. It is Truth. It is more than just a narrative with a fine plot and interesting characters; it is also a revelation of the way things really are. Consequently, if we are to understand Christian spiritual formation, we must begin within the heart of the Christian message itself.

How we understand this story is a big deal for our formation as Christians. Just recall for a moment: What was the gospel story within which you were raised? How did it affect your own Christian spiritual formation? In the fifth century, for example, there were Christians who told a story about our origins as pure intellects emanating from the Mind of the One.[1] The primary "fall" was not our earthly fall but rather a movement of spiritual beings prior to our earthly creation. What we call creation was, according to this story, the giving of bodies to semi-fallen spiritual beings. Earth and history then became the stage on which (and Christ, the hero through which) our return to spirit and the One is enacted. For these Christians, formation was about paying attention to the body in order ultimately to leave it behind. While some read a simple "body bad, spirit good" orientation in the writings of those with this view, other interpreters see a more nuanced respect for the body as the vehicle through which the spirit matures until it is free to transcend the body. In either case, the important matter is to see that formation, for this group, was often lived as a progressive purification of habits, vices, and other thought patterns.

Other Christians have seen the Christian gospel as a story about rebellion and forgiveness. Humankind rebelled against God's authority (sin and "fall") and deserved death as the result. God sent Jesus as the one to die in our stead and, upon that basis, forgave the sins of human beings. Those who believe in Christ Jesus receive the benefits of that forgiveness and look forward to being caught up with the Lord at an end-time rapture, spending eternity in heaven with God (that is, if they do not die and go to heaven first). For this group, formation is the ongoing application of "the cross" and the meaning of Christ's ransom for our lives. People accept the free gift of salvation and live in the context of gratitude for that gift and the love of the One who gave it. Love works its way out into Christian living and also inspires a sense of mission for the sake of those who are not heavenbound.

I am not taking issue with either of these stories. I present these two generalizations simply as illustrations of how our views of the gospel story can shape our approach to ongoing formation as a believer. Another interesting way to reveal how we tell the Christian story is to ask where different traditions place their emphasis: Is it on Jesus's birth and incarnation? On his death and atonement? On his resurrection and victory? Or on Pentecost and the outpouring of the Spirit? Again, I ask you to recall summaries of the gospel stories you have heard. How were these stories narrated? What did they *say*? What did they mean for your own formation or the formation of others? Whether we notice it or not, our formation as Christians is deeply embedded in the gospel story, however it is narrated.

For this reason, it is necessary to summarize the gospel story—the story of how God has brought about our salvation—for the sake of understanding Christian spiritual formation. As you will see, I try to be broad but bounded in my approach to these matters. I am captivated by the beauty of this story and by the significance of the gospel for our lives here and now. I see the gospel ultimately as *God's* story. True, it is in one sense *our* story: Scripture runs from the origins of humanity in creation to the completion of humanity in a new heaven and a new earth. But there are other members of the cast—angels, demons, and such—whom we know little about. And they *are* part of the story. Humans enter the stage in the midst of a larger story. Our story and this larger, cosmic story are somehow intertwined, though we can catch only hints of the outlines of the larger story. It is crucial to see that human beings enter the stage as participants in *God's* story, in *God's* plan. The story is bigger than us in the beginning, and it is bigger than us in the end. I call it the "all things new" story.[2]

The Beginning

The story begins in the first few chapters of Genesis, which were written as a prologue to the story of the family of Abraham, which itself was written as a prologue to the story of God's rescuing the Israelites out of Egypt and placing them in the Promised Land. Genesis 1–3 sets the stage for the story that follows by introducing the characters and revealing the plot.

The hero of this story is mentioned in the very first verse of the Bible: "In the beginning, *God*" (Gen. 1:1). Immediately, we learn something about this God. God is Creator, the ultimate source of all that is or comes to be. God is powerful, personal, creative, orderly, and "good."[3] Everything God creates is good.

The next character in this story is the world itself. I consider the world a character in the story because, truly, the world does not function in the gospel story simply as a passive stage on which the drama of salvation is played. Rather, as we will see, it is the God-world-human relationship, with all its interesting dynamics (especially as we consider humans to also be members of the world), that forms some of the primary features of the story itself. By the end of the first chapter, we meet the next players in the story: human beings, God's people—specifically, Adam and Eve. They are portrayed both as creations of God and as being in an intimate, conversational relationship with God. Furthermore, at the onset of this story God gives the human beings a mandate: "God blessed them and said to them, '*Be fruitful and increase* in number; *fill the earth and subdue it. Rule* over the fish in the sea and the birds in the sky and over every living creature that moves on the ground.' . . . The LORD God took the man and put him in the Garden of Eden to work it and take care of it" (Gen. 1:28; 2:15, italics added).[4]

In Genesis 3, we learn of another character in the story: the serpent. We are not told much about this serpent other than that it was "crafty." And indeed, this serpent craftily nudges humans in the direction of disobedience to God's instructions. They are banished from the garden. And the plot thickens. Will humanity recapture its place in the world as "very good" partners with God and corulers of the world?

By Genesis 17 and the story of Abraham, humanity is represented not as a simple family but as large tribal societies, even nations. God moves to fulfill his mission of creating a people to rule over the earth in full relationship with God (his person, values, and instructions) through a relational agreement (or covenant) with a single tribe: the family of Abraham. Abraham's descendants are to be a blessing to all peoples on earth. We now understand that "peoples" is the same thing as "the world" and that the purpose of humanity is to rule well not only over the plants and animals but also over one another. God reveals this relational covenant with Abraham, saying, "I will be your God" (Gen. 17:7–8).[5]

So this is how the story begins: God, world, God's people, and more—each playing its own part in the story of life.

The Ending

In the Christian Bible, the story ends with the last chapters of Revelation. These chapters were written to encourage struggling Christians who were facing the prospect of dying for the sake of their faith and who needed to know their life and death were not in vain. They were likely wondering where all this was heading. Much of Revelation documents the author's visions and encounters, the latter of which took him to the gates of heaven and the "end" of things as we know it. And, as a good story often does (and remember this is *the* story), the end recapitulates the beginning.

First, there is the hero God. This is not just God the Creator, whom we met in Genesis, but also God the Redeemer and Re-creator. This God is the one who finally sets things right. There is a final judgment (Rev. 20). Heaven and earth are rebuilt. The throne of God is reestablished. God's relationship with his people is restored in full intimacy, as that of a bride to her husband. God is revealed as both King and Lamb, both Ruler and Redeemer.

The tree of life is once again present, symbolic of a return to the garden of Eden. Natural light fills the land. God restores "a new heaven and a new earth" (Rev. 21:1). Those who fail to worship God are not allowed in this world and are condemned to the fiery lake (20:10–15).

The serpent, hardly mentioned elsewhere in the Bible apart from Genesis, is explicitly discussed in Revelation. In chapter 12, it is identified as a "great dragon, . . . that ancient serpent called the devil, or Satan" (Rev. 12:9), whose influence on earth is tied to some larger cosmic drama. In chapter 20, this serpent is mentioned again: "the dragon, that ancient serpent who is the devil, or Satan" (20:2). Now, at the end, this devil is condemned to torment "for ever and ever" (20:7–10).

As for those who choose to worship God, they are to inherit the fulfillment of God's relational covenant: "Look, God's dwelling place is now among the people, and he will dwell with them." We read, "They will be his people, and God himself will be with them and be their God" (Rev. 21:3).

And here, at the culmination of all things, God's people are restored to the purpose for which they were created. As it says in Revelation 22:5, "They will not need the light of a lamp or the light of the sun, for the Lord God will give them light. *And they will reign for ever and ever*" (italics added). God's objective—to bring humans (or more specifically, "a people") into intimate partnership with God while reigning over a richly productive earth in the context of forces beyond this earth—is now fulfilled. What was begun in Genesis and what God always intended to be has now come to pass. I believe "He who was seated on the throne" sums it up best: "I am making everything new!" (Rev. 21:5). This is the gospel story, an adventure of God, humans, and the world that leads ultimately (and wonderfully) to *everything made new*. A new nation, a new Jerusalem. No tears. Healing (Rev. 22:2). The serpent without influence. Nature producing and humans ruling once again in harmony with God and God's values. God in intimate relationship with his people—the "all things new" story.

In Between

Between the beginning and the end is the developing drama of redemption. God's life-giving mission in this drama is to create and re-create all things, every sphere of life. God carries out this mission by creating human beings, delivering them (again and again), reminding them of their identity, and then inviting them to share in the life of the personal Trinity. At each stage of this drama—and in the midst of various contexts and conflicts—God provides appropriate means by which God's people can join in God's vision and mission. Unfortunately, God's people usually ignore or reject God's invitations, often reinterpreting God's rich, relational initiation in terms of mere ritual commands, doctrinal specifics, or spiritual experiences. Nevertheless, God's visionary mission is also a *promise*, and God always perseveres toward its fulfillment. In the end (as we have already seen), God keeps this promise. God's redemptive actions, the elements of this drama, are frequently repeated in each of the key periods of history.[6]

Creation/Re-creation and Deliverance

Each key period of history presented in Scripture (e.g., creation, Abrahamic history, exodus and conquest, monarchies, exile, postexilic Judaism, intertestamental period, Jesus's lifetime, church age, final restoration) identifies both a historical context for the life of God's people and a narrative "chapter" in the gospel story. Each of these key periods establishes a setting for distinct expressions of God's restorative action, and, as we will see, each necessitates the provision of a somewhat distinct system for the formation of a people who will be in relationship with God and working toward God's purposes. As mentioned above, God is redemptively present through actions (or types of actions) that are repeated at various points in history. The first of these redemptive actions is creation/re-creation and deliverance.

It is the original action. If there is anything to be learned from Scripture, it is that everything begins with God: "In the beginning, God . . ." Yet God's initiative is not only characteristic of his role in the original creation; it is characteristic of God's work throughout history. God creates and re-creates through acts of deliverance, and each key period of history emerges from that re-creative and saving work.

We learned of the inception of the God-world-human relationship in the early chapters of Genesis. God later addresses a particular tribe, the family of Abraham, and relocates them in the land of Canaan, the Promised Land, in order to initiate a new beginning. Similarly—and more powerfully—God creates a nation through delivering the Israelites from the oppression of the Egyptians and reestablishing them in the Promised Land with a new leadership and a new law. The period of monarchy under David and his descendants was also the consequence of God's mighty acts of deliverance, saving God's people from the threats of the surrounding nations. Interestingly enough, the period of Israel's exile in and return from Babylon was also interpreted as a "new beginning" (Ezra 9:9; Neh. 1:9; Hag. 2:6–9): a re-creation of God's people wrought by the hand of God's judgment and mercy.

Needless to say, the emergence of Christianity following the birth, life, death, and resurrection of Jesus is understood throughout Scripture as a unique expression of God's saving, delivering, and re-creative work. Jesus accomplished what Adam, and the rest of Israelite history, did not. The deliverance provided by Jesus's death was like no other before accomplished. And with Christ, the hope of God's aims—a redeemed, re-created people living and ruling on earth in full relationship with God's person and will—was renewed with a rich, compelling promise. The four Gospels are vivid testimony to the aesthetic magnetism of the gospel hope expressed in and through Jesus.

Nevertheless, the person and work of Christ were not sufficient to bring God's mission to completion. It was necessary that Jesus leave in order that the Comforter, the Holy Spirit, might be released to equip God's people to fulfill God's will. The outpouring of the Holy Spirit at Pentecost marks another of God's delivering, re-creative acts. We are currently living within this period of history: a period established particularly on the foundation of Christ's work and the sending of the Holy Spirit to God's people. And as we have seen above, the end (as described in Revelation) is really itself a beginning. The final re-creation is itself another deliverance accomplished by the powerful hand of God.

The "all things new" story begins with God's creative, redemptive work, bringing us into being—as a family, as a nation, as a remnant, as a church, as a bride—and delivering us from those forces that threaten our extinction. God delivers the Israelites from Egypt, the remnant from Babylon, and all humanity from sin and Satan. Our formation as Christians, then, is made possible through God's action on our behalf. Just as the Old Testament law (and formation) can never be properly understood apart from a deep appreciation for God's delivering work through the exodus, so also Christians cannot grasp the meaning of Christian spiritual formation apart from a deep appreciation for God's delivering and re-creative work through Jesus Christ and the Holy Spirit. Everything begins with God.

Covenant Reaffirmation or Renewal

God fulfills his desires on earth by forging a relational agreement with humankind. This relational agreement—or more correctly, this kind of relationship—is described in Scripture as a *covenant*. In redemptive history, God reaffirms and clarifies the nature and arrangement of the divine-human relationship. Just who are we, and how do we relate to God? What does God expect of us, and what does God commit to us? These are the sorts of questions addressed by God's covenant renewals in history.

I have already mentioned God's covenants with Adam and Abraham. A similar covenant between God and God's people is reaffirmed in the context of God's delivering Israel out of Egypt. It is anticipated, for example, in Exodus 6:2–8 and is especially present in Deuteronomy 4–11. Thus God promises Moses in Exodus 6:7 that "I will take you as my own people, and I will be your God." Moses reaffirms this covenant identity at the end of their journey, as they are about to enter the Promised Land. In Deuteronomy 7:6, 9 he says, "For you are a people holy to the LORD your God. The LORD your God has chosen you out of all the peoples on the face of the earth to be his people, his treasured possession. . . . Know therefore that the LORD your God is God; he is the faithful God, keeping his covenant of love to a thousand generations of those who love him and keep his commandments." This same covenant identity is reaffirmed as God initiates a new stage of Israel's history with the kingship of David. The Lord declares regarding David that "I will be his father, and he will be my son" (2 Sam. 7:14). David, in turn, reaffirms this covenant identity regarding the entire nation of Israel in the same chapter in this prayer: "You have established your people Israel as your very own forever, and you, LORD, have become their God" (2 Sam. 7:24). The fulfillment of this very same identity is promised in Jeremiah's proclamation of a new covenant in Jeremiah 31:31–34. And, as we have seen, it is finally fulfilled in Revelation 21:3.

God's covenant renewals also serve to reestablish the people's understanding of God's person, of God's purposes, and of their own place within God's person and purposes. Christian doctrine as we understand it is not presented complete within any given stage of history or segment of Christian Scripture. Rather, Christian doctrine emerges from a careful reflection on the developing story of the faith itself. For instance, aspects of God's character revealed in prophetic history are not manifest elsewhere. Jeremiah's declaration of God's intention to forge a "new covenant" with his people was a fresh revelation of God's ways.

Similarly, the calling of God's people—as participants in God's mission—is clarified and developed along the way. Adam is charged with ruling over and taking care of the earth. Abraham's descendants are to be a blessing to the nations. The obedience of the nation of Israel was intended to serve as a model to the surrounding nations. Their practice of being God's people was a proclamation of the character and purposes of God to the entire world and, as such, acted as a magnet, drawing people to God (see Exod. 9:13–16; 19:5–6; Deut. 28:9–10), a function affirmed in the prophetic declaration of Isaiah that God's servant will be a "light to the nations" (Isa. 42:6; 49:6). The whole earth's restoration through the restoration of the peoples of the earth is part of the declared reach of God's person and purposes through the Holy Spirit–empowered church: "You shall be my witnesses in Jerusalem, in all Judea and Samaria, and to the ends of the earth" (Acts 1:8). We see God's mission fulfilled in the gathering of nations before the throne of God in Revelation and in the reign of humankind, as was intended in Genesis.

Invitation

Along with offering deliverance and renewed covenants, God invites us into new life. "Now, Israel," Moses declares to God's people in Deuteronomy 4:1, "hear the decrees and laws I am about to teach you. Follow them so that you may live and may go in and take possession of the land that the LORD, the God of your ancestors, is giving you." Near the end of his time on earth, Moses repeats this same invitation: "This day I call the heavens and the earth as witnesses against you that I have set before you life and death, blessings and curses. Now choose life, so that you and your children may live and that you may love the LORD your God, listen to his voice, and hold fast to him" (Deut. 30:19–20). Throughout the writings and the prophetic literature, God urges the Israelites, to "come," "listen," "return and repent," and "seek the Lord," and he invites them again and again into a path of life (e.g., Job 42:4; Prov. 9:5; Hosea 6:1–2; Amos 5:4–6).

The New Testament message is preeminently an invitation to life. "Repent, for the kingdom of God is at hand," Jesus announces (Matt. 4:17). He invites his audience, "Let anyone who is thirsty come to me and drink" (John 7:37). Again he calls them to himself: "I am the way and the truth and the life" (14:6). After Jesus's ascension and the outpouring of the Spirit, God offers a similar invitation to those who will hear: "Repent and be baptized, every one of you, in the name of Jesus Christ for the forgiveness of sins. And you will receive the gift of the Holy Spirit" (Acts 2:38). These invitations are often summarized in the simple offer, "Believe."

But God's invitation is always an invitation to a life in which God makes "all things new." Moses offered a new way of looking at the people's relationship with God, with one another, and with their own land. Amos invited God's people into a renewed sociopolitical life. Jesus, in the Sermon on the Mount, called his hearers to a fresh way of living in righteousness. The apostle Paul invited the readers of his epistles not merely to baptism and belief, but to an ever-increasing maturity in faith, complete with a transformed mind and a reformed pattern of behavior (see, e.g., Col. 3:1–25). God emphasized one or another aspect of "all things" as appropriate for each setting (tribe, nation, exiles, church). The full gospel of Christianity lies in the whole. God desires and invites us ultimately into a renewal of every area of life.

Provision for the Maintenance of Covenant Life

Along with the invitation *to* life, God provides the means *for* life, in every area *of* life. Let us look at the exodus from Egypt as an example. Along with inviting the Israelites to become a godly nation, Yahweh also provided them with a basic framework for the rehearsal and reorientation of their relationship with God. The tabernacle (and later the temple) served to organize the nation's ritual life: community worship events. Similarly, laws were established to govern the ethical life of the community and its participants. Gleaning laws, sabbatical laws, and family laws preserved God's values in the life of the Israelites, and with this they preserved the best possible life for the people. God also provided a pattern for the organization of the people themselves, including Levites, elders, judges, tribal divisions, and ultimately (responding to the demands of the populace) kings.

While the principles behind the Mosaic nation-community remained constant through various periods of history (e.g., the value of taking care of the powerless, of transmitting faith through family, and of giving no room for idolatry), some of the specific means God provided for the maintenance of the covenant people changed with the times. The tabernacle-temple served as the primary location of the presence and ritual worship of God within the old covenant, but Jesus himself became the focal point of God's presence under

Figure 2.1
The "All Things New" Story

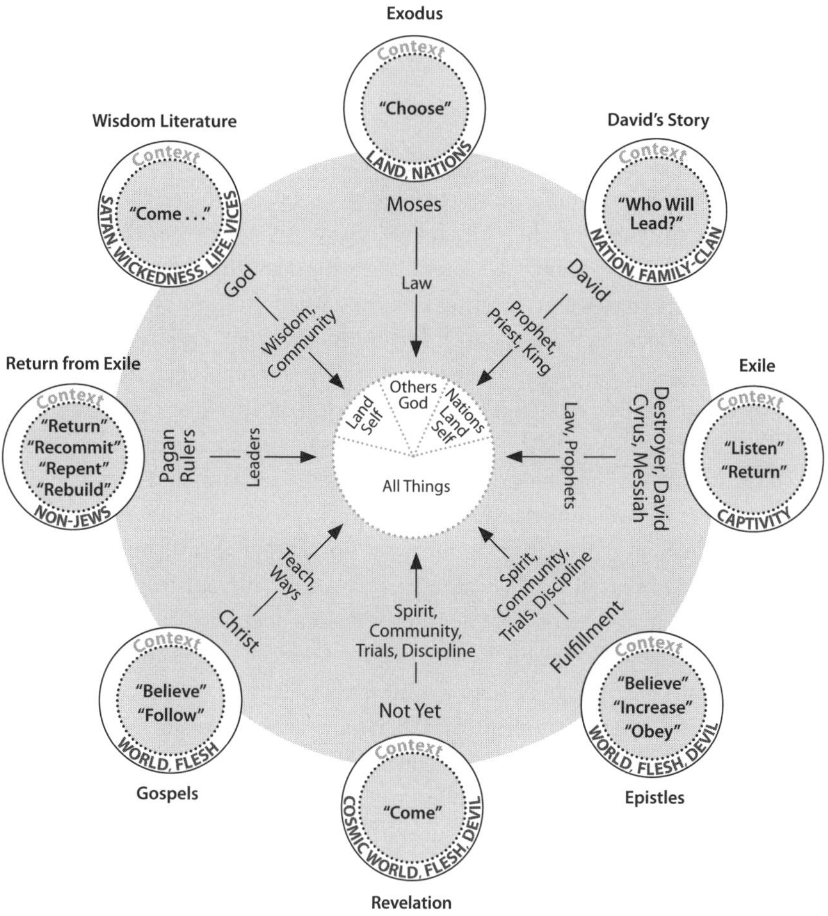

the new covenant. Likewise, while sincerely keeping the law enabled the old covenant Israelites to embody righteousness, under the new covenant, "the righteous requirement of the law" is fulfilled by those who live "according to the Spirit" (Rom. 8:4).

Along with the new beginnings made possible by God's deliverances and re-creations, the means by which God's people could thrive in each new historical period—as a people, in relationship with God and God's plan, and in the practical matters of political, economic, and ethical living—were also made possible by God.

Between the beginning and the end, God makes pathways into the "all things new" life. Through God's periodic re-creation, covenant renewal, invitation, and various provisions for covenant practice, God's people are graced with multiple opportunities to live into the fullness of the God-world-human relationship.

A Story of Formation

As I see it, this gospel story is a gripping narrative of God's offer of life—again and again. It is a breathtaking portrait of what might be (and what *will* be). And it is the Big Story within which and into which we are, and ought to be, formed. It is the fundamental context of formation; that is, the whole point of formation is that we are aiming toward a deepening relationship and an increasing conformity with the wonderful life, message, and mission of Jesus Christ. The Christian gospel is *the* story, *the* life and message, the truth about the way things really are. Therefore, the Christian gospel story seen as a whole is the framework out of which Christian views of formation must be derived.

But just how is this accomplished? What is the relationship between story and practice, between narration and formation? At a literary level, stories provide us with models to inform our own choices (heroes and heroines), plots within which we often see our own life (journeys, adventures), and images and phrases that summarize particular life events, feelings, and circumstances ("There's no place like home"). But the gospel story is also history, and we must take into account how history influences our formation. History both constrains and opens possibilities. Christ's death and resurrection made a new kind of relationship with God available. Christ's death and resurrection in first-century Israel also gave Christianity a distinctly Middle Eastern, Greco-Roman character. This geographic, historical character significantly shaped the development of the Christian view of formation. And, of course, history also produces things, like the Christian church itself. Furthermore, the Christian story is a paradigmatic story. (It is *the* paradigmatic story.) Paradigmatic stories are organizing centers around which a people define themselves; language and habits collect around the characters, phrases, drama, and meaning of the story.[7] Thus, not only did the Christian story produce the church historically, but it also forges the church in a literary fashion. We Christians form ourselves around the elements of the Big Story, a gathering point for our formation.

What is the object of the Christian story? Recalling the discussion of the object of formation in the previous chapter, we know the object identifies what formation (and here, the gospel story) is about. It is clear that the gospel story from beginning to end is about the God-world-human relationship. This is important to recognize because it means that the focus of Scripture is not merely personal entrance into heaven or even intimacy with God (though these are important). The object of God's story is the entire God-world-human relationship in the context of other, more cosmic (and less known) elements. It involves individuals, small communities, and larger configurations of peoples and environments. If this is the object of the Christian story, we must take it all into consideration as we develop our approach to Christian formation.

God's creation and re-creating redemption itself forms us. Our life is given to us. We have no choice in where we are born, who our parents are, and so on. We simply receive what we are given. The history of God's active presence and work both creates the environment within which we come to life and births life itself. The pattern of God's initiation and our response is built into the Christian faith. Our formation is rooted in this dynamic—for example, in the importance we ascribe to the art of discerning the voice and movement of the Holy Spirit. Furthermore, the complex of forces (nations, images, sentiments, and more) surrounding many peoples is shaped by the Christian story. This is especially true for those who inhabit the so-called Christian West. The Christian story provides part of the historical and religious context within which we are formed. Remember, the Christian story is a community story, and this community is two thousand years old. Formation is about change, and the factors that make for the changes of Christian spiritual formation are set within the Christian story.

Of course, the story provides us with the aim of formation. We are being formed into God and the gospel. As with many stories—and paradigmatically within the Christian story—the end (finish) of the story defines the end (goal, aim) of our formation into the story. The aim of formation, the gospel end (both finish and goal), is making "all things new." Orthodox belief alone is a false gospel. Random acts of kindness, no matter how sweet, are insufficient of themselves to express the fullness of the gospel aim. True religion is the presence of a sincere and full relationship with God, making its way into every area of life.[8] The Christian story also identifies our *identity* as Christians in formation. More than psychological tests or past experiences, our covenant relationship with God defines who we really are. Our invitation into formation comes through the Christian story. As I mentioned, we are currently living in the period of the ministry of the Holy Spirit. Our place in the story determines the chief *agent* of our formation (the Spirit of Christ) and the provision of *means* of our formation (the body of Christ, the sacraments, preaching, the shape of personal prayer, and so on).

The point of all this is to see that Christian spiritual formation is necessarily embedded in the larger Christian story, which means that our breathtaking vision of an "all things new" gospel must inform our approach to formation at every level (agents, means, aim, and so on). We cannot understand Christian spiritual formation without understanding it within the "all things new" story of the faith. And the reverse is also true: we cannot understand the Christian gospel unless we understand it as a story of formation—an adventure of creation, redemption and re-creation, and a continual formation of fresh, new expressions of God's heart until the time when those who love God are bathed in God's light and reign with him for ever and ever.

One Formation Example

Subsequent chapters will address how all this is worked out in practice. That is what Christian spiritual formation is: changing into the likeness of the person and story of Christ. Nevertheless, it might help at this point to see a taste of how this "all things new" story influences our approach to formation. Here's my own story.

Like most people, I wonder about my "calling." It gets a bit complicated sometimes. You see, I do not have a full-time job, and my wife's responsibilities (educating our daughters, raising the food we eat, helping with her parents' ranch) do not bring in an income. I've just pieced our income together here in Colorado by helping repair fences on a ranch, teaching one class a semester at the local community college, writing articles and books, and leading a few retreats and spirituality seminars. My time is often divided between manual labor, study, prayer, and time with people. Sometimes I find myself spending time doing things that seem less meaningful than teaching or pastoral work. Several years ago I got to thinking, "What *really* is my 'calling' anyway, and why do I spend so much time doing stuff I never felt 'called' to do?" As I considered this question, I concluded that one view is, for example, that ministry in spirituality is my calling and the rest is just stuff I have to do because of other obligations. But this option did not seem fair to other parts of my life. So I could say that I am called to be part of a family, for instance, and that this calling necessitates other kinds of work. But once again, it still made the work itself only a negligible calling. It just did not feel right.

As I examined my understanding of God and the gospel more carefully, I began to catch glimpses of what was going on. In the end, I wrote the following in a document that I've returned to often:

> God invites all of humanity into "all things new." Yet this invitation is comprehended and embodied in natural concentric circles of relationship. First, God invites all of humanity *as humans* to follow his creator/rulership—and there is a natural mandate to care for the planet. This natural human mandate is lived out in the sociocultural spheres of family, polis, and nation. Individual human life is nearly always embedded and lived out within the lives of families or other similar, immediate living environments, towns or tribes, and nations or larger structures. God calls not only individuals, but also communities and nations. Consequently, my personal calling and formation are only adequately discerned within a broader discernment of God's work within these larger frameworks. An individualist approach to spiritual formation is simply unfaithful to Scripture and God's formation. Furthermore, God also invites his followers in a special way together to live out the model of his way of life and to express his heart. We call this God-follower-together-relationship "church." Finally, God invites individuals particularly through the work of the Holy Spirit and community into particular means of conformity to Christ. Consequently, the development of a personal rule of life must be undertaken with deep sensitivity to the *who(s)* within which one has their being. Spiritual formation *is*, but is not *just*, about me.

I began to see that I was called—sincerely invited by God as part of God's people (according to old and new covenants)—to be a caretaker of this earth. I began to see that I was called to be a just citizen of the country where I lived. I began to see that no matter where I was living, I was called to be an agent of the kingdom of God. However I made my income, however I spent my time, *this* was my scriptural calling. When I worked on the ranch, issues of animal care and care of land were important; they were part of my calling. When I spent time writing, how I used my computer was important; it was part of my calling. Ultimately, I identified six biblical mandates that communicated for me the breadth of this calling. You can recognize each of these in my account of the Big Story above. I wrote them into my rule of life as my general calling:

God invites us through biblical mandates to become

- caring servants (Gen. 1–2 and beyond);
- a model people (the exodus story and beyond);
- followers of Jesus (see the Gospels and beyond);
- loving neighbors (see Jesus's teachings and beyond)—love God, love neighbor;
- a holy church (consider the work of the Spirit); and
- agents of the kingdom (again, this is the work of the Spirit).

I concluded that my calling was not a particular *task* in the world (like teaching or evangelism or work for justice or healing, for example). Rather, it was a set of *roles* I am to play in this world. No matter what my task, my job, or my career may be, these are the roles I am to play as a human recipient of God's invitation and restoring activity.

The real, practical consequence of my study and discernment was that, using this list, I developed a little Celtic-style prayer I try to remember to say when I begin each general activity of the day. When I sit down to write, for example, this is my prayer:

Here I am. Evan. Beloved.
By the Father—a caring servant participating in a model people,
By the Son—one of the followers of Jesus and a loving neighbor,
By the Spirit—a member of a holy church and an agent of the kingdom.
I hereby give to you this time of writing: within You and for You. Amen.

My life, even my own spiritual formation, is not only about me. Part of my very spiritual formation—the improvement of my relationship with God—involves my obligations to family, church, city, and land. And yet the aim of my formation is not simply for the sake of others. God desires every aspect of my life—and every aspect of the lives of the people all around me—to be ever new also for my own sake and simply for the glory of God. This is the story of formation. And I am learning to see my own calling, and my own formation, in light of this story.

Going Deeper

1. In this chapter, we have addressed God's vision for "all things new" from the perspective of the biblical narrative: how the Scriptures develop

a story of the fullness of our salvation through the work of Father, Son, and Spirit over time. But what would it be like if we were to take a different perspective? What might our view of God's plan and our formation look like if, for example, we summarized God's vision for the universe from the perspective of systematic theology? Go ahead and give it a try. Summarize the key doctrines of the Christian faith (such as the doctrines of Christ or salvation), and see what view of Christian spiritual formation develops from this approach.

2. The gospel story develops in the context of one conflict after another. We have seen that conflict is constant. Whereas some people develop an interest in spiritual formation, hoping that practices like contemplative prayer and private retreats might facilitate a bit of distance from the chaos and conflicts of ordinary life, we find the biblical perspective is that even in our times of private retreat (see Luke 4, for example) we face conflicts: spiritual, social, personal, and more. What conflicts are present in your own personal or congregational contexts? What might the "all things new" story have to say about these conflicts?

3. This chapter has rooted Christian spiritual formation within the Christian Scriptures. We have learned in this chapter how to see the depth and breadth of spiritual formation within the overall story of the Bible. But we usually do not read the Bible all the way through. Oftentimes we sit with a short passage of Scripture in order to be nourished by a small, bite-sized portion. How do we (or how do *you*) interpret the small bites with a view toward the Big Story, such that the whole forms you through the reflection on a part? How does Scripture influence formation?

4. In the start of this chapter we asked about our own hearing of the gospel, the stories we were raised within. One practice that helps us see our own story in dialogue with the larger biblical story is keeping a journal. Through entries in a journal, we record our story from the perspective of our sense of the gospel story. We can even use a journal to remember our own appropriation of the gospel in previous seasons of life. For example, I might record the time when I studied about worship and was moved to think of God not merely as a friend but also as an Almighty Ruler. Give journaling a try. Document the story of the Christian message as you understood (or misunderstood) it through the history of your life until the present. What do you learn about Christian spiritual formation from such an exercise?

PART TWO

THE ELEMENTS

3

....

The Fullness and Aims
of Christian Spiritual Formation

Overview

Having viewed the aim of formation from the perspective of the grand, divine story, we will now look at this same aim from the human perspective. Just what *is* a person or a community, and what does it then mean for *this* person or community to be formed into the likeness of Jesus Christ? In this chapter, we will survey the breadth and depth of human experience. We will consider what it means to be simultaneously embodied and spirit and what it means to function with intellect, emotions, and will. We will examine both the flow of human experience and the web of relationships that give human experience its characteristic interpersonality. Each of these dimensions of human experience can be seen in various layers of depth, which we will investigate.

Then, having summarized a broad view of the key characteristics of human experience, we will explore the significance of taking this view with regard to the aims of Christian spiritual formation. What is spiritual formation about? What does it try to accomplish? We will look at a few terms that have often been used to identify these aims: *holiness, sanctification, deification, obedience, kingdom of God, increase*. By the end of this chapter, we will discover that the "all things new" vision of the gospel story and our vision of the fullness of human experience transformed in Christ are really the same vision: a profound foundation for Christian spiritual formation.

When we meet someone and have occasion to get to know them a bit more closely, we often say, "Tell me your story." We mean by this phrase that we wish to hear something of their past, but we also want to know how they themselves interpret that past, such that we learn from their telling who they see themselves to be in the present. That is the nature of "telling our story."

In the previous chapter, I told the story (so to speak) of Christian spiritual formation to give a sense of where it has come from, where it is heading, and, consequently, a little bit about what it looks like in the present. When we grasp the nature of Christian spiritual formation through the lens of the gospel story of Scripture, we see a compelling vision of a restored God-world-human universe. The gospel is a story of formation: the formation of a people of God and of persons for God. It's a story of "all things new"—God's desire to restore every aspect of life: our relationship with God, with others, with ourselves, with nature, and more. We touch the "all things new" story when we hear the particular stories of Sarah and Abraham, Moses and Miriam, Hosea and Gomer, Mary and Joseph, Jesus, and Paul. Each chapter of the story builds on the previous ones, revealing—piece by piece—the fullness of the salvation offered us through Christ and the Spirit, which will finally be fulfilled in the eschaton.

We encounter this same fullness of formation, this same invitation to "all things new," more concretely through getting to know other Christians over time. Perhaps you have encountered something like this scenario. You develop a friendship with someone, even a close, spiritual friendship. You share your ideas about Christianity, the feelings of your Christian experience, the decisions each of you are exploring. Then, one of you begins to change. (For this scenario, let's say it's you—though it could just as easily be your friend.) It might be some passage of Scripture that starts you on a new journey, or perhaps it is an experience of God, or an encounter with pain. However it starts, the point is that down the road, one of you is into "something new" and simply cannot shake it. This something new is not taking you away from the Christian faith. (Yes, apostasy does happen, but it is not what I am talking about here.) Indeed, quite the opposite—for the person who is changing, this season is a journey deeper *into* Christian faith. You may rant about the state of the church and its lack of this or that. You may gush about your own healing and urge your friend to pursue the same. You might find you have an insatiable appetite for Scripture, outlining whole books of the Bible, and learning doctrines you had never dared think about before. Whatever the something new is, it is experienced as an invitation into a deeper relationship with God (though you may not consciously express it this way). Christ is becoming Lord over more of your life.

We might wish that we all went through this journey of ever-increasing growth and maturity at the same pace and with regard to the same aspects of life. No such luck. We are stuck with the complications of learning to love one another in the midst of our incomplete and interwoven conversions. I will be speaking of conversion more in chapter 5. What I want you to see here is simply that the fullness of the "all things new" gospel confronts us again and again as we relate to our fellow believers over time.

And, of course, this can happen at the level of community as well as at the individual level. In this scenario, a congregation or a small group is led by this or that into a new direction. The members explore new things and experience new things. They feel that, through these practices, they are progressing into a loving relationship with God. But others may wonder: Is this heresy? Is this maturity? How does one evaluate it? (We will address discernment in chap. 11.) Without elaborating on this scenario further, let me point out that these new ventures can contribute to our maturity. God can invite us into new and unexplored aspects of our relationship with God, into a new, fresh, and challenging alignment with an ever-growing vision of God's person and plan. I have seen scenarios like those described above many times.

Just underneath such encounters lie the breadth and depth of human experience itself. Throughout history, Christians have understood Christian maturation as involving an ever-broadening and ever-deepening influence of Christ and the gospel into various aspects of our experience. People writing about Christian spiritual formation today are increasingly approaching it from a holistic perspective and realizing that spiritual formation cannot but involve—to some extent or another, at some time or another—the fullness of what it means to be human.[1] We are learning that in order to comprehend Christian spiritual formation, we must know something about the fullness of human experience. Through examining the character of human experience, we become uniquely acquainted with the fullness of the formation offered us through Christ and the Holy Spirit. For this reason, whereas chapter 2 explored the trajectory of spiritual formation "from the top" (the divine story), the present chapter will cover something of the same territory "from the bottom"—that is, from the angle of human experience.

I will first present a summary of the breadth and depth of human experience. Then we can examine what human experience, in relationship with Christ, might be formed *into*—for that clarifies the aim of Christian spiritual formation. We will look at some of the terms that different Christian traditions use to identify these aims: *holiness, sanctification, deification, obedience, kingdom of God*, and *increase*. Finally, we will see how grasping the fullness of Christian experience shapes our approach to these aims and to the "all things new" life.[2]

The Breadth and Depth of Human Experience

Human experience is a rich tapestry of diverse threads woven together into a single reality we identify as a "self" (we use the terms *we* or *I* to identify the corporate or personal self, respectively). When we pull apart the fabric a little and look at the different threads independently, we gain an appreciation for the breadth and depth of all that God desires to make new through Christian spiritual formation and all that is involved in a growing relationship with God through Jesus Christ in the Holy Spirit.

Embodied Soul

Human experience is both embodied and spirit (some speak of a "soul" or "heart").[3] That is part of the unique character of humanity. Whereas angels are essentially spiritual beings and worms are essentially material beings, humans are composite beings, manifesting both physicality and spirituality. We experience ourselves as both body and soul. While there are moments when our bodies seem disconnected from life (dreaming, for example), these are rare. The fact is, our bodies structure our souls. Brain development, body shape, and hormonal predispositions all contribute to the character of one's soul. The soul also constitutes itself through the body. This is what a gesture is all about. It is one thing to read the words of a worship song silently to ourselves; it is quite another to sing those words with our voice in the context of a church gathering. The apostle Paul offers a final blessing to the Thessalonians in his first letter: "May God himself, the God of peace, sanctify you through and through. May your whole spirit, soul and body be kept blameless at the coming of our Lord Jesus Christ" (1 Thess. 5:23).

Intellect, Emotions, and Will

Human experience tends to manifest itself through the development of distinct operational systems, sometimes called *faculties*. Just like the digestive and the nervous systems in our bodies, each of these systems is made up of a unique set of parts and has a distinct manner in which these parts work together. One common way of dividing our operational systems is to think of human experience in terms of intellect, emotions, and will.[4]

Our intellect is especially oriented to the structure of our environment. It incorporates such operations as inquiry, insight, comparison, and deduction. Verbal and spatial intellectual processing combine to produce language, architecture, and more. And our intellect is an important part of our worship: Romans 12:2 urges the brothers and sisters to be transformed "by the renewing of your mind."

Emotions inform us about the meaning of our person-environment relationship. For instance, you see a snake, hear a rattling sound, and respond with fear—because your well-being is threatened. A stranger risks life or limb to rescue my beloved child from an oncoming car, and I, upon hearing of the event, cry tears of gratitude. Emotions integrate our appraisals of a situation with our physiological processes (heart rate, tear glands), our tendencies to action (the inclination to flee, hug, etc.), and other factors (like an existential feeling or sense of an emotion). The psalmist in Psalm 139:21 proclaims, "Do I not hate those who hate you, LORD, / and abhor those who are in rebellion against you?" By using the parallel terms *hate* and *abhor*, the psalmist shows that emotional responses, even negative ones, can be a reflection of conforming to God's own person and plan.

The will operates with regard to human experience itself. We choose to attend to a particular noise, decide to take a particular action, or allow ourselves to experience the fullness of an emotion ("letting ourselves go"). We adopt a theory (will and intellect) or nurse a grudge (will and emotion). The will moves human experience from one moment to the next. The will oversees our habits, and forming godly habits is precisely what Paul considers his vocation when he speaks about persuading the gentiles to the "obedience that comes from faith" (see the various translations of Rom. 1:5; 16:26).

Each of these three systems may have distinct elements and perform distinct functions, but they work together as a whole. The emotions and the intellect interact with each other while the will drives the movement forward. I emphasize this in my account of Christian spiritual formation because transformation of our relationship with God (*spiritual* formation) must—as a spiritual *formation* of ordinary human experience—involve changes in our ways of thinking, feeling, and acting.[5]

Stages and Movement of Experience

Furthermore, in general, human experience tends to flow in a given direction and through stages, employing distinct activities. I have identified six of these: being aware, experiencing, understanding, evaluating, deciding/acting, and integrating.[6] These illustrate the rich unity-in-diversity found both in human corporate and personal experience and in Christ's church, where distinct but coexisting and cooperative expressions together communicate the mind and life of Christ. It may be helpful to understand the relationship of these activities to Christian spiritual formation and the body of Christ by a comparison with Richard Foster's *Streams of Living Water*. Let us imagine the mind (so to speak) of the church. We can acknowledge how contemplative traditions have nourished the self-awareness of the body of Christ throughout history.[7] Charismatic traditions have enriched our experience of God. Progressive traditions have posed important questions to the body of Christ, facilitating our understanding of God. Evangelical traditions have kept us close to the center of our beliefs, supporting the church's practices of evaluation. Holiness traditions and social-justice traditions have stressed practical life, nourishing the body's deciding and acting. Finally, by representing the whole ("one, holy, catholic and apostolic church") through liturgy and art and life, sacramental traditions promote integration of the body of Christ.

Just as one's knowledge and life are made up of the warp and woof of the stages of human experience, so too the church requires the cooperation of various traditions in order to cultivate a healthy knowledge of and life in God. I do not want to be overly specific about how each tradition may or may not fit into a given category. Rather, I present these six stages to illustrate how God invites us—in God's own way, in God's own timing, and by means of the whole church in all its various expressions throughout history—into a rich and diverse formation, the fruit of which is increasing conformity with the spectacular beauty of God's own life and plan. We will learn about how God does this in the chapters ahead.

The Web of Relationships

Another way to see the fullness of human experience is to examine our relationships. Human experience apart from relationships simply does not exist. Being human is, by definition, to be related to others—related on many levels.

But just what is a relationship? In mathematics, we can say that −3 and 3 bear a similar relationship to zero. We cannot say such things about the relationship between −3 and the phrase *black dog*. Thus, when terms or entities have the capacity to coordinate with one another, we can say they are in a relationship. Some entities are related not simply as coordinates but also by interaction. For instance, chemists speak of different kinds of bonds as atoms interact: ionic bonds, which involve the transfer of electrons from one atom to another, and covalent bonds, which involve the sharing of electrons between atoms.

As we move from atoms to molecules to compounds and beyond, we are confronted with ever more complex and profound levels of coordination, interaction, and sharing. Biologists describe various forms of symbiotic relationships, wherein the lives of organisms are mutually dependent. Often modes of communication are employed to facilitate shared experience, as with the dancing used by some species of bees. Coordination, interaction, adaptation, shared experience, symbolic communication, and more—all are important aspects of relationship.

Humans are related at many levels. First, we are related to nature. We are creatures. Human beings are distinct from God and dependent on God for life itself, just as are the other products of God's creation. We interact with nature through our senses, including touch, sound, and speech. We have learned to adapt to the presence of other creatures and even to share our life with them, to a certain extent, such as when we relate to an animal through the use of symbols and language. Our very function on this planet, our role as stewards, involves how we navigate this relationship with nature.

Second, we participate in interpersonal relationships. These exhibit the characteristics noted above, but they do so with even greater complexity, depth, and significance. Remember, a person is not merely a physical thing, but rather a whole that comprises body, emotions, decisions, and more. That being the case, interpersonal relationships involve the sharing of all of these.

To explore interpersonal relationships further, we must add this piece to the model of human experience presented above: the process of human experience is also a process of knowing. The development of human experience—from being aware to experiencing and then to understanding and so on—is a process of adapting our thoughts and life to our world. In common parlance, we say we know something when our thoughts (and life) correspond or cohere in some fashion with that something. We often distinguish between *knowing about* something and *knowing* something. While I may speak of knowing about a famous person, having read articles in magazines or watched interviews on the internet, it is quite a different matter to say that an individual or community knows that same person. Much more of human experience is involved in the latter.

It is within the context of knowing another that we live in interpersonal relationship. An interpersonal relationship, then, is the mutual experience of another along with the shared knowledge of that experience. I am experiencing your feelings. You are understanding my decision. We share events together, such as when my wife and I enjoy watching one of our hens with her brood after she has hatched out a few chicks. Furthermore, as we declare a thing to be both common and part of our individual identities, we begin to have a corporate self. It is then that we begin to talk of *our* experience, *our* conclusion, *our* chicks.

Third, humans also possess a relationship with a self. I will speak of how we construct selves in the following chapter. I simply want to state here that we do perceive a self, one we define and interact with. Our own thoughts and feelings and habits can become the object of our own thoughts and feelings and habits. We can find ourselves experiencing our own thoughts. We can decide about our own patterns of emotions. Sometimes, despite our efforts, we can't seem to get rid of certain thoughts. We undertake programs of self-improvement and (rightly) repent from our sins of self-hatred. All of this is part of what it means to be in relationship with ourselves. Human experience is deeply personal, and we can explore this vast universe of self-to-self relationship through the psychological fields, if we wish.

Fourth, the Bible presents the story of human experience as one embedded within a larger story of other spiritual realities. While there is much we don't know about angels and demons and such, we are wise to at least acknowledge that we exist within the interaction of a variety of forces. Indeed, we have some kind of relationship with them. Angels have been known to bring information through dreams or visions, and we seem to have the power, in Christ, to rid ourselves from the influence of demonic forces. Christians throughout history have understood what is often called spiritual warfare to be an important part of their formation.

Finally, we are in relationship with God. The Christian God is a personal God who reveals himself: God is knowable, and we can know God. God has condescended to human capacities of understanding such that authentic relationship between God and humans is possible. This means our relationship with God is like any other interpersonal relationship: sharing experiences, knowing another, and so on. But the Christian God is not like any other person. Our God is all-powerful, all-knowing, infinite, and the One we value above everything. Thus, while our relationship with God is interpersonal, it is unlike our other interpersonal relationships, because it is a relationship of worship, within which we offer reverence and complete devotion to the Other.

This combination of our special makeup as humans (both physical and spiritual) and the unique character of God (both personal and transcendent) makes our relationship with God so fascinating. Our relationship with God through the new covenant is the source of our formation as Christians. God invites us to change through the gospel and the Spirit. Our relationship with God is also the primary aim of our formation: it is exactly what we are maturing into when we are formed. Spiritual formation is not just about a change in our character, although it may include this. It is fundamentally

Figure 3.1
A Model of Human Experience

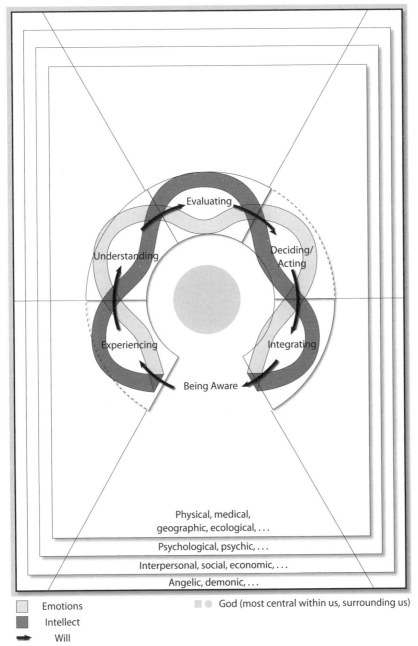

a change in our relationship with God—a change in how individuals and communities communicate, share experience, and participate in the life of the Trinity.[8]

Human experience is lived out in the context of a broad web of relationships. And herein we find another illustration of the breadth of human experience and the fullness of Christian spiritual formation. For if relationships are essential to what it means to be human, then the formation of human experience in Christ must involve change—to some extent, at some time—in those relationships that make us human. God created us to cogovern the earth in harmony with God's own loving care. This is the purpose fulfilled in Revelation 22:5: our relatedness to nature is restored. This restoration is also offered with regard to our relationships with self, others, spiritual realities, and God. The "all things new" gospel of Christian spiritual formation includes our participation in setting right every framework of human relatedness. Personal healing, gospel evangelism, spiritual warfare, sacramental recovery, political justice—all are part of the restoration of our relationships through our transforming relationship with Christ, the Father, and the Holy Spirit. Figure 3.1 (p. 51) illustrates how these various systems (emotions, intellect, and will; the stages of human experience; and the web of our relationships) all interact and fit together.

Depth

And all of this change takes place in various elements of human experience, and it happens at various depths. Sometimes it is something small—a mere thought, a feeling, or a single action—such as when I choose to discard my initial harsh evaluation of a stranger as we meet, preferring to think the best. We may find that changing a single thought is a significant step in our Christian spiritual formation. But often, change happens at a deeper level. Beneath our thoughts are our beliefs. Beneath our feelings are patterns of emotions. Beneath our actions are habits. And just as God can change a thought, God can also change a belief (e.g., the belief that Jesus was only a wise human being and nothing more or that homeless people are lazy). When beliefs change, our habits and patterns of emotions might change as well.

Change can go even deeper. Beneath our beliefs are worldviews. Beneath our patterns of emotions are basic emotional concerns, as is the case when compulsions and addictions point to deeply hidden emotional needs.[9] Beneath our habits are lifestyles. Sometimes God invites us into some pretty deep changes. When a lifestyle is re-formed, it is bound to have an effect on our emotions and our point of view. Likewise, there are times when God remodels the whole way we see things, and suddenly we find ourselves getting excited about things we never imagined—or upset at things we never imagined.

But it can go still deeper. Sometimes God reaches into the very core of our being, the place where intellect, emotion, will, relationships, and decisions all seem to come together. Both the classic accounts of Christian spirituality and my own personal experience of spiritual direction confirm that God can (and does!) do some deep work of transformation in some mysterious center of our being. Figure 3.2 illustrates something of how these levels of depth work together.

Figure 3.2
The Depth Dimension

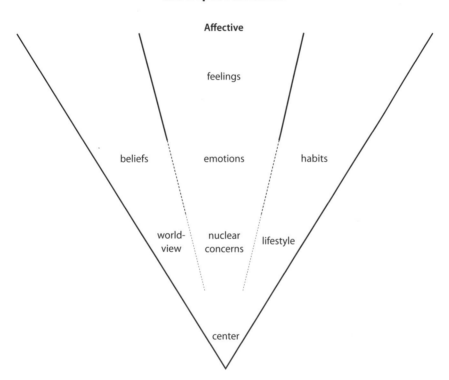

Although many of the examples given here involve a human individual (because it is easier to grasp a concept if we see it from an individual standpoint), similar examples can be found for communities or corporate selves. Communities have relationships with others; consider how a group may relate to a particularly bothersome but powerful outsider or to a rival group. Communities can change in matters shallow, such as a softening toward a certain style of music, or in matters deep, like when God's Spirit seems to pour over the congregation for a month, yielding new fruit of the Spirit.

The fullness of Christian spiritual formation has both breadth and depth. While we cannot predict—and we ought not prescribe—the ways the Spirit works, we can see from this outline of human experience the range of possibilities we might find in ourselves and others. Knowing something of this richness equips us to recognize and accept God's invitations to formation when and where they arise.

The Aims of Christian Spiritual Formation

"OK," you might say, "I accept that human experience is indeed both broad and deep. It's actually pretty complicated. But that brings me to a new problem. With all these relationships and operational systems and stages and such in play, I've lost the target."

It would be simpler if we all could talk about "growing closer to Jesus" or learning to "live the Christian life." And in one sense, those are the goals of this book: to help us to grow closer to Jesus and to live the Christian life. Yet another question surfaces: Just what does it *mean* to grow closer to Jesus and to live the Christian life? To answer this, let's revisit what it means to be a human community or individual.

I stated in chapter 1 that "formation always has an aim." Such is the nature of formation. Particles attract and repel, resulting in new atomic configurations. Flowers bloom and trees grow to maturity. People form—and want to be formed—into something. I stated in the same chapter that Christian spiritual formation is oriented toward conformity with the life and gospel of the Christian God—a good summary of its aims. But, again, what does this actually mean? When I serve as a spiritual director for someone, how and in what ways do I hope that individual will mature? If I am the senior pastor of a congregation, what do I want that church to become ten years down the road, and what will I do to facilitate this?

Chapter 2 presented the story of Christian spiritual formation: God is inviting us into significant changes so he can make "all things new." So formation is about growing closer to Jesus, though this means a whole lot more than we might have assumed. Our identity as a corporate people of God is involved. Our relationships with others and with nature are involved. Social change often both contributes to and flows from a formation that is truly of the Spirit and, given the elements of human experience discussed in this chapter, has only magnified this breadth and complexity.

Again, we are struggling to find a definition for spiritual formation. So much is involved. Just what are we aiming at when we pursue spiritual formation? Once again, our target seems to disappear.

Or does it? In one sense, the target or aim of Christian spiritual formation (both as defined and as lived) just grows. As the Epistle to the Ephesians says about God's purposes, God seeks "to bring unity to all things in heaven and on earth under Christ" (Eph. 1:10). God will gather up "all things." When the target grows, it means that everybody hits it somewhere and nobody hits it everywhere. I think this is a little of what it means for us to "know in part" (1 Cor. 13:12). The aim of formation is perhaps too grand for any of us to reach or even understand fully on our own. And perhaps that is exactly the point. Formation is ultimately God's work, as suggested by some of the terms used to describe it, including *holiness, deification, the obedience of faith, the kingdom of God,* and *increase.*[10] Let's investigate those terms.

Holiness and Sanctification

One term frequently used to identify the ultimate aim of spiritual formation is *holiness*. In fact, the word *sanctification* (Greek *hagiasmos*) has its origins in *holiness* (Greek *hagios*, Latin *sanctus*). First Peter affirms the aim of holiness clearly: "But just as he who called you is holy, so be holy in all you do; for it is written: 'Be holy, because I am holy'" (1 Pet. 1:15–16).

The idea of holiness carries nuances of religious purity (being set apart for a special purpose), of righteous living, of personal integrity, and a quality of being touched with the power of God. The very first entry in Jonathan Edwards's collection of "miscellanies" is on holiness.

> Holiness is a most beautiful and lovely thing. We drink in strange notions of holiness from our childhood, as if it were a melancholy, morose, sour and unpleasant thing; but there is nothing in it but what is sweet and ravishingly lovely. 'Tis the highest beauty and amiableness, vastly above all other beauties. . . . It makes the soul like a delightful field or garden planted by God, with all manner of pleasant flowers growing in the order in which nature has planted them, that is all pleasant and delightful, undisturbed, free from all the noise of man and beast, enjoying a sweet calm and the bright, calm, and gently vivifying beams of the sun forever more: where the sun is Jesus Christ; the blessed beams and the calm breeze, the Holy Spirit; the sweet and delightful flowers, and the pleasant shrill music of the little birds, are the Christian graces. . . . How, if one were holy enough, would they of themselves and as it were naturally ascend from the earth in delight, to enjoy God as Enoch did![11]

At times in the history of the church, holiness became identified with a narrow range of behaviors, such as sexual abstinence or gifts of mystical prayer. But when the church has been at its healthiest, it has realized that holiness is ordinary human experience being increasingly conformed to Christ and Christ's values. For example, 1 Peter follows the command to be holy with a discussion of our relationships with others, saying believers should cultivate "sincere love for each other" (1 Pet. 1:22) and rid themselves of "all malice and all deceit, hypocrisy, envy, and slander of every kind" (2:1). After describing Christians as "a holy priesthood" (2:5) and a "holy nation" (2:9), the author urges the readers to "abstain from sinful desires" (2:11) and to "submit . . . to every human authority" (2:13). True holiness, at least to those writing and reading 1 Peter, encompasses emotions, relationships, political strategies, and more. It is both wide and ordinary.

Deification

Many Christians, especially those in the Orthodox traditions, use the term *deification* (*theosis*) to identify the ultimate aim of spiritual formation.[12] Theologian John Meyendorff writes, "In deification man achieves the supreme goal for which he was created."[13] The roots of this idea can be found in the encouragement in 2 Peter 1:4 that through the promises of God we "may participate in the divine nature." In light of this understanding, Bishop Kallistos Ware discusses deification in answer to the questions, For what am I saved? What is my end point or final aim? "To be saved," he proclaims, "is to share with all the fullness of human nature in the power, joy, and glory of God."[14] But what does it *mean* for humans to participate in God's nature?

Some Christians reflect on deification as our becoming more Christlike, in that the human and the divine are united in Christ. Just as Christ possesses both human and divine natures, each communicating with the other without mixture or confusion, so we through deification share in God ever more fully, yet without changing or violating our own human nature. Others emphasize our sharing of God's energies as opposed to his essence. However expressed, deification is understood not merely as an imitation of Christ but rather as a full sharing of the life of Christ insofar as humanly possible. Deification happens when we begin to share Christ's compassion for the weak, when we participate in Christ's own resistance to temptations, when we see the beauty of the Trinity. Deification, though "realized in its fullness only in the age to come after the resurrection of the dead," is "fulfilled ever more and more even in this present life, through the transformation of our corruptible and depraved nature and by its adaptation to eternal life."[15]

Obedience

Paul identified the aim of his own missionary work as bringing the gentiles to the "obedience that comes from faith" (Rom. 1:5; 16:26).[16] Paul is simply following the lead of Jesus, who in his Great Commission commands his followers to make disciples, "teaching them to obey everything I have commanded you" (Matt. 28:20). It is essential that the one worshiping is in a posture of obedience to the One being worshiped—as both Jesus and Paul model and reiterate in their ministries. John Calvin writes that the Holy Spirit was given to us "for sanctification, that he may purge us from all iniquity and defilement, and bring us to the obedience of divine righteousness."[17] But just what does it mean to obey?

To obey is simply to conform our experience to a standard revealed to us by someone else. Let's say a military superior commands me to carry supplies to a given destination. To obey, I must actually pick up the supplies and take them to that location. My act conforms to my superior's command. Jesus commands us, in the Sermon on the Mount, to monitor the thoughts and feelings that arise (anger, lust, rejection of enemies, and so on). To obey is to pay attention to my thoughts and feelings and to reject those of which Jesus disapproves. Because obedience is a matter of both actions and the heart, the aim of true obedience, as with deification or holiness, is not identified with the presence of a powerful experience or with moral precision. Rather, obedience is really an increasing conformity of the breadth and depth of human experience to the life and values of God in Christ.

The Kingdom of God

The phrase *kingdom of God* communicates God's corporate aims for spiritual formation. J. Heinrich Arnold, speaking to his flock of Anabaptists known as the Bruderhof, pleads,

> I sometimes wonder whether our community has not completely forgotten the kingdom of God, and whether the distinction between personal salvation and the kingdom is clear enough to us. Both are of great importance. Eternal salvation is very important—it is wonderful to experience the nearness of Christ and to be redeemed by him. But the kingdom of God is still greater![18]

The kingdom of God is one of the primary metaphors used in the Gospels to describe God's purposes. The idea of a kingdom or realm of God suggests a sphere within which the influence and authority of the living God are welcomed and recognized. God's kingdom may include the fullness of individual life (hence we can think of God having sway over every area of personal life), but a kingdom is primarily a corporate ideal. The Jewish apocalyptic expectation—and the Christian fulfillment of that expectation—pointed to the coming of a divine king who would bring safety and a new presence of God into the lives of individuals; in addition, this divine king would reclaim a people for God and initiate a new corporate life of peace, justice, and righteousness. This has begun with the outpouring of the Holy Spirit of Christ on the followers of Jesus. The presence of Christ the King establishes a visible king-oriented and king-ordered society.

As a metaphor for the ultimate aim of spiritual formation (formation in and by the Spirit), the ideal of the kingdom of God urges the church into maturity. The church is the "community of the king," a collective body of subjects ordered around and expressing the character of their king.[19] Though he did not specifically use the language of kingdom in the first chapters of Acts, Luke clearly saw the beginnings of the fulfillment of Christ's desires for a community (or family) of the king in the life of the early church (Acts 2:42–47).

From this perspective, the passions to be mastered by obedience en route to the ultimate aim of spiritual formation are not simply the private vices of individual sensuality (greed, lust, avarice, and the like) but also the public vices of "hatred, discord, jealousy, fits of rage, selfish ambition, dissensions, factions and envy" (Gal. 5:20–21). Just as Ignatius of Loyola can speak of "disordered affections" inhibiting an individual's discernment and following of the will of God, so we may also think of "disordered" patterns of corporate life inhibiting a community's discernment and following of the will of God. The aim of the kingdom of God, then, is to see the deification, the holiness, and the perfection of corporate life—the restoration of the community of the King.[20]

Holiness, deification, obedience, kingdom of God—however one designates the aim, it points toward our growing likeness, in any and every element of human experience, to the fullness of Christ's person and gospel message. All of our faculties and relationships are in the jurisdiction or are the territory claimed by Christian spiritual formation.[21] And, consequently, Christian spiritual formation cannot be the preserve or domain of any one Christian tradition (the contemplative tradition, for example). Instead, it is nourished by the whole body of Christ, in its full-orbed breadth and diversity.

Increase

Should this goal of "all things new" seem too vast, too far beyond practical Christianity, I offer a more modest proposal: *increase*. In the New Testament, increase is important. John the Baptist "grew and became strong in spirit" (Luke 1:80), and Jesus "became strong" and "was filled with wisdom" (2:40). When the Holy Spirit was acting on the church, "the Lord added to their number daily" (Acts 2:47), and "living in the fear of the Lord and encouraged by the Holy Spirit, it increased in numbers" (9:31). (See also Acts 4:4; 5:14; 6:1; 11:21, 24; 12:24; 16:5; 2 Cor. 4:15.) Paul encourages his readers' love to increase (1 Thess. 3:12; see also Phil. 1:25), noting that they will be "transformed into his [Christ's] image with ever-increasing glory" (2 Cor. 3:18). In 2 Peter 1:5–8 (a passage that summarizes our theme nicely), believers are exhorted to

> make every effort to add to your faith goodness; and to goodness, knowledge; and to knowledge, self-control; and to self-control, perseverance; and to perseverance, godliness; and to godliness, mutual affection; and to mutual affection, love. For if you possess these qualities in increasing measure, they will keep you from being ineffective and unproductive in your knowledge of our Lord Jesus Christ.

Consider the phrase *every effort*, which presses us to find the appropriate means and relationships that will foster ordinary increase in relationship with God. There is a tension to respect here. On the one hand, God is personal Holy Mystery, transcending our every model or formula. Relationship with God is sacred ground, traversed in its own time and manner, subject to no personal or communal plan. On the other hand, we have received a divine mandate to increase and to participate in one another's increase by the intentional use of particular means. Spiritual formation is neither a random effort nor an oppressive assigning of guilt to one another. It is rooted in an authentic aim, in a vision. Christian spiritual formation is *intentional*. This means formation, whether for individuals or for communities, is about taking the next appropriate step forward—with a real idea of what that entails. Consider this account of Russian spiritual master Nil Sorsky:

> The monk had to have a conscious understanding of the goal of perfection and the means most suitable to attain it, along with a willing determination to arrive at that end. Therefore, the individual monk had to understand and be convinced of the instructions given him. Then, by force of conviction, he had to put them into practice in his life. So with Nil, as with the ancient Fathers, no step of perfection was reached unless the monk had grasped for himself with his intellect the importance of a given teaching and then with his will moved his whole being to attain the proposed goal by choosing the best means.[22]

Needless to say, this pursuit cannot happen without the grace of God nor, in nearly all cases, without the support of our communities. Yet there is something about having a vision, an aim, that compels us to increase practices of devotion in our lives. I have heard it said that if you aim at nothing, you are sure to hit it.

What piece of the fullness of human experience is a priority for you? Which are you pursuing these days? Which are you avoiding? In contrast with physical fitness or academic training, spiritual formation seeks to transform a single, identifiable aspect of human life: one's spiritual life, one's relationship with God. But how can God develop a transformational relationship with us without that change influencing other aspects of our life?

In the chapters ahead, I will try to honor this distinction. This is not a manual on social change or evangelism. Many wonderful books on these topics have been written, and I believe that social change and evangelism each will—at some point in time, to some extent—be a part of our maturing in Christ as communities and individuals. But my goal in this book is to acquaint you with the dynamics of relationship with God and spiritual formation such that you will be able to notice the connections between God's invitations and the fullness of your experience, both as a community member and as an individual, and respond appropriately and wisely to God's invitations in the contexts of prayer, community life, mission, and other aspects of your life in Christ.

Going Deeper

1. We have been looking at the various parts of human experience: the different components that make us who we are. And as we have seen, each of us—each individual, each community—possesses a unique configuration of these components. Just as our physical systems are distinctive to us (such that one person's stress is experienced in the digestive system while another's is experienced in neck and shoulder muscles), so too the systems of our soul are distinctive to each of us, whether as individuals or communities. So ask: Am I more intellectual or more emotional? Am I more oriented toward relationships with people or with nature? Does my congregation or other faith community of significance tend to pay attention to experiencing, to evaluating, or to acting? At what level of depth does the community generally express faith when meeting and talking about this or that aspect of relationship with God? Spend a few minutes reflecting (and perhaps journaling) on the character of your

own experience as an individual or community. Who are you, and how does who you are affect your own formation in Christ?

2. We considered a few terms used to identify the aims of Christian spiritual formation. Theologians have pondered and debated the nature of each of these concepts. Theologians have also pondered and debated the wisdom of using several of these terms. Whereas some traditions might urge us on to entire sanctification, others would question the value of this notion. While some consider deification a central doctrine of the Christian faith, others are concerned that it leads us astray from a biblical understanding of our relationship with God. How might we compare each of these terms and the respective traditions that have championed them? Is there a way to reconcile the positive and negative features of these varied yet similar aims of formation? How might our affinity for one or the other of these terms affect our approach to Christian spiritual formation in practice?

3. We have considered not only the implications of the fullness of human experience in personal and corporate expression, but also the unity of the church of Christ more generally. This chapter proposed a model of the unity-in-diversity of Christ's church—a necessary coexistence and co-operation of the body's distinct expressions (contemplative, charismatic, sacramental, social justice, and so on). What do you think of this idea? Is this ecumenism really the answer? What is the relationship between the different traditions of the church and our formation as individuals or communities in Christ? In what ways do we, within our own church or personal spiritual practice, encourage (or discourage) the mutual coopera-tion of traditions or the inclusion of elements from various traditions?

4. One practice that has helped many Christians in their maturing faith is imagining the aims of formation. Whether we speak of holiness or the kingdom of God or simple increase, we can benefit from devoting time and attention to picturing what the achievement of formation might look like in real life. A gymnast might visualize the perfect execution of a complicated routine; likewise, a believer could picture the execu-tion of compassion or other virtues. Just as a mechanic might imagine the best solution to a structural problem in the driveshaft of an old but valued piece of farm machinery, so too devoted Christians can imagine how a life of holiness might best be expressed in the midst of a divided congregation's structural problems. Give it a try. Take some time this week to think about the aims of formation in your life or in the life of your community. What do you discover? How does this simple act (or habit) of reflection shape your formation into Christ?

4

· · · · · · · · · · · · · · · ·

The Contexts and Agents
of Christian Spiritual Formation

Overview

In this chapter, we begin our review of the various elements shaping the nature of Christian spiritual formation and take a brief tour of the contexts within which we are formed. After noting the significance of culture, we consider three types of context that are especially significant for Christian spiritual formation: the home, the congregation, and those countermovements that appear on the fringes of Christianity. Yet even as we consider these contexts, we raise the question of whether these are fully appropriate categories for describing our contexts in twenty-first-century society.

After surveying some important contexts of our formation, we will discuss the agents of our formation—those individuals and communities that take active and responsible roles in our spiritual formation. First, we will set our eyes on the Holy Spirit, the primary agent in Christian spiritual formation. Then we will explore our own role (that is, our own agency in spiritual maturity) before taking a look at the role of others in our own formation, particularly through the ministry of spiritual direction. Finally, we will close with a few words about the counteragents in our spiritual formation: those forces that actively influence individuals and communities to move away from Christlike maturity.

Context

The context surrounding the formation of a flower is really quite simple. There is the soil, which is a blend of nutrients, acids, phosphates, and other chemicals; the proximity to other flowers, which attract pollinators but also facilitate the spread of disease; the insects sharing the ecosystem, which can pollinate or devastate a developing plant; and the climate, comprising heat, precipitation, wind, and so on. If the context is ideal, a flower may thrive easily. If the context is harsh, it will survive only if it is of a hardy variety. Even though my own garden seems ever so mysterious, there are actually a limited number of factors to consider when thinking about the context in which a flower is formed.

The context surrounding the formation of a human being, however, is another story. There is the "soil" where we are raised, though people can be "transplanted" over and over again. We have likely all heard the idiom "raised on foreign soil," which English speakers use to compare how human beings can develop in places that might be unfamiliar. Our use of phrases like *transplanted* and *foreign soil* testifies to the complications of human contexts: the plant-human analogy works, but only to a certain extent. We do not grow in soil the way a plant does. Our relationship to geography is real, but it is not as singular or as involved as that of a flower. (Human contexts are not as firmly "rooted" in the dirt as plants.) Our consumption of nutrients often has less connection to our geography and more to do with culture, whereas a flower needs soil. Human formation depends a great deal on our early development in families, much as a flower's growth is influenced by the plants around it. Human beings struggle to survive in the midst of both a physical climate and a social climate—including education, social status, and employment—similar to a plant's hardiness zone.

The context surrounding the formation of a Christian human is still another story. We must take into consideration physical, cultural, and spiritual climates. Spiritual climates have connection to cultural climates, just as there is still something of England in the Episcopal and Anglican churches in America. Nevertheless, spiritual climate influences our relationship with God; for example, a season of spiritual revival is very different from a season of spiritual drought. Each of these spiritual contexts uniquely affects formation in Christ. (I know. I came to faith during the Jesus movement.)

We are wise to pay attention to the contexts surrounding our formation as humans and as Christians. When failing to take context into consideration, a new youth worker may, for example, encourage those in her care to explore a discipline of fasting, unaware that some may be suffering from eating disorders.

When failing to notice context, newcomers to a new worship culture, say, may attribute energetic worship solely to the ministry of the Holy Spirit, without recognizing the cultural influences. The *intention* of formation must be balanced with the *wisdom* of formation, the latter of which attends to context. Let's look first at our broader cultural contexts before exploring the more particular contexts of home, church, and fringe movements.[1]

Culture

In chapter 1, I described formation as involving a complex of forces. One of the forces influencing the shape of spiritual formation is culture. Shared activities, values, aesthetics, and habits of relating are among the factors that combine to form a given culture. All of this affects how Christians in different cultures experience spiritual formation. Take spiritual direction as an example. Some cultures understand helping relationships such as spiritual direction very hierarchically. People in other cultures would be reticent to receive guidance from spiritual directors outside appropriate kinship relations. One's sense of spiritual experience (whether valued and welcome or dangerous and suspicious), sacramental presence, and virtues of mature faith are all deeply informed by the cultures within which we dwell.

We are wise to take our cultural contexts seriously when attempting to foster mature spiritual formation in Christ. Our cities and workplaces, and therefore our relationships and even our own sense of identity, are increasingly multicultural, so our efforts toward Christian spiritual formation must acknowledge this.[2] We need to be open to the unfamiliar, just as the Jews opened themselves to the unfamiliar when welcoming gentiles—with all their gentile practices and assumptions—to the faith.

Which spiritual disciplines are appropriate? Which are actually counterproductive? How do we structure worship services to glorify God and edify the congregation? What kinds of relationships should be promoted for the best formation of groups and individuals? What does authentic revival look like? All of these questions must be addressed with our cultural contexts in mind.

Lay Spirituality: The Context of the Home

We are formed not only in the broad context of culture but also in the midst of more specific contexts. Dutch Carmelite Kees Waaijman, in his masterful *Spirituality: Forms, Foundations, Methods*, distinguishes between three different forms of lived relationship with God, each of which is realized in its own particular context: lay spirituality, realized in the context of the family;

schools of spirituality, which manifest themselves in the public domain; and countermovements, which occur outside of the cultural and religious consensus.[3] I have long considered Waaijman's categories to be a helpful survey of the basic forms of lived spirituality. And yet, just in the time since the publication of his work, the forces of change have made it necessary to adjust his categories and thus to reexamine the fundamental contexts of Christian spiritual formation.

In the book of Genesis, we read about families and homes. Abraham and Sarah move from Ur to Canaan. We are told where Isaac, Jacob, and Esau lived and whom they married. We also learn where Leah, Rachel, and their many children lived and died. Family life is the context in which their relationship with God was formed. This is lay spiritual formation: a life lived primarily in the midst of work and family, survival and death. Lay spirituality has not received a great deal of attention, but it is a fundamental expression of lived relationship with God. And the home is a significant context of our spiritual formation.

The home is usually where life begins. Even if one is born in a hospital, this new person soon goes home. Our earliest images of God often emerge in the context of our home. This is where we are nurtured—or abused. This is where human experience is shared most deeply with others—or where we are neglected. In many cultures, rituals are performed at home to celebrate key transitions in people's lives. Dwellings are sometimes arranged and decorated to honor the presence of God. At home, among family, is generally where we know one another from birth to death. A special kind of spiritual formation is contextualized over such a time with such an intimate group. And there is tremendous untapped potential for spiritual formation in the context of the ordinary home.

Yet I use the word *home* instead of Waaijman's term, *family*. Times are changing. In much of the West, adults are more likely to be single than married. So-called broken homes are commonplace, even normal. Many people live together in shared arrangements, though they are not a family. In many non-Western cultures, the extended family is the source of life and nurture, though we are seeing how globalization has brought and popularized changes to traditional ways of living family life everywhere. The relationship between parents and children and the degree of independence one has from family members are among the issues being negotiated within the context of globalizing ambiguity.

All of this affects spiritual formation. One family environment will model the love of Jesus differently than another, perhaps in the way each resolves conflict and defends that form of resolution with Christian teaching. The

difference in modeling Christlikeness will in turn influence the spiritual formation of the members of these different families. Consider a few questions:
What does *discernment* mean in a family context in which tradition in the
country of origin dictated that a child submits to parents' decisions, but the
culture of the country in which the family now resides is more progressive
toward a child's freedom to decide and is more openly "Christian" than the
country of origin? Where are spiritual disciplines found in a family life that is
Christian in name but functionally secular? What does home spiritual formation look like in an environment in which family members spend all their time
either working or hidden in their own private worlds of entertainment? These
challenges demonstrate the significance of home for our spiritual formation.
Home is a setting for powerful spiritual formation, but it is also a context
undergoing a great deal of change.

Schools of Spirituality: The Context of the Congregation or Parish

Waaijman defines schools of spirituality as "historical syntheses," naming
the Benedictine centuries, the mendicant orders, and Reformational spirituality as examples.[4] The denominations, orders, and traditions of the Christian
church all can be generally identified as schools. Each started from a "source
experience," and each synthesized a perspective on life and established communities of followers, often creating congregations.[5]

Congregations, or parishes, have been organizing centers of spiritual formation since the beginning of the Christian church. Education, fellowship,
liturgy, and outreach have often been coordinated within the context of a
local congregation or a cluster of congregations in the same denomination.
Congregations have their own networks of supportive and nurturing relationships as well as their own versions of what the aims of Christian spiritual
formation might look like (entire sanctification, baptism in the Spirit, growth
in the Christian life). Therefore, the school or congregation in which we are
formed has a significant influence on our formation itself. I might not learn
about speaking in tongues in a high-church liturgical environment; I might not
learn about the various dark nights of the soul in a Pentecostal environment.
Congregational context both informs and forms. Furthermore, a congregation
supplies the context of individual members' spiritual formation, and that is
important, but the congregation itself is also being formed into Christ as a
unique corporate self. Programs of Christian education, pastoral care, worship planning, and the like contribute to the formational ministry of a local
congregation.[6] Consequently, it is vital that we take the congregational context
into consideration as we understand and practice Christian spiritual formation.

But are local congregations the center of formation they once were? For some people they definitely are, but not for all. Some maintain their faith identity without participating in the life of a local congregation. Many people are networking their spiritual formation these days. One listens to sermons on his iPhone. Another does daily devotions through the website pray-as-you -go.org. Still another attends a Precepts Ministries Bible study with women from several area churches. For better and worse, many Christians around the globe are shopping for the components of their own spiritual formation. And what is delivered through this networking is not a single school of Christian spirituality; it is a collage of viewpoints and practices that is more or less integrated by the individual Christian. Local congregations may have been the central context of spiritual formation in years past, but this may not be the case for many Christians today.[7]

Furthermore, each school of spirituality—as well as each local community and even each individual—possesses a unique blend of skills, attitudes, habits, and values characteristic of its community. Scholars of Christian spirituality use the term *charism* to refer to this blend of approaches to being in relation- ship with God.[8] The notion of charism, which has its roots in the biblical notion of the gifts (Greek *charisma*) with which God graces individuals within the church, is used by students of church history to identify distinct personalities or cultures visible in schools of spirituality and in individuals. We can, then, speak of the differences between a Benedictine and a Franciscan charism. Be- cause charism is part of our context, it is important to acknowledge charism when we approach spiritual formation. By respecting the agency of the Spirit to work through charism, we avoid the dangers of reducing formation to, for example, spiritual disciplines or perseverance in trial. By attending to charism, we recognize the rich and diverse character of formation.

Countermovements: The Contexts of the Margins

"Some people are so profoundly touched by the Absolute that they are drawn outside the cadres of the prevailing cultural and religious consensus," writes Waaijman. "Their intense passion then challenges the established order. Their 'counter-game' deregulates its dominance. Their intransigence breaks its power."[9] Waaijman divides such countermovements into six categories: liberation spirituality, devotion, "ant-agonists" (who live seemingly foolish lives), uprootedness, spirituality of martyrs, and eschatological spirituality. Joan of Arc, Symeon the fool, desert fathers and mothers, and the martyrs are among the case studies he presents. Countermovements challenge the pre- vailing consensus (liberation). Or perhaps they are simply drawn to separate themselves from that consensus (uprootedness). There are simply some who, for God's sake, don't fit in.

Our spiritual formation is conducted not only in the midst of established contexts but also within an awareness—however weak or strong—of the possibilities of what could be. We are aware of a group out there that talks about regularly performing miracles. We are aware that many Christians die as martyrs for professing their faith in Christ. We are aware of Christians who think of church very differently than we do. Our own sense of who we are, of how we are formed, is developed alongside our awareness of where we will go spiritually and where we choose not to go.

Somewhere between schools and countermovements are experiments in consecrated religious life.[10] The Franciscan school of spirituality, with its distinctive viewpoint and practices, began not as an established school but as a countermovement. Many reform movements don't necessarily fit in but choose to stay in proximity in order to serve the church from the edges. Unlike congregations, monastic expressions and outreach movements do not need to provide a full range of sacramental and pastoral services to their membership, and this freedom enables them to be pioneering forces for experimentation. As such, they have the potential to be quite intentional about formation. Indeed, as discussed in chapter 1, one of the earliest contexts for using the phrase and concept of *spiritual formation* was among nuns and monks. I suspect that experimental expressions of religious life today will also serve as powerful creative forces, fostering our formation, as individuals and communities, into the gospel of Christ.

In any case, some elements of the countermovements we've heard about make their way into our own spiritual formation as communities and as individuals. We wonder what experimenting with a season of solitude or praying for miracles might be like. And perhaps one element from a countermovement becomes part of our own pursuit of the faith and influences our formation. Ideas, practices, and perspectives are introduced through awareness of a countermovement toward which we may choose to be formed. One could also simply decide to abandon all tradition and join a countermovement completely or sneak off to the cutting edge and join a new monastic expression. Christian spiritual formation is lived out, however consciously or unconsciously, in the context of both mainstream and uncommon expressions of Christianity.

We pursue our formation in Christ as individuals and communities within the cultures, homes, congregations, networks, and countermovements that surround us, presenting a set of forces within which we discover and live out our growing relationship with God. These contexts form the setting within which the unique gifts or charisms of individuals, communities, and even traditions are discovered and expressed. When we pay attention to these forces, we are better able to make wise choices about how to explore formation. We will address this further in chapter 8, when we consider what it means to be formed together.

Agents

Teachers form young students. The novice mistress of a convent forms the novices. As Christians, we are all subjects of the guidance of the Holy Spirit. Furthermore, we ourselves are actively involved in our own formation, responding to the leading of other people and God. Thus Christian spiritual formation is both a Spirit- and human-led process. By understanding the key agents of spiritual formation and the roles each plays, we equip ourselves to navigate the relationships that will prove most valuable for our formation in Christ. In what follows, I will introduce three separate agents with whom we are in relationship: the Holy Spirit, ourselves, and the spiritual director.[11]

The Holy Spirit

I briefly mentioned the Holy Spirit in the first chapter as I explored what Christian spiritual formation might look like. There I described *spirit* as referring to the core of our person, to the Third Person of the Trinity, and to that which has to do with our relationship with God. It is the second of those references—the Holy Spirit, who is the Third Person of the Trinity—that I am concerned with here, although, as we will see, language for *spirit* and *Spirit* can be a little hard to pin down.[12] That is the way it is with the Spirit of God.[13]

God's story is also a story about the Spirit. The story of the gospel, the "all things new" story, is also a story about God's Spirit, who is for Christians the primary agent of newness. This story begins in the first verse of Genesis, where we read that the Spirit of God (or "wind from God") was hovering over the waters (Gen. 1:2; for spirit as "wind," see Hosea 8:7; 12:2; John 3:8; Heb. 1:7). In the next chapter, we find that the Lord God breathed into Adam the "breath" of life (Gen. 2:7 uses a synonym to the word for spirit used in Gen. 1:2). From the very beginning, we were given spirit from God, and this spirit brings us our life, a life that is truly "in God" (see Job 12:2–10; Ps. 104:29–30; Luke 8:55; James 2:26). The same terms are also used to describe the core of God's personality or self, as is the case in Genesis 6:3, where God says, "My Spirit [spirit] will not contend with humans forever" (see also Ps. 104:29–30). Writing about the use of *spirit* in the Old Testament, theologian Max Turner notes, "If one were to ask Jewish readers of the Hebrew Bible, most would have been liable rather to explain the Spirit as God's *own* life and vitality in action, just as a person's 'spirit' is his or her own 'vitality' or 'life.'"[14] Furthermore, others—even others who do not follow Yahweh—can recognize the influence of this spirit/Spirit in God's people (Gen. 41:38; Dan. 5:11–14).

The Spirit is present at the key periods of history: distributing the power that was on Moses to a group of elders (Num. 11:17–29; see also 27:18) as well as empowering individuals to perform acts of deliverance (Judg. 3:10; 6:34; 14:6, 19) and service (Exod. 28:3; 31:1–3; 35:30–35). All through this history, we see the Spirit of God contributing to the formation of a people conformed to the image of God's person and plan. Unfortunately, God's people repeatedly failed to welcome the Spirit.

Eventually the prophets of Israel began to speak of a time when a fresh work of God's Spirit would characterize the renewal of God's people. The "servant of the Lord" described in Isaiah will be specially equipped by the Spirit (Isa. 42:1–7; 48:16–17). The Spirit of the Lord will rest on the shoot from the stump of Jesse (11:1–2). The ministry of the Spirit of God will equip God's people to follow God, who has provided ways to maintain relationship with God and God's plan (59:21; 61:1–2). As a matter of fact, this new relationship between God's people and the Spirit will be more than a means of maintaining relationship with God; it will be part of the new covenant identity and will be, in itself, the lived reality of that relationship with God (Ezek. 37:1–14).[15]

Jesus was the first to fulfill these prophecies. He was conceived by the power of the Spirit, and his divine birth was confirmed by Spirit-filled prophets (see Luke 1–2). Jesus's baptism was an encounter with the Spirit, after which he was led by the Spirit to be tempted and then returned, full of the Spirit, to proclaim and demonstrate the kingdom of God (Luke 3–4). His life was characterized by a profound sensitivity to the presence and activity of the Spirit of God.[16] Jesus both modeled the new relationship with God's Spirit and promised the same to his followers (John 14–16).

But it took the outpouring of the Spirit at Pentecost for the fullness of the ministry of the Spirit of Christ to be realized. This outpouring was the delivering, re-creating event, giving birth to the Christian church. The new covenant identity was an identity of relationship with the Spirit. "Repent and be baptized," Peter exhorts, "and you will receive the gift of the Holy Spirit" (Acts 2:38). Again and again we hear that receiving the Spirit is essential to Christian identity (8:15; 10:44; 19:1–2). The very invitation to those who might become Christians asks them to welcome this Spirit.

But most significantly for our purposes, the Spirit is the key to the maintenance of relationship with God and formation into conformity with Christ's life and purposes. As we have already seen, the Spirit is the very source of re-creation and new life. We call it being "born again" in the Spirit (John 3:5–8). This itself is a profound work of formation, but there is more to come. The Spirit is also an aim of formation. It is *spiritual* formation that we are after—life in ever-deepening relationship to the Spirit of Christ. If the Spirit of God is the presence of God in our midst, then relationship with God is relationship with the Spirit of God. Learning to walk in the Spirit—in all areas of life—is really another way of describing what Christian spiritual formation is all about.

This brings us, then, to an account of the Holy Spirit as an agent of Christian spiritual formation. The Holy Spirit is both personal and divine.[17] Consequently, my relationship with the Spirit of God is a relationship with One who can initiate communication, effect change, and foster increasing conformity with the person and plan of Christ. But how is this done?

The Spirit is a revealer of truth. The Spirit of God introduces the thoughts of God into our mind and heart, bringing illumination, conviction, and confirmation of God's truth (John 14:16–17; 15:26; 16:13; Acts 15:28; Rom. 8:16; Eph. 3:16–19; 2 Tim. 1:14; 1 John 4:6; note both the communal and individual contexts reflected in these passages).

The Spirit is also an agent of moral renewal. While seldom mentioned in the Old Testament (yet see Mic. 3:8; Isa. 4:4; 32:15; Ps. 143:10; Ezek. 11:18–20; and [significantly] Ezek. 36–37), this theme is prominent in the New. Our baptism in the Spirit is an immersion into a fire of renewal (Luke 3:16; John 1:33). The Spirit will bring to mind the things of Christ (John 14:26), reminding us of the instructions from the Sermon on the Mount and other truths. The Spirit leads and prompts us toward the good (Rom. 8:14). When living "in the Spirit," one dwells in a sphere in which one's habits and desires are under divine control rather than being directed by the flesh. The Spirit fills us, indwells us, and sanctifies us. Remember, we are dealing with a *Holy* Spirit.

The Holy Spirit is also an agent of righteous relationships. We are baptized through the Spirit into one body (1 Cor. 12:13). We experience, through the Spirit, occasions wherein our relationships with others are nurtured and developed (Acts 2:4, 42–47; 4:31–35; 13:2; 15:28; Eph. 5:18–19). The Spirit fosters interpersonal virtues (Rom. 14:17; Col. 1:8). The Holy Spirit edifies and equips the body through distributing gifts (1 Cor. 12:4–11). And, finally, the Spirit unites us as communities of God's people (Eph. 4:3–4; Phil. 1:27; Jude 19).

The Spirit of Christ empowers us for the mission of Christ, part of which entails the Spirit's being present in the very act of making us new in character, habit, and relationship with God; making us righteous in relationships; making us grow in truth; and making us a "light to the nations" (Isa. 51:4).

But further—or more specifically—the Spirit also arranges evangelistic appointments and strategies (Acts 8:29; 9:17; 13:2), empowers both the proclamation of the gospel in word and the demonstration of the gospel in deed (Luke 4:18; Acts 4:8; Rom. 15:16–19; 1 Cor. 2:4; 1 Pet. 2:12), completes the effectiveness of words and deeds (Acts 1:8; 10:38; 1 Thess. 1:5; Heb. 2:4), convicts the receivers of the message (John 16:8–11), and regenerates those who believe (John 3:5–8).

Finally, we can speak of the Spirit as the agent of our formation in worship. Jesus describes the purpose of the Holy Spirit as bringing glory to God (John 16:14). Again and again the Holy Spirit prompts acts of worship (Luke 1:35, 41, 67; 2:25–32; Acts 2:4; 10:44–47; 13:52; 19:6; Rom. 8:15; Eph. 5:18–19). The Holy Spirit responds to our worship (Acts 4:31; 13:2). The Spirit (or a God-oriented spirit) is described as the sphere within which we worship (John 4:23–24; 1 Cor. 14:2, 15; Jude 20) and as the One who stimulates emotions appropriate to worship (Rom. 5:5; 8:6–27; 12:11; 15:13; 2 Cor. 3:17; Col. 1:8; 1 Thess. 1:6; and many other places).

The above outline is sufficient to show that the Holy Spirit is the central agent of formation for Christians. Our formation as Christians is truly a formation "in the Spirit." The steps we take toward "all things new" in this life are made under the leadership of the Spirit of Christ. What we have not developed yet is just how the Spirit does this. We will explore this in the chapters ahead.

Ourselves

Though it is the primary agent in Christian spiritual formation, the Holy Spirit is not the only agent. We ourselves play distinct roles in our own formation as Christians. We live in the Spirit. We attend. We notice. We discern. We respond. We integrate and live again. When we learn to follow the lead of the Holy Spirit, we can find the momentum of our formation and learn to stay with it, for the benefit of our own maturity and for the gospel of Christ.

Consider too how embedded within our ways of thinking and speaking about ourselves are guiding values, emotional concerns, and well-established habits that govern our lives at a just-conscious or just-below-conscious level. Though Joe may not have thought about the philosophical ins and outs of the meaning of life, he can probably tell you that getting ahead in life is one of his guiding values. Adriana may not be able to unearth her emotional history, but she can probably tell you that safety is a concern of hers. Sometimes our values, concerns, and habits are not really distinct. Values are established, in part, to protect emotional concerns (which may, in turn, be shaped by deeper, unconscious, unmet needs in our past). Emotional concerns may function to maintain well-established habits, even habits we wish we did not have. Basic habits may be formed in the context of deeply rooted values. Our own self-image and self-development are exceptionally complex, arising from the interplay of historical, geographic, cultural, and spiritual factors, among others.

Yet—and here is my point—the construction of an individual self is not just a passive coalescing of various forces (mere conditioning). It is also an active crafting. Certain patterns of thoughts, feelings, or actions gain dominance in our lives through our choices: they become habits. This self-invested patterning of human experience leads to the development of inclinations toward thoughts, feelings, relationships, and the like. As research in neuroplasticity reveals, "neurons that fire together, wire together."[18] We establish tendencies to make decisions in certain ways, and one might call this a form of will. In the blend of forces surrounding us, we synthesize a sense of what is important, and from here our aims, motives, and expectations arise. I call this the activity of current self-construction.[19]

Furthermore, this self-construction is accomplished within basic orientations. As we learned in our discussion of feelings, humans tend to develop concerns that, consciously or unconsciously, shape our actions. What I did not mention there is that we also establish basic orientations that guide the character of our concerns. Self-orientation, for example, organizes experience around aspects of self-concern, such as concern about advantage or the perceived fulfillment of a deep need, the latter of which may drive one to lead a private life despite great risk. Yet we can also act out of an other-orientation—acting strictly from a sense of the worth of, the value of, or our obligation to another. "You are my everything," one proclaims to the beloved and proves it by manifesting rage when someone hurts that loved one or by making a habit of waking up early (contrary to our natural tendencies) just to spend some time together before the workday starts. This is not about what we get out of it. Rather, it is about our sheer appreciation for the other. Over time, our admiration for the other leads to sharing the other's values, viewpoints, concerns, and habits. In other-orientation reasoning, emotional inclinations, arousal, personal motives, and such develop within the context of a fundamental arrangement of our concerns around another value or person. And this orientation develops by our own chosen participation and investment. We are, even as simple human beings, agents of our own formation.

Now we can begin to understand the self's roles in our own Christian spiritual formation. I will summarize by describing two separate roles, the first with reference to the aims of spiritual formation and the second with reference to the agency of the Holy Spirit.

First, our role in our own formation is to see with the eyes of faith and to act—even aggressively—into that sight. Christian belief is not a passive acceptance of a set of intellectual propositions; it is a life-changing reorientation toward the truth of the gospel. This is a fundamental framework of Pauline ethics: the relationship between the indicative (who we are in light of Christ) and the imperative (how we are to live).[20] For example, Paul declares in Ephesians that we are saved through faith (Eph. 2:8) and goes on to remind his readers of who they were (separate, far away) and who they are now (brought near, included), adding that God's "purpose was to create in himself one new humanity" (2:15). Again Paul reminds them that they are no longer strangers, but fellow citizens being built together (the transition to ongoing formation) "to become a dwelling in which God lives by his Spirit" (2:22). This is the indicative, who we are. And Paul urges his readers to see their identity—and to concretely think of themselves, to construct themselves—in light of this truth.

Then, after a prayer in Ephesians 3, comes the imperative: "I urge you to live a life worthy of the calling you have received" (Eph. 4:1). What is that calling they have received? To become a dwelling in which God lives by his Spirit. This is part of the "all things new" gospel as expressed in Pauline language and could be paraphrased as, "Become what I have made you (by the life and work of Christ and the ministry of the Holy Spirit) to be." Paul follows this with a list of instructions and exhortations: "You must no longer live as the Gentiles do." "You were taught . . . to put off your old self, . . . to be made new, . . . to put on the new self." "Walk in the way of love." "Live as children of light" (4:17–5:8; notice also the instructions in these passages). The choice to embrace a corporate or individual identity, which has been provided for us through Christ, is active and even aggressive ("Have nothing to do with the fruitless deeds of darkness," 5:11). Our ongoing self-construction happens in the light of a fundamental orientation to the Holy Other, the trinitarian God, making use of whatever means are appropriate to our context. We assume that our connection to Christ will bring forth a transformation (whether suddenly or gradually) of our values, our habits, our relationships—indeed of any or every aspect of our human experience. Our job is to see by faith and to act accordingly.

Spiritual writer Richard Lovelace describes this living by faith as appropriating "primary elements of continual renewal."[21] You live into who you are: you are accepted (justification), you are free from bondage to sin (sanctification), you are not alone (the Holy Spirit dwells within), and you are in command (authority in conflict). As we read about in the previous chapter, Russian monk Nil Sorsky "had to have a conscious understanding of the goal of perfection and the means most suitable to attain it, along with a willing determination to arrive at that end. Therefore, the individual monk had to understand and be convinced of the instructions given him. Then, by force of conviction, he had to put them into practice in his life."[22] This is living by faith. Philosopher and spiritual writer Dallas Willard—using a framework of vision, intention, and means—posits that our role in spiritual formation, at least with regard to our aims, is to see our calling (vision) and to act (intention) into that calling, making use of whatever methods (means) are most appropriate. This too is living by faith.

Second, regarding the agency of the Holy Spirit, our role in spiritual formation is to attend to the active presence of the Holy Spirit and to respond. In this present age, the Holy Spirit is the chief initiator of our formation in Christ. Once again, this is a primary theme in the Pauline Epistles: we are to live by the Spirit. The New Testament urges Christians to receive the Spirit and then to set our mind on the Spirit. We are exhorted to follow, to obey, to be led by, and to walk in the Spirit. All of this requires a certain degree of attention to the thoughts, feelings, inclinations, and such that the Holy Spirit uses to initiate transformation in our lives as communities and individuals. We must open ourselves to the active presence of the Spirit, placing ourselves within those environments where the Holy Spirit is frequently manifest. We must learn to notice and to discern the voice of the Spirit. And we must soften ourselves to respond with consent to the Spirit's leading. We fulfill our role with regard to the leading of the Spirit when we are most carefully attending and most radically obeying. We construct our selves in each moment, each activity, each habit of thought or feeling—all in response to our perception of the Spirit's influence in our life. And, as with our approach to the aims of Christian spiritual formation, we are obliged to make good use of whatever means are most appropriate for us to fulfill our role. This is living in the Spirit.

The Holy Spirit is the Christian's primary agent of spiritual formation, and yet we too play a role in our own ongoing formation into the fullness of Christ. We live by faith, recognizing (believing) who we are and acting in such a way as to live into the "all things new" vision. We live in the Spirit, paying attention to the active presence of God through the Spirit and responding appropriately. In both of these roles, we make use of various means through which we perceive the Spirit, see our calling and charism, and respond to God's invitation. We will explore the means of formation in chapter 6.

Spiritual Direction

Obviously, other people also play a role in our Christian spiritual formation. Parents influence children over years of intimate contact. We may receive prayer from a friend for some issue only to receive far more than just prayer. Others shape our formation in subtle, informal ways as we sense their approval or disapproval. Teachers, pastors, and other leaders also play more formal roles as agents of our formation as Christians. In this section, I will introduce one type of agency that is common among Christians and that has been a significant contribution to Christian spiritual formation since the relationship between Jesus and his beloved disciple: the one-on-one helping relationship, which I call the spiritual direction relationship.

This kind of relationship has not always been called spiritual direction, and there are a few different relationships that have some kind of family resemblance to what I am calling spiritual direction. In fourth-century Egypt, people used the term *getting a word* to describe the wise counsel received from an Abba or Amma (a spiritual father or mother, respectively). In the medieval West, it was common to have a person, often a priest, to whom one confessed and from whom one received counsel and absolution; this person was known as a *confessor*. The phrase *cure of* or *care of souls* (Latin *cura animarum*) was commonly used to describe the ministry of one-on-one assistance to people regarding matters other than physical well-being. Puritan divines encouraged believers to meet privately in what they called a *conference*. Of course, the phrase *spiritual direction*, common throughout much of Christian history, expressed relationships that might appear different to people in various eras.[23] People today use the terms *Christian counseling*, *discipleship*, *coaching*, and *spiritual direction*, and each has its own particular nuance. Figure 4.1 (p. 78) provides a simple outline of the features of some of these one-on-one relationships. My intent is not to quibble with vocabulary but rather to look at the general ministry of one-on-one helping relationships. I will use the term *spiritual direction* in this text, insofar as such a relationship includes some kind of spiritual goal and uses spiritual means to accomplish certain ends.

Authors William Barry and William Connolly, both Jesuits, offer one of the better definitions of spiritual direction: "We define Christian spiritual direction, then, as help given by one Christian to another which enables that person to pay attention to God's personal communication to him or her, to respond to this personally communicating God, to grow in intimacy with this God, and to live out the consequences of this relationship."[24] This definition emphasizes the personal intimacy aspect of Christian life, perhaps to the neglect of other aspects of the Christian "all things new" gospel. Nonetheless, it provides a clear outline of the main features of a spiritual direction relationship.

First, a spiritual direction relationship is one of help or care. As a spiritual director, I give what I have in order to help the directee's formation in Christ

Figure 4.1
One-on-One Relationships

	Friendship	Spiritual Direction	Evangelism	Mentoring	Counseling
1. Orientation of the relationship	"play"	"presence"	"position"	"plan"	"problem"
2. Goals of the relationship	mutual	spiritual	spiritual	spiritual/ practical	psychological/ spiritual
3. Means used in the relationship	varies	spiritual plus	varies	practical/ spiritual	psychological plus
4. Mode of relating	sharing	being/watching	persuading/ demonstrating	equipping	restoring
5. Does one of the people come for help with a problem?	both	no	yes	perhaps	yes
6. Duration of the relationship	varies	long, varies	varies	varies	until problem ends
7. Frequency of meetings	often	varies	varies	varies	regular
8. Setting of the meetings	varies	carefully chosen	many	varies	usually office

through the Holy Spirit. Sometimes all I have to offer is a listening ear. How many people have someone who will listen for as long as it takes as they pour out themselves freely, revealing weaknesses right and left? In today's busy world, the art of unrushed listening is a precious treasure. This listening is especially valuable if it is done in stereo, so to speak; that is, you can learn to listen attentively (with your ears, eyes, heart, and body) to another person even as you are also listening for the voice of God's Spirit. It is from this stereo listening that insights, or words of salvation, come.

But there are other forms of help we can also offer. Often spiritual directors are those who have walked the journey a bit further and a bit longer than the ones they are directing. That experience, especially when supplemented by good education, enables the director to notice traps from the accuser as well as openings, invitations, and subtle signs of the Spirit. Directors offer help to directees when they share—at the right time, in the right manner—what they have learned. Directors can offer guidance, support, and encouragement and can be present to celebrate directees' recognition of the active presence of the Spirit, even in the smallest feature of life. Directors rehearse and share the vision of the gospel: you are accepted, you are free from the bondage to sin, you are not alone, you are in command, and all things can be made new. They ask good questions at the appropriate times, and they accompany directees through long trials, listening to their rants and lamentations. Directors remind directees what they said last week about what they deemed important and, at their request, hold them accountable for the steps they intend to take.

Different people and different models tend to emphasize slightly different elements of the spiritual direction relationship. For one director, it may be a charismatic ministry of prayer. For another, it may be standing beside directees through thick and thin. For still another, direction may look like instruction, with the director using the classics of Christian spirituality to illuminate a directee's experience. Each director employs a variety of skills and activities—listening, probing, encouraging, setting goals, discerning, prophecy, healing, teaching—while offering one-on-one help. This variety is reflected in the many images of the spiritual director: doctor, counselor, intercessor, mediator, host, teacher, midwife. But in any case, the point of a spiritual direction relationship is that a person comes alongside another to offer help, given in love.

Second, a spiritual direction relationship is centered on a person's relationship with God. This is perhaps the strongest distinction between spiritual direction and mentoring (though the terms overlap at times). While mentoring often involves facilitating some particular element of life (such as one's leadership skills), spiritual direction is primarily focused on our relationship with God. But of course this gets complicated, because—as we have already learned—every aspect of life is implicated in authentic relationship with God. *All* things are being made new. Nonetheless, the ministry of a spiritual director is to help the directee to draw connections between God and life, watching for subtle signs of the Spirit. The spiritual director acknowledges grace when it is present. An informed director brings history and theology to bear when it is the right time to do so. And finally, and perhaps most importantly, a director intercedes on the directee's behalf.

Finally, the spiritual direction relationship helps a directee to respond, to live out the consequences of being in relationship with God. Often it is not enough, at least in the long run, simply to pat someone on the back and affirm God's presence in our lives. As an agent of spiritual formation, a director helps others respond to the Spirit and act out their vision of the gospel in their lives. Thus directors learn not only to walk with directees but also to lead them to green pastures. There are times when a spiritual director—who has earned this right in relationship with a directee and in the Spirit—must issue a warning. There are times when others ask a director for ideas about disciplines, practices, relationships, expressions, experiments, and so on. And there are times when a director is asked to hold a directee to account for disciplines and practices and so on. These are aspects of walking with another on a spiritual journey.

The burden of a spiritual director is great. If you seek to become one, be prepared to cry. You must be "prayed up" or "soaked in prayer," as some traditions say, if you are to take on this ministry. It is a ministry of agency that is (and should be) usually recognized and initiated by others' spontaneous requests and informal acknowledgments. You may suspect that you have the gift or role of spiritual director because others keep asking you to listen, to offer a word, to tell your story. It is not enough to take a class or read a few books before announcing that you're available for spiritual direction. The anointing of a spiritual director comes from the Spirit. Yet there are two kinds of authority connected to this ministry of agency. Most fundamentally, there is the authority of the Spirit. Those whom we respect as spiritual directors carry this authority and do so humbly, and we can perceive it in their ministry. It is apparent in the way they love, in the way they listen, and in the way they act. In addition, directors may be under a formal institutional authority. Some are appointed to oversee the development of others in their community. Pastors, novice masters, ministry coaches within an organization, and the like have some element of formal authority connected with their role and agency as a spiritual director. The nature of this authority, including the origins of the relationship itself—namely, who called whom—shapes the character of that relationship. This is the mix of both agency in and context of Christian spiritual formation.

Whether formal or informal, the work of spiritual direction is a wonderful ministry. The body of Christ needs many more people who are willing, sensitive, and trained as spiritual directors. Intimate spiritual guidance is one of the present generation's deepest needs. The agency of the Holy Spirit and the agency of the self often need help working in tandem. Bringing that about is the role of a good spiritual director.

Counteragents

We have established that the Holy Spirit, the self, and others—particularly in the ministry of one-on-one spiritual direction—are agents of spiritual formation. Many more agents could have been included: wise grandparents, prayer groups, and such. Still, the agents presented provide a sufficient sense of what it means to be an agent of spiritual formation. Nevertheless, preparation for spiritual formation should include a discussion of counteragents.

Just as we can talk about countermovements, which are expressions of Christian spirituality that do not always conform to the current consensus on how Christian life is to be lived, so also we can speak of counteragents. But whereas countermovements are forces supporting the Christian cause, however unusual their expression, counteragents are agents (specific individuals or groups with particular roles in our formation) whose role is to drive us *away* from formation in Christ. They act *counter* not simply to current Christian consensus but to the gospel itself. It is important to recognize that we are influenced both by the work of agents that support the gospel and by forces acting counter to the gospel—identified throughout Christian history as the *world*, the *flesh*, and the *devil*. An extended section on our response to these counteragents will come in chapter 9 when I address spiritual warfare.

Going Deeper

1. We have learned in this chapter that wise spiritual formation attends to context. But how do we do that? How do we recognize the influence of the contexts of a culture, home, congregation, or countermovement in the life of a community or in our own life? How do we discover or name the charism of a given individual or community? More particularly, what steps can you take to practice the art of discerning contexts in your own life and in the lives of others?

2. Should we even be concerned with context? Doesn't Christ transcend context? Shouldn't all Christians simply grow closer together, no matter what culture they identify with, as they grow in Christlikeness? Rather than paying attention to culture, aren't we wiser still just to point people to Jesus?

3. Discussions of the contexts of home, school and congregation, and countermovement—along with the idea of the agency of another person—almost of necessity include the question of authority. The authority exercised in these contexts can be oppressive on one extreme or laissez-faire on the other. Needless to say, our experience of authority deeply influences our formation in life and in Christ. Is there a right way to exercise authority in a home, a congregation, or even a countermovement such that it best facilitates Christian spiritual formation? How best can we foster our own (or another's) formation in various authority conditions?

4. Describing context is a practice that has nurtured the spiritual growth of many. Imagine, for example, struggling with a particular vice or

personality characteristic that seems to be an obstacle on the path of spiritual maturity. Sometimes it can be helpful to sit down (alone or with a spiritual director) and examine every element of context and how it may have influenced your present situation. Are there physiological components to this situation? How do they affect your life here and now? How have you developed socially? What kinds of expectations from the world have you (consciously or unconsciously) believed? What doctrines have been important to you or to the tradition within which you have developed, and how do they affect your sense of this situation? What models in community have you witnessed, and what have they spoken to you? If you continue this line of probing, you may find a rich perspective from which to view your own current place before God.

5. Another practice that flows from the insights of this chapter is that of relationship. Different cultures "do relationship" differently, and so no single, simple model of appropriate spiritual direction relationship can be given. And yet some basic principles—including regular communication, careful and prayerful listening, spiritual focus, and practical aims—can be encouraged in perhaps every culture. Experiment with spiritual direction by meeting for a season, either formally or informally, with someone you trust. Talk to that person about your spiritual life. What does she notice as she listens to you? How does God speak or touch within this relationship? What do you learn about your relationship with God or about spiritual formation from this time of relationship with a spiritual director?

5

The Process of Transformation and the Task of Formation

Overview

In this chapter, we examine two more primary elements of Christian spiritual formation: the process and task of formation. The process brings about transformation, involving both the divine and the human. So we will begin by pondering the broad and ongoing character of Christian salvation and the implications of salvation for our ongoing transformation. This grand approach to salvation and transformation then leads us to consider Christian maturity as an idea and an experience, particularly those stages of ongoing Christian growth recognized throughout Christian history.

Having learned something about most of the primary elements undergirding Christian spiritual formation—aims, contexts, agents, and process—we will take a closer look at the task of Christian spiritual formation itself as understood from the perspective of the human participant. We close the chapter by defining the task of formation and suggesting a number of steps or activities frequently associated with this task.

Christian spiritual formation is ultimately about change: transformation and conversion. We have all heard the stories, or testimonies, as we call them. We tell people stories about how our lives have been changed by the transforming work of Christ and the Holy Spirit, testifying to the reality of the

Christian faith.[1] When someone asks me to tell my story, I frequently recount some of my "conversions": from a lonely junior high school boy to someone with a "special best friend," to a young man who experienced God through social justice, to a man committed to a life of contemplative prayer, to a pastor ministering under the power of healing prayer, and on and on. Each conversion added a new layer of experience to my previous sense of what relationship with God was all about. (Hint: he was making "all things new"!) Each conversion also introduced new experiments in formation. I discovered new aims, connected with new agents, and employed new means of growth that were appropriate for each season of my Christian life. Because Christian spiritual formation combines divine initiation and human response in a re-creative process that involves both the transformation of God and the task of Christian communities and individuals, the Spirit's transforming work guided my own spiritual formation work.

This chapter is about that connection: the process of transformation and the task of Christian spiritual formation. To get our bearings, however, let us review what we have covered so far. In the first chapter, we worked our way to a definition of Christian spiritual formation, one that would guide the development of the rest of this book. I defined Christian spiritual formation as a Spirit- and human-led process by which individuals and communities mature in relationship with the Christian God and are changed into ever-greater likeness to the life and gospel of this God. In chapters 2 and 3, we explored the big vision of Christian spiritual formation—the "all things new" story of the Christian faith—and the fullness of human experience. These chapters provided a sense of the aims of formation—namely, what this likeness to the life and gospel mean. In the previous chapter, we discussed the contexts and agents of Christian spiritual formation. We reflected on how our formation in Christ is lived out amid cultures and forms of lived relationship with Christ (lay, school, countermovement) and among the agents of our formation (the Holy Spirit, ourselves, spiritual directors). And we discovered something about what Spirit- and human-led processes of formation might look like. In the chapter ahead we will explore the means of formation: the activities, conditions, and relationships that foster growth in Christlikeness.

In the present chapter, then, we look at the process, the change of formation itself. As I mentioned in our first chapter, everything is changing—is being formed—all the time. But a special kind of change happens when communities and individuals are influenced by the Christian God. This is the change we want to examine more closely in the present chapter. This change is transformation. Then, once we have examined the process of transformation, we can describe the task of Christian spiritual formation.

Transformation

Transformation is the change from something that was into something different that is. Perhaps my favorite image of transformation is a simple chemistry demonstration that I saw when I was young and that I recently reconstructed. I took a test tube (an old glass bottle I found in the recycle bin), cleaned it, dried it, and poured in two spoonfuls of white sugar. Then I turned on the Bunsen burner (our gas cooktop), held the "test tube" over the "Bunsen burner" using tongs, and observed what happened. Sure enough, in a couple of minutes, the bottle broke and I had sugar and broken glass all over the stove.

Once I cleaned up the mess I tried again, this time with the sugar in a different test tube (a metal measuring cup). I also turned the flame down a little, so that the heating would occur more slowly. As the sugar began to absorb heat, I saw the crystals on the edges start to melt little by little. First the liquid was clear, then yellow, then brown, getting darker all the time. The liquid area started to bubble, first just a little and then more. I watched as the amount of bubbling liquid increased and the amount of crystallized sugar decreased. A stinky gas rose from the mixture (so I ran to open the door and turned a fan on to clear the smoke out of the kitchen). The bubbling mixture got darker and thicker; there was a time when you couldn't tell just what it had been or what it might become. It bubbled up and formed a kind of balloon inside the measuring cup. (I thought it was going to drip out over the stove for a moment.) Then the bubbling died down and the mixture got drier. Soon the stuff seemed to stabilize: a black, hard, dry, airy substance that looked kind of like the surface of the moon. Cool! One moment I had pure white sugar, and now I had this black ball inside my measuring cup. Transformation!

Another enduring image of transformation is that of a pilgrimage—a journey from the starting place to a holy destination, a journey wherein the person who finishes the journey is different than the person who began it. During a pilgrimage, one encounters catalysts, forces that stimulate change. Just as happens in chemical transformations, there may be times when it is not clear to the pilgrim who she is or what she is becoming. Small changes at one point could end up fostering great changes further down the road. But good pilgrimages, like good lab demonstrations, move ultimately from uncertain identity to a new, certain identity.[2]

The point of these illustrations is that transformation is a process of change. Whether we are talking about chemicals or a personal pilgrimage, transformation is about change over time. Sometimes the change is slow, even barely perceptible. A pilgrim who concludes the journey is a different person than he was when he began, though he may not be able to say just when that change took place. In other seasons, we may be keenly aware when the heat reached its peak and everything suddenly changed. As a process of change, transformation—such as Christian spiritual formation—involves a variety of factors that influence one another: the heat of the Bunsen burner and the material of the container, the expectations of the pilgrim and the dangers of the road, the sovereign grace of God's Spirit and the unique personality of the congregation. The process of Christian spiritual formation is rooted in the interplay of divine and human. The preached Word strikes your mind just as you were seeking truth about a matter, and you understand, and then live out, your faith differently. You experience, through the care of a community in a time of great pain, a living demonstration of God's love and, consequently, permit yourself to really believe, deep inside, that God can love you for who you really are. Formation assumes the ongoing work of transformation. And a belief in ongoing transformation assumes something about salvation.

So our next task is to contemplate Christian salvation.

Salvation

The theological term for this transformational change is *salvation*. When we learned the story of formation in chapter 2, we found that we cannot understand Christian spiritual formation apart from a knowledge of the Trinity, redemption, and so on. Certainly the doctrine of salvation (known as *soteriology*) is relevant to our practice of Christian spiritual formation. But just what is salvation? And what does it mean for an individual's ongoing development in Christlikeness or for life as the people of God? Salvation is another way of looking at the "all things new" story. We inhabit this salvation story as we appreciate the greatness of human experience and move from tragedy to restoration.[3] As Christians, we inhabit the framework of salvation somewhere in the midst of initial and ongoing salvation.[4] Thus, keeping in mind these markers of where we are, I will focus our soteriological lens on a couple of issues that are especially relevant to pursuing Christian spiritual formation.[5]

The first issue is the very inclusion of ongoing transformation as part of salvation. Some Christian traditions see deification (our participation in the life and nature of Christ; see chap. 3) as the essence of salvation, in which justification and sanctification are not clearly distinguished.[6] Others distinguish carefully between an initial justification and a subsequent sanctification.[7] What is relevant here is that however one parses these, ongoing transformation into likeness to Christ must be considered part of Christian salvation. This is precisely how the New Testament uses the word *salvation*. In some of the Epistles, we read that we were saved when we first made a commitment to Christ and received the Holy Spirit. "He saved us," we read in Titus, "not because of righteous things we had done, but because of his mercy. He saved us through the washing of rebirth and renewal by the Holy Spirit" (Titus 3:5). Yet elsewhere the Epistles remind us that we are saved by the gospel, if we hold firmly to the apostles' teaching (1 Cor. 15:2). The great theological synthesizers of the late patristic period (such as Maximus the Confessor in the East and Augustine in the West) recognized ongoing participation (Maximus) or perseverance (Augustine) to be an essential component of authentic salvation in Christ.[8] Protestants discuss which component should be placed in which order, but all recognize that faith, repentance, sanctification, and perseverance are part of a single "order of salvation" (Latin *ordo salutis*).[9] Following Scripture and tradition, our approach to Christian spiritual formation must see spiritual formation as part of God's larger work of salvation.

The second issue regards the breadth of salvation. Some see salvation as a matter of our personal appropriation of God's forgiving work on the cross. Others speak of salvation in terms of social justice or charismatic healings. Which is it?

The Greek words for salvation (*sōzō*, "save"; *sōtēria*, "salvation") are used throughout the New Testament, with various meanings. In Acts 16:31 Paul and Silas encourage their jailer to "believe in the Lord Jesus, and you will be saved [*sōthēsē*, from *sōzō*]." In Luke 7:50, we find a sinful woman receiving forgiveness when Jesus tells her, "Your faith has saved [*sesōken*, from *sōzō*] you." Jesus also says the same words to a man who received his sight: "Your faith has healed [*sesōken*, from *sōzō*] you" (Luke 18:42). And in the very next chapter of Luke we find a repentant Zacchaeus redistributing his ill-gotten gains. Jesus responds to Zacchaeus's act simply by saying, "Today salvation [*sōtēria*] has come to this house" (Luke 19:9). Biblically speaking, the notion of salvation refers to the restoration of any aspect of the fullness of human experience.

Just think of the word *saved*. To be saved is to be saved from something. Humans are inescapably captive to sin, lost under the guidance of the devil, oppressed by systemic evils.[10] We are not capable of rescuing ourselves. And the breadth of this tragedy is as wide as human experience itself. We are alienated from God, from one another, from ourselves, and from our rule over creation. Regarding our relationship to creation, the Reformer Martin Bucer writes,

> With the loss of the knowledge of God we have lost also the knowledge of creatures. As we no longer wish to live to serve God, His creatures were rightly taken away from our service. . . . Thus the whole creation, which should have been used for the praise and glory of its Creator and for the preservation and

profit of men, has been disgraced, profaned, and depraved by our diabolical use and self-seeking.[11]

Our thoughts tend toward error, our feelings are governed by self-centered concerns, and we choose our actions from avoidance or rebellion rather than consent to God. All of our relationships are twisted. Rather than being a light to the nations, we've become an institution of darkness. From the shallows to the very depths of our experience, we are in need of a savior.

And this is precisely what Christ has done for us. When we were lost, Christ showed us righteousness through his life. When we were captive to sin, God forgave our debt through Christ's death and made us victorious through the Spirit. When we were oppressed by the devil and by evil social structures, Christ gave us authority over Satan and instituted the church. As we have learned in the previous chapters, our Savior has opened the way to restoration in every aspect of human experience. Bucer goes on to describe the final restoration:

> Then shall the creatures also become free from serving corrupt existence in order to share the glorious freedom of the children of God. . . . When the created shall again stand in its original order, when each creature shall be directed to the other for its utility, joy, and blessedness, then God, with His elect, will again look with favor at His creatures, at the entire creation, which, as at the beginning, shall be very good.[12]

Christian spiritual formation is the ongoing process we undergo to live into that future salvation. This has implications for our sense of acceptance by God. It also has implications for our own relationship with the creatures of the earth. The future informs the present. The indicative, as I noted above, informs the imperative. Bucer concludes, "From all this it is clear that no one should live for himself, because God created all things so that they might contribute not to their own good but to that of others, and be an instrument and evidence of the divine goodness which all things should express and spread forth."[13] This, then, is our salvation insofar as it informs the practice of spiritual formation. Salvation is the freeing up of the people of God in order that we might rejoin the mission of God for the sake of the glory of God, the benefit of the world, and the profit of our own life. When we, as communities and individuals, begin to think like Jesus, to feel for others like Jesus, and to love and to heal like Jesus, then formation, mission, and community join in one expanding experience of salvation.

The breadth of God's salvation ushers us, therefore, into an ongoing life of broad transformation. The Spirit touches this aspect of our lives, and then that one, and we respond. Ongoing salvation will address different aspects of our lives at different times. In a sense, we may experience many conversions in our lives: moments or seasons in which we reencounter the gospel or fresh aspects of the gospel. Monk and theologian Thomas Merton writes, "We are not converted only once in our lives, but many times; and this endless series of large and small conversions, inner revolutions, leads to our transformation in Christ."[14] Similarly, following the lead of Jesuit scholar Donald Gelpi, I have identified a number of forms of conversion: moral, religious, affective, intellectual, social, and ecological.[15]

With regard to Christian spiritual formation, the point is this: we are wise to pay attention to the breadth of transformation. (I described the range of my own conversions at the start of this chapter.) But how do we engage this as ministers of formation? For example, let's say you are a new pastor in an old and shrinking congregation. As you listen to members of the congregation tell their story, you learn that long, long ago, the congregation went through a powerful season of spiritual renewal and congregational unity. This local body clearly experienced some kind of affective conversion, engaging their emotions. But that was long ago, and members are now older and, honestly, drier. They have weathered doctrinal controversies admirably and been faithful to follow the Lord's lead into community service. But as you hear their stories, you sense a longing for the experiences of earlier times. Just what is this longing you perceive? Is this merely nostalgia, or could this be the spark of a divine invitation to a fresh affective conversion? What should you do as shepherd of this flock? They have experienced intellectual conversion. They have expressed a social conversion toward their own neighborhood. What may be next? The issues in such a situation are complex. Nevertheless, whatever you choose to do in such a situation, the important task is to attend to the breadth of conversion in any community, any individual.

Transformation

We must remember that our ongoing salvation is not of our own making. God does not save us initially so that we might then use our own efforts as individuals or communities to "make it happen." Not at all. Both our initial and our ongoing salvation are initiated by God. To see how this works is to observe the ways of transformation.

Transformation is the way that salvation is manifest concretely in the lives of believers. It is change. We live like we are accepted by God. We demonstrate authority over the devil. We show ourselves to be a community of unity. In the framework of the new covenant, this means that, within our contexts as communities and individuals, the Holy Spirit invites us into—and produces—change. An idea seems to carry a special weight as we're brainstorming. I feel a nudge to let an offense go. Someone's body is physically strengthened as they receive prayer. And we are led into something new. This is the agency of the Holy Spirit. Our job, then, as cooperative agents of spiritual formation, is to notice and to respond. One constructs a self in view of the beauty of the gospel and in response to the Holy Spirit. This is the Spirit- and human-led transformation available in the new covenant: to see it, to believe it, and to live into it.[16]

Maturation

Our salvation is experienced uniquely by each community, each individual. Each grows at its own rate. The sovereign will of God and our varied contexts combine to make some kind of one-size-fits-all approach to Christian transformation—and consequently, to Christian spiritual formation—impossible. Community size, gender, and personality type are among the many factors that influence the ways that transformation will be experienced in any given situation.[17] I want to address one factor commonly discussed with regard to transformation and its relevance to spiritual formation: the stages of maturation.

Throughout the history of the Christian faith, spiritual writers and scholars have noted that Christians develop through identifiable stages of maturity. Models of the stages of Christian growth are often helpful. They give us a sense of where we are in relationship with God: the kinds of struggles we may expect, the lessons we may need to learn, the experiences common to a given stage. Pastors and spiritual guides use models to help discern the signs a person gives of their maturity and to target their ministry to the needs of that particular individual or group.

At times, however, viewing the Christian life from the perspective of a particular model of Christian growth can be very unhelpful. We are pressured into certain experiences just because they are considered necessary for a certain stage of growth. We are made to feel inadequate because we don't show the expected signs of a stage of growth. Sometimes we are (wrongly) praised because we do exhibit the right signs when, in fact, we really are not all that mature—and that feels odd too. And there are times when a spiritual friend misunderstands our struggles because he has labeled us in the wrong stage of growth. Models of the stages of Christian growth are powerful tools that both enable the wise surgeon to cut to the heart of a person's need and permit the unwise to wound another and leave her to bleed.

These models are rooted in Scripture. Paul writes in 1 Corinthians 3:1–2, "Brothers and sisters, I could not address you as people who live by the Spirit but as people who are still worldly—mere infants in Christ. I gave you milk, not solid food, for you were not ready for it. Indeed, you are still not ready." Ephesians 4:13–14 speaks of God giving ministers to the church "until we all reach unity in the faith and in the knowledge of the Son of God and become mature, attaining to the whole measure of the fullness of Christ. Then we will no longer be infants, tossed back and forth by the waves, and blown here and there by every wind of teaching and by the cunning and craftiness of people in their deceitful scheming." Likewise, the author of Hebrews writes, "Therefore let us move beyond the elementary teachings about Christ and be taken forward to maturity, not laying again the foundation of repentance from acts that lead to death, and of faith in God, instruction about cleansing rites, the laying on of hands, the resurrection of the dead, and eternal judgment" (Heb. 6:1–2). Children to adults, milk to solid food, immature to mature, basic teaching to perfection—the stages may be simple, but the message is clear: people develop spiritually through recognizable stages. Those at one stage need different kinds of teaching and treatment than those at another require. It is reasonable to assume that one's spiritual life can be assessed in terms of a continuum between the beginning and end points of their metaphorical models. The essence of Christian growth is moving as close to the mature side of the model as one can here on earth.

In the centuries that followed the completion of the New Testament, a number of Christian maturity models gained the respect of many Christians. Origen of Alexandria, an early Christian ascetic, suggested that the soul passes through stages of learning virtue, reflecting on reality, and contemplating God. Bonaventure, a thirteenth-century Franciscan philosopher, promoted an influential threefold schema that distinguished between stages of purgation, illumination, and union. Dominicans such as Thomas Aquinas, a contemporary of Bonaventure, preferred a simple division of beginners, the proficient, and the perfect.[18] While Protestant Reformers were often wary of models of spiritual growth, later Protestant theologians engaged in debates regarding the *ordo salutis*. Other influential models include Carmelite saint Teresa of Avila's seven mansions, which she outlined in *The Interior Castle* and, more recently, the Holiness and Pentecostal movements' discussions of entire sanctification and the baptism in the Holy Spirit.[19] And the model making continues to this day.[20]

The many different—and at times conflicting—models surrounding us originate in a number of different settings, draw from a variety of different influences, and suggest different expressions of wisdom in practice. So how do we separate what is helpful from what is unhelpful? One valuable suggestion is to emphasize what is clear and minimize what is not. Just as we are wise to pay attention to the breadth of Christian transformation, so too we are wise to attend to stages of Christian maturation.

For example, while many will be able to appreciate the *descriptive* value of theories such as Bonaventure's threefold way, I think we are in danger when we promote it as a *normative* pattern for all Christians. The pattern of purgation, illumination, and union, for example, is not taught clearly in Scripture. Likewise, we are in danger when we try to determine too exactly the nuances of a Protestant *ordo salutis*. Precise schematization of an *ordo salutis* may require a systematic evaluation beyond the evidence of what is given clearly in Scripture. While we can biblically affirm that there are stages of growth, each requiring different teaching and pastoral treatment, we must be careful of the degree of specificity in those patterns claimed to be normative.[21]

Similarly, we must be cautious when identifying so-called required experiences. That we are to experience the Holy Spirit seems clear from the New Testament. But just which experiences are normative—that is, all Christians must have these in order to advance to a particular stage of growth—seems beyond what we can confidently determine. Certainly we are all called to maturity, but whether that maturity is necessarily characterized by an experience of "infused contemplation," a "baptism of the Spirit," or a moment of "entire sanctification" is less clear. Scripture and tradition affirm, rather, the diversity of giftedness and experience within a general framework of growth. The goal is to develop descriptive wisdom about what we see (in ourselves, in others, in our community) while situating this wisdom within a larger, and appropriately minimal, normative vision of maturity. The challenge is to appreciate the place of suggestive, descriptive micromodels of growth within a larger, more distinctively Christian macromodel. The macromodel must be broad enough to encompass the growth of Christians in general yet narrow enough to assert real categories. Figure 5.1 (p. 93) presents my own outline of a four-point macromodel, drawing somewhat from the biblical metaphor of spiritual growth from infancy to adulthood, accompanied with a few descriptive micromodel comments about each stage.

Stages of corporate spiritual maturity have not been as richly explored and sketched out as have the stages of personal maturity. Nonetheless, an approach to transformation that embraces the whole of the Christian gospel will embrace corporate as well as individual dimensions of the gospel. If we think of groups as being independent selves, we could employ figure 5.1 to identify stages of development in communities of faith. We might distinguish between young congregations, which are just beginning to identify

Figure 5.1
Stages of Ongoing Christian Salvation

1. Reaching, Standing, Walking: The First Year of Life	To proceed from this stage, believers generally require • an understanding of basic Christian truths; • a felt sense of identity with Christ; • a few basic Christian habits; • a fundamental break with the past; • a sense of the body of Christ as one's community; and • formal initiation into the Christian faith and community.
2. Playing, Learning: Solid Growth as a Child of God	During this stage, one usually acquires • an increased, deeper awareness of the machinations of one's heart, mind, and life; • a basic perception of and participation in the basic cycles of Christian discipleship (e.g., God's initiation, our response, God's response or God's presence, life as lesson, our action and God's action, integration); • a way to assess the health and biblical foundation of a theology, community, or identity; • an initial understanding of four primary means of grace: Holy Spirit, ordinary events of life, planned disciplines, community (see chap. 6); and • a growing sense of and involvement in Christian service.
3. Climbing, Dancing, Journeying: Exploring the Christian Life	This stage often involves developing • a broader and still deeper understanding and experience of God; • an acquaintance with different traditions in the church; • an exploratory attitude toward the breadth of Christian transformation; • a familiarity with a wider range of means of grace; • a life of active service and giftedness in the body; and • a practice of Christian discernment and reintegration (see chap. 11).
4. Active Resting, Restful Acting: Living a Mature Christian Life	This stage—which typically follows a season of exploration and is usually characterized by an integration of what has been gained and lost in one's Christian life—is likely marked by settling into • a lifestyle of exploration, discernment, and reintegration; • a sense of identity, call, and rhythm; • one's community and theology; • both possibilities and limitations; • a way of navigating crisis and resettling; and • short- and long-term investments.*

* I have not incorporated a particular season of not sensing God's presence into this outline, simply because I see a variety of forms of darkness influencing believers at each and every stage of development. Believers and spiritual directors need to discern the particular form of darkness being encountered and an appropriate response in the situation at hand. For more on experiences of darkness or desolation, see, e.g., *The Ascent of Mount Carmel* and *The Dark Night of the Soul* in John of the Cross, *The Collected Works of John of the Cross*, trans. Kieran Kavanaugh and Otilio Rodriguez (Washington, DC: Institute of Carmelite Studies, 1979).

themselves in the faith and solidify both their collective sense of the basic truths of the faith and their collective sense of experience of God, from more mature congregations, which have "been through it," have experienced various trends and ideas, and are now settling into a healthy, integrated rhythm. Or perhaps we could use the language common to group research on stages of growth (the terms *forming, storming, norming,* and *performing,* for example, are common) and explore the roles that God may have to play as Christian groups move from stage to stage.[22] Many of the models from group research, however, are models of group identity—not models of group maturity in relationship with God. This is an area that deserves more investigation. The New Testament Epistles were written to communities, and it is time that we reflect on what it might mean for our communities of faith to mature and that we ask what stages we might journey through on the way to corporate maturity in Christ.[23]

Just as business managers are more successful at integrating employees into a corporate vision when they respect that different staff members are at various developmental stages, so also those who wish to facilitate the spiritual formation of a community or individuals into the life and gospel of Christ will have greater success when keeping in mind the stages of maturity achieved by those for whom we care. This is one of the ways models of growth are helpful. In this light, let us look at one example of how the stages outlined above might assist us as we facilitate another's maturity in Christ.

Imagine that you a rising college senior. Next year you will graduate from a well-respected Christian college with a degree in theology and ethics. You have explored the trendy questions and the classic ones, been exposed to a wealth of experiences and interpretations of the Christian faith, and have enjoyed dancing on the edges of tradition with your peers. These years of study have been valuable for your journey of faith. You see a much bigger God now than you did when you first entered college. You hope someday to put your education in theology and ethics into practice in some form of compassion and social-justice ministry. So you volunteer for a summer internship working with the homeless.

After a few weeks, you find yourself leading a small group of men, all older than you, who have lived on the street for many years. Most of them have responded to altar calls at soup-kitchen presentations of the gospel. Yet they are new in the faith, just beginning to stand, one could say. And now you have a whole summer to nurture their maturity. What will you do? If you are excited about what you are learning in your own spiritual life (a look at fig. 5.1 [p. 93] reveals that you're at stage 3), you might lead discussions about faith and social issues. You might tell these men about a wide range of probably unfamiliar practices through which they might grow deeper with Christ. You might try to get them involved in active service on the streets, a way of developing relationships that might be spiritually fruitful for all. And perhaps some of this might truly be helpful.

But some of it might not. You might introduce questions that they have never asked and that, without prior exposure to the faith, they are incapable of properly addressing at this point. The ambiguity might be valuable for you, but these are new believers, and you may have rocked their boat without giving them a way to stay afloat. Unless you can provide ongoing guidance, these unfamiliar practices may confuse them more than serve them. And by sending them back to the streets to minister to others, some of whom may have substance-abuse problems or other unhealthy behaviors, you may be sending these men right into temptation. Of course, this is all a matter of wisdom and discernment, but you get my point. One is wise to respect others at the faith stage they've reached instead of the one you've reached or the one you want them to reach.

So you, being wise, choose to serve them where they are. You lead Bible studies on the basics of the Christian faith, patiently responding to their questions with clear answers. (Yes, you can be clear and not cliché at the same time.) Together you make a list of some basic Christian habits, like prayer and Bible reading, and then you train them in these habits. You support them as they make a fundamental break with the past by listening to their stories again and again, by going with them to Alcoholics Anonymous meetings, and by refusing to accept their reasons for needing a drink right now. After a few weeks, all this baby Christian stuff might seem a bit boring and unsuccessful. It seemed cutting edge when you volunteered, but it feels different now. Nevertheless, by the end of the summer, you have invested in a few believers. By God's grace, you have rescued a few from danger. You have cared for their immediate needs. They feel like your little Bible study group really is "their people." They have reached out and now are standing on their own, and you have fostered that by respecting their development. This is Christian spiritual formation informed by a sense of the stages of faith.

Task

We have now seen something of the process of Christian transformation—the change that manifests the ongoing work of salvation in the people of God. Transformation is the concrete working out of God's mission in its fullness among the people of God for the sake of the world and the glory of

God. Our understanding of transformation, then, brings us to a place where we can identify the task of Christian spiritual formation. Whereas viewing things from the perspective of salvation gives us a God's-eye view of change, and describing transformation blends the divine and the human perspectives, identifying the task of formation shifts our perspective toward the human agents. Aware that any particular program of formation in Christ is part of the Spirit's larger work of transformation, we still choose to take positive steps toward nurturing our growth in Christian maturity. Monasteries have formation directors, Christian organizations send their staff to classes or seminars on formation, and churches hire pastors of formation with the idea that these pastors will be responsible in some manner for the spiritual growth of the congregation or individuals within that congregation. There must be a task of formation that names the work being done in these situations by directors, formation pastors, and the like. Furthermore, our identifying this task ought to be tied to our understanding of salvation and transformation. They are all necessarily connected.

As an agent of formation, the self sees with faith and acts, while attending and responding to the Spirit. When we link these roles to the more tangible world of transformational change, we move closer to understanding the task of Christian spiritual formation. In chapter 1, we defined Christian spiritual formation as a Spirit- and human-led process by which individuals and communities mature in relationship with this God and are changed into increasing likeness to the life and gospel of the Christian God. When we look at Christian spiritual formation from the point of view not of one observing the process in general but of one's own self participating as an agent in that process, we can say that the task of Christian spiritual formation is simply *the active cultivation of appropriate Christian transformation.*

First, the task of Christian spiritual formation is active. Christian formation is what we do in light of what Christ has done and the Spirit does now. We listen to others' stories and discern the Spirit's work, helping them to celebrate and appropriate that work in their lives. We use this insight to design a series of sermons for a congregation, conscious that this is the tender edge of growth for this particular community. Or perhaps we prepare ourselves to weather the storm ahead, opening ourselves to receive what this season of suffering may have to offer us. In each of these we are actors: we choose thoughts, actions, sentiments, and such that we hope will contribute to a fruitful end.

Second, the task of Christian spiritual formation is a form of cultivation. Other words could be used to describe this aspect—*nurture, facilitate, promote, foster*—but I like the agricultural analogy. Like a farmer, we pay attention to the soil and the weather. We add nutrients, pull weeds, plant seeds. The fruit just appears. We cannot make things grow, but we can cultivate. That is the task of formation: to cultivate godly change.

Third, the task of Christian spiritual formation aims at Christian transformation. We explored this already when we talked about the aims of formation, the work of salvation, and the process of transformation. I'm revisiting transformation because the task of formation deals with the particular elements of change that are present in an individual or community's life here and now. And this is transformation. Elsewhere, I have talked about this task as one in which we put off, put on, or put into practice the gospel.[24] However it is worded, the task of Christian spiritual formation is to encourage change, to foster a maturing of relationship with God and an increase in likeness to the person and gospel of Christ.[25]

Finally, the task of Christian spiritual formation is to cultivate appropriate transformation. As a spiritual director, I exercise the wisdom of paying attention to context. I notice stages of maturation and survey areas that have the potential for transformation for signs that they are ready for new growth. I facilitate the relationships that will best encourage, instruct, support, and challenge here and now. I design rituals that confirm the good intentions of a group or an individual, cooperating with what we see the Spirit doing in our midst. Christian spiritual formation is not simply the oversight of a program. It is the combination of wise insight, patient care, and courageous action—at just the right time.

The task of spiritual formation often involves a series of acts and attitudes that together integrate the context, agents, aims, and means of formation. And, whether for communities or individuals, that task will include steps such as these:

- Help oneself or others gain a clear *vision* of the aims of spiritual formation. In general, this is accomplished by acquiring knowledge of (and attraction to) the greater glory of God and the ultimate aims of spiritual formation. But that vision must move beyond the general to the particular. What would the gospel of God look like in this directee's life, in this place and time? What are some realistic proximate aims of this congregation's spiritual formation? What does appropriate increase look like in this or that situation?

- Promote in oneself or others a strong *determination* not to give up the process of growth—even if things don't appear to be "working."

- Nurture *community support* to facilitate Godward reorientation and rehabituation.

- *Identify* where a directee may be suffering from de-formation, disorientation, or ill habituation. Consider what he must "put off." What must he "put on" instead—not just generally, but here and now?
- *Select* disciplines, practices, rules, circumstances, relationships, sentiments, experiences, and the like through which one hopes to introduce or reinforce a new, Godward orientation or habit.
- Give careful *attention* to the nuances of one's own context such that selection and revision are made in light of one's own real situation.
- *Implement* an intentional program of activities or cease certain unhealthful activities.
- *Experiment* and revise the ongoing process as needed.

Ultimately, I call this *play*, and I mean it. We grow through our own ability to play with things. We build forts and learn planning and construction. We play house and learn how to navigate relationships. We will grow in our relationship with God as we find the freedom to play with our practices, relationships, and more, always reflecting, with God's help, to see what our play teaches us.

The task of Christian spiritual formation, then, is to employ steps such as those outlined above in order to cultivate the transformations that God desires here and now. We cannot change every part of our life and achieve perfection today, yet we are not doomed to wallow in our own fallenness or the oppression of the enemy. The task, then, is to concretely place ourselves in the Spirit's path, to see the appropriate change ahead, and to cooperate with God, using practical steps to cultivate an increase in likeness to Christ and the gospel. We will explore just what this looks like in the chapters ahead.

Going Deeper

1. In the process of exploring the process of transformation, we have been obligated to consider the very nature of Christian salvation—what the Christian God has accomplished for us and how we appropriate that work. But, as we all know, Christians sometimes differ with regard to views about salvation. What are the primary differences with regard to Christians' views of salvation, and how might one's view of salvation influence one's approach to Christian spiritual formation?

2. Transformation develops over time and, often, even through various seasons or stages. What season or stage are you (or your church) in

currently? Spend some time looking over figure 5.1 (p. 93). Are you walking, playing, dancing, or resting? Where have you already been? Different areas of life can be in different stages. Can you identify various areas of your life and the stages they are in? Reflect and respond to the outline as a way of reflecting on your own or your community's spiritual development. What do you see, and how might your insights affect your own approach to spiritual formation at present?

3. When we talked about the task of Christian spiritual formation, we learned about the appropriate next step. What does this term *appropriate* mean? How is Christian spiritual formation entwined in the discernment of what is appropriate, and how does this approach differ from other approaches you have known? How does what you have learned about the other elements of formation (context, aim, agents, and so on) inform your own understanding of appropriateness in a given instance of formation? Perhaps you can think of a current personal example.

4. One practice that communicates the elements of process and task clearly is the practice of testimony. Through offering our testimonies, we recount how salvation has been encountered over time. As we listen to the stories of others, we compare them to our own and learn how the basic framework of salvation is lived out in the ongoing transformations among individuals and communities. Spiritual directors listen to the story (the testimony) of another in order to discern how they might encourage spiritual progress. After you've read and reflected on some of the writings on testimony cited in note 1 on page 257, gather some people and share your stories—give testimonies. What do you learn about the participants, about God, and about spiritual formation during this time together?

6

....

The Means of Christian
Spiritual Formation

Overview

We now take a look at the final basic element of Christian spiritual formation: the means of formation. We will begin by examining the work of the Holy Spirit as both an agent and a means of formation, which reveals the ways the Spirit of Christ influences us toward Christ and the ways by which we, through responding to the ministry of the Spirit, cooperate with that influence. Then, after an aside on the role of nature in spiritual formation, we will consider spiritual disciplines: their character and their healthy use in formation. We'll turn next to consider community as a means of grace, looking at how worship gatherings and the communication of the Word act as means of grace for individuals and congregations. After that, we will discover that the trials of everyday life can be means of grace when we approach them with wisdom. Finally, having surveyed the various means of grace, we can apply our insights by reflecting on how they may be employed in the context of congregational worship.

III

When I want to chop vegetables for a meal, I pick up a knife. The knife is the instrument I use to chop the vegetables. When a group of musicians decide that they want to become a symphony orchestra, they might hire a conductor to lead them. Their relationship with the conductor becomes one of the means (along with the music books, the instruments, and their rehearsals) by which they become an orchestra. A veteran might recount a story of a time when he was taken captive and imprisoned. When he tells this story, he explains to his hearers that the hardships he endured in prison "made me the person I am today." The experience of hardship was a means by which his sense of self was re-formed. Change often comes about through the use of means.

Christians sometimes speak of the means through which God's presence becomes real and active in our lives. John Wesley, founder of the Methodists, called them "means of grace." In a 1777 sermon on this topic, he defined the means of grace as "outward signs, words, or actions, ordained of God, and appointed for this end, to be the ordinary channels whereby he might convey to men . . . grace."[1] Whereas the aims and the task of Christian spiritual formation are definite and universal, the means of formation vary and are personal. In one sense, God has provided the means of sustaining covenant relationship in the Christian era by sending the Spirit, by inspiring the Scriptures, and by instituting the church, so there is a defined set of distinctly Christian means that Christians employ to cultivate growth in their relationship with God. In addition, Scripture and the church treat a variety of other kinds of activity as means through which God works transformation into us—for example, fasting, singing, self-examination, and testimony. Since Christians are commanded to "make every effort" to support our faith with goodness and so on (2 Pet. 1:5–8; see also Luke 13:24; Rom. 14:19; Eph. 4:3; Heb. 4:11; 12:14; 2 Pet. 1:10; 3:14), the reasonable conclusion is that, in this effort, we would be making use of a wide range of means.

I repeat: the means of formation vary. Practices, possessions, relationships, attitudes, and more all can be employed as vehicles through which God's presence is welcomed. One culture will be more familiar with some means than another culture. Consider the Asian church's practice of praying aloud simultaneously in corporate meetings. Something is experienced and communicated through this means that is not experienced when we take turns to pray in meetings, as is common in the American church. For some, this all-at-once group prayer is uncomfortable; for others, it is simply normal. Such is the way with means. Collected in the eighteenth century, the Large Minutes of the Methodist Society (essentially the denomination's rules and regulations) distinguished between instituted and prudential means. The former includes praying, studying Scripture, sharing in the Lord's Supper, fasting, and taking part in Christian conference (fellowship). The latter comprises making use of particular rules for personal growth; attending class, band, or other meetings; watching against the world, devil, and besetting sins; denying oneself useless pleasures and needless food or drink; taking up one's cross and willingly bearing whatever is grievous to our nature; and exercising the presence of God through always setting God before us.[2] Different needs, different means.

In this chapter, we will explore the means of Christian spiritual formation with a fourfold division: the ministry of the Spirit (including a note regarding the place of nature), spiritual disciplines, the community of believers, and the trials of ordinary life.[3] Then, having surveyed this outline of the means of grace, we will turn our attention to the ways that our corporate and individual personalities make use of means.

Means and the Ministry of the Holy Spirit

The Spirit of God is the life-giving force in creation. In the Christian era, the Holy Spirit is God's provision for maintaining ongoing covenant relationship with God. The Holy Spirit is the revealer of truth, the initiator of moral renewal, the mediator of righteous relationships, the One who empowers us for mission, and the stimulator of holy worship. In all of these works, the Spirit acts as the primary agent of our formation, initiating an "all things new" formation. But just how is the Holy Spirit not only an agent but also a means of our formation? Exploring this will get at the nature of our experience of the Spirit.

Consider, for example, a spiritual direction relationship. We might say, "After I met my spiritual director, I was never the same." This spiritual director serves as both an agent (having a particular role facilitating my spiritual life) and a means (a vehicle through which change is experienced). When we speak of relationships as means, we highlight our experience of that relationship and the influence of that relationship on our lives. So also with the Holy Spirit. It is one thing to affirm what the Spirit does as agent (initiator of change). It is another to describe just how that influence is perceived and how we cooperate with it.

The Scriptures use a variety of expressions to describe the ministry of the Spirit. The Spirit is "sent" or "given" to God's people (Rom. 5:5; Gal. 4:6; 1 Thess. 4:8). God "baptizes" us in, with, or by the Spirit (Mark 1:8; John 1:33; Acts 1:5; 11:16; 1 Cor. 12:13). A number of these expressions are spatial metaphors. The Spirit fills (Luke 1:15; Acts 2:4; 9:17), flows from within (John 7:38–39), comes on (Acts 10:44; 19:6), is "poured out" (Acts 10:45), and "dwells in" (1 Cor. 3:16; see also 2 Tim. 1:14). We also can be "in" the Spirit (Rev. 4:2). The metaphors depict the kind of influence the Holy Spirit has in our lives. You do not have a literal "inside" that the Holy Spirit fills. Rather, the term *fill* describes the kind of experience (especially in Luke and Acts) or the theological meaning (especially in the Epistles) of the Spirit's influence as encountered by the people of God.[4] The term *filled*, for example, implies that the Spirit exercises powerful control over some measure of human experience: in this case, giving Paul the impulse and courage to speak a curse upon Elymas (Acts 13:9–11) or inspiring the church to sing while under the influence, so to speak (Eph. 5:18–19; a similar description of those filled with the Spirit being accused of drunkenness is in Acts 2:13).

Terms like *filled*, *baptized*, and *poured out* describe the influence of the Holy Spirit with relation to human experience generally. Yet a number of Scriptures teach us about the Holy Spirit's influence with respect to specific operations of human experience. God's Spirit inspires ideas, images, or words in our minds (e.g., Num. 24:2–3; 1 Sam. 10:10; 19:20–23; Neh. 9:20, 30; Isa. 48:16; Ezek. 11:1–5; John 14:26; Acts 4:25; 1 Cor. 2:10–14; 2 Tim. 1:14; 2 Pet. 1:21). The Holy Spirit's influence triggers the presence of or shifts in our emotions (Rom. 5:5; 8:15; 15:13; 2 Cor. 3:17; Gal. 4:6; Eph. 5:18–19; 1 Thess. 1:6; Titus 3:5–6). When we are led by the Spirit, our inclinations or wills are influenced by the Spirit (Mark 1:12; Luke 2:25–27; Rom. 8:2–6). The Spirit speaks through an inner voice (Acts 8:29; 11:12; 15:28, with a communal context; Rom. 8:14; Gal. 5:16–25) or a dream (Acts 10:19). Sometimes this influence of the Spirit is spectacular—extraordinary in its manifestations or impact. At other times, the work of God's Spirit is simply to provide or to enhance ordinary abilities exercised by faithful followers (see Exod. 31:1–5; 35:30–35; Dan. 5:11–14; Rom. 12:4–8).[5]

Sometimes we perceive the Spirit acting on us like a human friend would, persuading us to think or choose in a way that might please Christ. Perhaps this is one way we might understand how the Spirit glorifies Christ: by making what is Christ's known (John 16:14). At other times, we find ourselves sharing the thoughts and feelings of Christ without any special moment of revelation. We participate in Christ (2 Pet. 1:4), consciously or unconsciously, and we acknowledge that this is part of what it means to live "according to the Spirit" (Rom. 8:1–9). And we may also recognize the presence of the Spirit through the fruit of the Spirit. You have somehow become, in this or that area of life, more like Jesus. We, as a congregation, proclaim the gospel by our corporate life more than we used to. And we declare, as we admit this change, that we "are being transformed into his image with ever-increasing glory, which comes from the Lord, who is the Spirit" (2 Cor. 3:18).[6]

What does all this mean for spiritual formation? In order to cooperate with the work of the Spirit, we must learn to attend to the quality of our own experience, for that is where the Spirit works. Just as we can, by attending to our experience, learn to recognize the influence of caffeine on our thoughts and impulses, so also we can learn to recognize the influence of the Holy Spirit. Just as you can learn to perceive when the presence of a particular person in a meeting is shaping the way you behave in that meeting, so too you can learn to perceive when the presence of the Holy Spirit is shaping your experience in a meeting (or is perhaps shaping the character of the meeting itself). Have you ever been in a gathering where a word was spoken—whether a sermon, a prophetic utterance, or just a statement of common sense—and it gripped the gathering in such a way that nearly all knew that this was the Spirit speaking to them? We actively employ the Holy Spirit as a means of spiritual formation when we choose to attend to this influence and to recognize the movements of the Spirit so that we might respond appropriately.

And respond we must. Our relationship with the Holy Spirit is not simply a matter of perceiving which way the wind blows. The Spirit's breath is not merely a touch. It is also an invitation. The Spirit is not simply some vague force. It is also personal: the Third Person of the Trinity. The presence of the person of Jesus required a response among those who encountered him; the presence of the Spirit invites our response today.

Our response to the Spirit's influence can be consent. We choose to "receive" the Spirit (John 20:22; Acts 2:38; 8:15–19; 10:47; 19:2), to be compelled by the Spirit (Acts 20:22), or to act "in" or "by" or "through" the Spirit (Luke 4:14; 10:21; John 4:23–24; 1 Cor. 14:2, 16; Phil. 3:3). We "walk by" or "according to" the Spirit (Rom. 8:4; Gal. 5:16). We "live by" the Spirit (Gal. 5:25). Characteristic of these positive responses is our openness and willingness to step into the flow of the Spirit's influence.

We can, however, also choose to respond to the Spirit's influence with resistance. We "resist" the Spirit (Acts 7:51). We "grieve" the Spirit (Eph. 4:30). We "quench" the Spirit (1 Thess. 5:19). We can choose to "lie to" or "test" the Spirit (Acts 5:3, 9) and "blaspheme" or "insult" the Spirit (Matt. 12:31–32; Heb. 6:4; 10:29). While responses of consent exhibit a kind of softness and pliability when encountering the Spirit's influence, responses of resistance exhibit a hardness, an unwillingness, or an avoidance when faced with the Spirit's active presence in the life of a community or an individual. The Spirit is always an *agent* of spiritual formation: initiating, bringing thoughts to the mind or impulses to the heart, inviting us into newness in this or that area of life. Yet it is only when we choose to pay attention and then to respond to the Spirit's presence with an attitude of consent that we actually make the Spirit a *means* of our formation and an instrument through which we cultivate an increasing likeness to Christ and the gospel.

A Note on Nature

These days, when I ask people where they find God or what they are doing when they notice God, they often respond by telling me about moments involving nature. One saw a sunset. Another was walking in a park or watching animals. Pastor Sam Hamilton-Poore, speaking about a place in Iowa, summarizes well what I often hear: "It's not so much that I went out to Willow Creek and then found a spot to pray; it's more accurate to say that every time I came within sight or sound of the river, I found myself in prayer."[7] Nature and the creatures of God's creation seem to function as vehicles through which God is mediated. And yet so little is said about nature as a means of grace. None of the disciplines listed in figure 6.1 (p. 109) mention nature. Only one of the sixty-two spiritual disciplines identified by spiritual director Adele Ahlberg Calhoun has any explicit connection with nature, and this discipline (which she calls "care of the earth") is more directly related to action on behalf of the environment than on contemplation while in nature. Why is it that so many people seem to make a significant connection with God while spending time in nature, and yet we do not see nature as a means of grace?

Perhaps nature is more a *context* of grace than a *means* of grace. You can study the Bible in nature just as you can in an office. You can practice solitude indoors or outdoors. You can offer hospitality in your backyard just as easily as you can in your dining room. From this point of view, nature is the environment within which some disciplines are exercised. But if that's so, then perhaps we who write about spiritual disciplines and spiritual formation have done the body of Christ a disservice by not speaking more about how valuable our environment is as a vehicle of grace and by not training people to appreciate Christ (and their disciplines) in the context of nature.

Furthermore, I think that another reason for our negligence lies in the condition of modernity. The rise of interest in and writings about spiritual formation reflects a turn to historical sources of the Christian faith, most of which were written centuries ago. Many of these writers simply assumed the context and value of nature, though they mentioned it only periodically. For example, a philosopher asked how Anthony of Egypt, a desert father who lived in the third and fourth centuries, got along without books. Abba Anthony replied, "My book is the nature of created things, and as often as I have a mind to read the words of God, it is at my hand." Similarly, the Reformer Martin Luther wrote, "All creation is the most beautiful book or bible, for in it God has described and portrayed Himself."[8] Perhaps whereas our forebears lived closer to the world of nature, we today suffer from "nature-deficit disorder."[9]

Consequently, we are more keenly aware of the precious environment that nature offers for our spiritual health.

Christian writers are only just beginning to speak about nature with a sense of its formation potential, and this book is no place to develop the field.[10] Yet I feel obliged to offer a few brief suggestions by way of pointing Christians toward a nourishing practice of developing relationship with God through nature.

First, recount the story of your own relationship with nature and its impact on your spiritual life. Have there been any places that have been special to you? Why? Have you done things in nature that have—either in a single event or over a period of time—nourished your spiritual life? Again, why? How has nature played a part in your own developing growth in likeness to Christ?

Second, welcome the awe. Nature is vast, magnificent, breathtaking. Both microscopic and cosmic, it captures us with its all-encompassing character, and we feel awe. "How majestic is your name in all the earth!" Psalm 8 proclaims as it begins a litany of natural phenomena. Researchers have discovered that 75 percent of human awe is inspired by the natural world.[11] Nature is a stimulus to worship. It was meant to be. Puritan Jonathan Edwards, minister Agnes Sanford, and author Richard Foster each had powerful experiences of God in nature. We must give ourselves permission to make the effort to get to that beach, to hike up that hill, to walk in that park and notice the divine. Nature truly is a sanctuary.

Third, consider nature as a teacher of theology. Proverbs 6:6 encourages us to "go to the ant." Jesus directs us to "consider the lilies" (Matt. 6:28 KJV). The apostle Paul declares in Romans that God's "invisible qualities . . . have been clearly seen, being understood from what has been made" (Rom. 1:20). We learn about God's care, the nature of life, the interconnectedness of causes and effects, and so much more by attending carefully to the world of nature. Some of the lessons are in the form of analogies. Other lessons come as we simply learn about the way things are—the way that God made them to be.

Finally, make room for the special kind of contemplation that happens outdoors—including the reflection that comes when doing repetitive activities. Jesus seems to have walked to solitary places as a matter of his ongoing spiritual life. Personally, I have found good hard work outside to be a life-giving practice. I would even say that walking, working, and doing simple things in nature and with nature can be a spiritual practice. And I am not alone in thinking so.[12]

Spiritual Disciplines

Spiritual disciplines, duty, ascetical practice—the language varies. The Greek word *askēsis* is often translated as "discipline." Greeks used this word to describe athletic training, and it is also employed to describe the ascetic exercises of early nuns and monks. Thus Eastern Orthodox Christians, who are more directly connected to the Greek language, talk about "ascetical practice." Puritan divines tended to speak of "duty." I have heard people talk about undertaking a "discipline" (such as inviting guests for dinner each week) as a way of nurturing the "practice" of hospitality. In this section (and through the rest of this book), I will use all of these terms to mean the same basic thing: the act or habit of intentionally constraining one's own human experience in the context of God's active presence to achieve spiritual ends.[13]

The essence of a spiritual discipline or ascetical practice is that it is an act or habit that functions as a constraint on one's own experience. Some speak of a struggle or some kind of renunciation, but the term *constraint* seems to fit more broadly how asceticism affects human experience. The sorts of acts that Christians consider to be means of cultivating or expressing likeness to Christ and the Christian gospel vary a great deal. One congregation encourages both individual members and the congregation to explore seasons of fasting. Another finds that the practice of regular community hospitality nudges the congregation just where it needs to be growing. Each practice constrains or focuses experience in its own way. Needless to say, the possibilities are endless.[14]

A discipline is an intentional act toward one's own human experience. Practices that are compelled or accidental are not really ascetical in the proper sense. The very character of a discipline is that it accompanies a particular intention of the person or group who chooses it. Furthermore, both the performer and the recipient of ascetical practice are the same, whether individuals or communities. It is one's own experience that is ultimately in view. Ascetic individuals or communities may have a subsidiary aim of influencing or effecting change with regard to a wider sphere, but the direct object of their asceticism, as asceticism, is their own experience.

Finally, spiritual discipline is performed for the sake of Christian ends and in the conscious context of God's active presence. Whether we are boldly waging war with one of the seven (or more) deadly sins—say, abstaining from the use of products manufactured in a setting of conflict or oppression, or keeping a regular time of public devotion—Christian asceticism, as Christian, is never simply a matter of self-improvement or cultural interaction.[15] The Triune God, present and active in history and creation through Christ and by the Spirit's movements, is the primary actor in any ascetical performance. The objective of spiritual practice is a spiritual end.

There are healthy and unhealthy ways of approaching our relationship with spiritual disciplines. One of the unhealthy ways is the way of *legalism*, in which one identifies a few "required" practices that all "good Christians" engage in

Figure 6.1
Outlines of Spiritual Disciplines in Selected Christian Literature

Celebration of Discipline	Spirit of the Disciplines	Soul Feast	Spiritual Theology	Evangelical Practices	Path to Salvation
Inward Disciplines	*Abstinence*	spiritual reading	*Fundamental Means*	Scripture	*Rules for Preserving the Zeal for God*
meditation	solitude	prayer	sacraments	read	being within
prayer	silence	common	meritorious	study	vision of another world
fasting	fasting	worship	good works	meditiate	remaining in feelings that lead
study	frugality	fasting	petitionary		to resolve
	chastity	self-examination	prayer	*Sermons*	
Outward Disciplines	secrecy	confession		preach	*Exercises for Confirming the Believer in Goodness*
	sacrifice	awareness	*Aids to Growth*	hear	
simplicity		spiritual	presence of God	read	mind—read, study, ask, talk
solitude	*Engagement*	direction	examination of		will—submission to church,
submission	study	hospitality	conscience	*Family Worship*	civil order, God,
service	worship	rule	desire for	*Song*	conscience . . .
	celebration		perfection	*Intercession*	heart—church, prayer, icons,
Corporate Disciplines	service		conformity to	*Small Group*	holy customs
	prayer		God's will	*Revival*	body—guarding senses,
confession	fellowship		fidelity to grace	*Meeting*	tongue, abstinence and
worship	confession		plan of life	*Testimony*	fasting, moderate sleep . . .
guidance	submission		spiritual reading	*Sabbath*	outward ordering of life—
celebration			holy friendships	*Journal*	abandon evil customs
			spiritual	*Writing*	purge relationships and such
			direction		determine new order
					rearrange duties to fit new life
					establish order in family
					govenie
					completing ascetical labors
					receiving the sacraments
					Rule for War without the Passions
					freely choosing and loving good
					reviewing our enemies
					rules of spiritual warfare

Richard Foster, *Celebration of Discipline: The Path to Spiritual Growth,* 20th anniversary ed. (San Francisco: HarperSanFrancisco, 1998).

Dallas Willard, *The Spirit of the Disciplines: Understanding How God Changes Lives* (San Francisco: Harper & Row, 1988).

Marjorie J. Thompson, *Soul Feast: An Invitation to the Christian Spiritual Life* (Louisville: Westminster John Knox, 1995).

Jordan Aumann, *Spiritual Theology* (London: Sheed & Ward, 1980).

Joseph D. Driskill, *Protestant Spiritual Exercises: Theology, History, Practice* (Harrisburg, PA: Morehouse, 1999).

Evan Howard, "Evangelical Spirituality," in *Four Views on Christian Spirituality,* ed. Bruce Demarest (Grand Rapids: Zondervan, 2012), 181–85.

Theophan the Recluse, *The Path to Salvation: A Manual of Spiritual Transformation,* trans. Fr. Seraphim Rose (Platina, CA: St. Herman Press, 1998).

regularly, and then, guided by this rigid standard (and neglecting to consider context), one either values or devalues other members of Christ's church. By such means, we subtly impose some disciplines on others, effectively dividing the body of Christ and fracturing the gospel of grace. The opposite danger is known as *antinomianism* or, at times, *quietism*: the error of withdrawing from disciplines or any kind of intentionality altogether. This results from believing that either the Christian life is identified solely with forgiveness or that the Spirit is the only agent and means of our growth in maturity. Hence, there is no concern for such practices as personal devotional times or attendance at the sacraments. While there is some wisdom (for some, at certain times) in letting go and letting God, people who take this approach can be in danger of simply "letting go."

We need to appreciate the beautiful art of wisely appropriating Christian practice. To show what this might look like, I will share two examples of the healthy use of disciplines (and, in the first, nature). Furthermore, in order that you might see how the task of spiritual formation makes use of the means of spiritual formation, I will situate each of what I'll call case studies within my survey of the task of spiritual formation outlined in the previous chapter: vision, determination, community support, identification, selection, attention, implementation, experimentation.

Case 1: John

Let me introduce John, who can't seem to discern his next step in life. He has been a successful businessman for many years. He has given himself faithfully to providing for his family, serving in his local church, and volunteering for Christian mission efforts. Recent events, however, have shaken the ground John has stood on for decades and forced him to start over.

The first two events were positive and expected. His youngest child, a daughter, graduated from college and immediately found placement into a promising career. In the very same week his daughter graduated, John was offered a promotion to vice president of the corporation where he was employed. He suspected for a full year that this offer might be coming, but he wasn't quite sure what to make of it. Would he enjoy the responsibilities of this position? Was this promotion God's will?

The third event was heartbreaking and unexpected. One month prior to his daughter's graduation, his wife of twenty-eight years suddenly died of a heart attack.

John was simply lost. His nest was empty—no, more than empty. He had no wife or children at home to share life with, and this career opportunity now seemed surreal. What was it all for? Perhaps he should retire early and volunteer for a mission organization instead. John simply had no sense of a next step or of some particular vision for his life. For the first time, John felt like a deer in the headlights, unable to move.

John knew he needed help from God. But where was he to find this? His faith had always been practical: reading the Bible and doing what it says was the discipline he had always depended on. Love those nearest to you and help where you can. These were all wise words, but they were insufficient for the present need.

Unable to come up with some particular vision for his life that would determine his response to the job offer in the near future, he realized that he needed to reassess his relationship with God. And with only this little understanding, he took the next steps: he had determination and sought community support. He went to his weekly men's Bible study and told them what he thought. "I just can't give the company a final answer right now," John declared. "I don't know and I probably won't know for a while. I need some time to work things out. I need some time to work things out with God. You know, my wife was the spiritual one of the family. But now I have to step into this somehow. And I need your help." The men sympathized with John's dilemma and expressed their concern. One of them had read a lot about the spiritual life and volunteered to help John explore some disciplines (devotional reading, contemplative prayer, trips to retreat centers) that might help him go deeper with God.

John met with his friend a few times and even read a few pages of the mystics, which his friend had recommended. In the end, John identified working in the garden and going on long walks along the beach as the activities during which he most often felt God's presence accompanying him, if he could explain it that way. So he simply chose to go on walks and work in the garden.

Unfortunately, this was not as easy as it might seem. The company president wanted to make the promotion attractive and thought that John might respond to interesting new tasks. Some folks at church were afraid that John was secluding himself from the fellowship in his grief and urged him to be more social. His mystics-reading friend thought he was avoiding the hard work of pressing forward into a deeper relationship with God. John, however, was attentive to all this. He felt the tugs this way and that, even amid his confusion. But he knew his own personality, his own needs, his own charism, and so he implemented his disciplines of walking and gardening. When he needed a walk, he just took it. He worked in the garden nearly every day. He only accepted a few of the new tasks at work, refusing the rest. Over time, the men at his Bible study understood—largely because he never stopped attending—what he was and wasn't doing, and they began to ask him what he noticed on his walks. At first, John would speak of noticing the pelicans or the other people. But then John began to speak of noticing how much he cared about the younger employees at work. As vice president, he would have freedom to mentor and even to minister Christ to them.

It had been six months now, and his boss was more than ready for his decision. So John met with him and asked for another six months of revised responsibilities, so that he could test out whether he was capable of serving the company well as vice president. If he were to move up into this responsibility, John wanted to be sure he could give his all. John also told his boss that he would not sacrifice his personal life—time to go on walks and work in his garden and be alone with God. His boss agreed, the six-month experiment was a success, and, in the end, John continued serving his company and his church, visiting with his daughter, and volunteering with the mission organization. In his later years, he reread writings by one of the mystics his friend had recommended and was inspired to began a practice of meditative Bible reading (also known as *lectio divina*).

Case 2: Chi-won

When Chi-won signed up for spiritual direction sessions, she had no idea where it might lead. Spiritual direction, at least under this name, was new to her church circle in Seoul, Korea. A student at one of the seminaries in Seoul, she was exploring fresh ideas and new experiences. Spiritual direction? Sounds interesting! Why not?

From the very beginning, Chi-won found the environment comfortable. Her director was a Korean woman who had received training in the West, though she had thoroughly adapted her practice of spiritual direction for the Korean culture. The bow, the meeting rituals—everything was just right. But what was so special was the way this woman listened to Chi-won's story. She had never been heard in this way before. Chi-won found herself sharing more than she had expected.

As she talked about her relationship with God, Chi-won also mentioned her financial problems. Her bank account was often nearly depleted. "But why?" her director asked. "You have a fine job." Chi-won did not answer at that time, but two months later, she brought it up. "I shop too much, you know," Chi-won said in the middle of talking about something else. Over the next few sessions, her director learned that Chi-won was actually addicted to clothes shopping. Chi-won was terribly embarrassed, but she admitted everything. Her meetings with this spiritual director gave her the hope that perhaps something might change.

Eventually, her hope shifted to determination. Chi-won looked her director in the eye and said, "I think God would be happy if I could learn to live with the clothes I have. Could you help me?" The director explained that change was ultimately God's work, but that if Chi-won sensed the invitation of God's Spirit, perhaps this was the time to do something about it.

This conversation led to a few sessions in which Chi-won talked about her past history and how she felt about herself. She was the least capable of her family members, all of whom excelled at everything they did. Her peers were into the newest trends, and when she was able to get the latest and most expensive clothes, Chi-won could tell that they admired her. To change her shopping habits meant risking her feelings of acceptance. Chi-won's director knew that Chi-won needed to get in touch with God's unconditional acceptance of her, so she taught Chi-won how to picture herself in the middle of Gospel stories. Using the Gospel of Luke, Chi-won began a practice of imagining herself present in the moments when Jesus meets people who are neither successful nor respected. It was as if she were there as Jesus lifted up the bent-over woman (Luke 13:10–17), as he healed the woman with the hemorrhage (8:42–48), and as he shared a meal with Zacchaeus in his home (19:1–10). Chi-won's spiritual director also taught her how to talk back to the enemy using Scripture—much as Jesus did in the wilderness (4:1–13)—when the temptation to go shopping was strongest.[16] She also introduced Chi-won to a confidential prayer circle of Christians who could support her. Chi-won politely declined this last offer and said that she would prefer to be accountable to her spiritual director, who understood Chi-won's reluctance.

They experimented with these disciplines for a season. Chi-won made a list of Scripture passages, such as Matthew 6:28 ("Consider the lilies . . .") and Philippians 4:11–12 ("I have learned to be content . . ."), that served to speak against the voices and emotions that plagued her when she wanted to shop. Chi-won also added a discipline of avoiding shopping centers, going only when the most dire need demanded it. Window-shopping was just too tempting. But the most powerful change in her life came through the imaginative Bible reading. When she could experience Christ's love, she did not need the approval of her friends as strongly as she once had. She could simply admit that she didn't need the newest shoes. And, aware of God's love, she learned to live with the change in her peers' responses.

Spiritual disciplines can be employed for a variety of reasons. We make use of a particular discipline to address a particular situation, like a shopping addiction. At other times, we have no idea what change is needed, so we employ a discipline (like gardening or going on walks) that will help a directee to just *be with* God. Still other times, we use disciplines not to *facilitate* change but rather to *express* change. It is important to recognize that using spiritual disciplines for the purpose of Christian spiritual formation requires sensitivity to context, history, agents, aims, and other factors. It is an art form, not a formula.

The Community of Believers

Formation in Christ is for both individuals (Paul writes letters to Timothy) and communities (Paul writes letters to the Corinthian church). The Big Story of God's mission is about the redemption of individuals and the restoration of a people. The rich transformation of the "all things new" gospel is available for families and churches and Christian communities, just as it is for individuals. The community of believers is a context for our formation. Community members can become agents in our formation. Yet community is also a means of formation, and therefore it is appropriate to mention a couple of features of community life that are frequently understood as means of grace in Christian spiritual formation. Because I will return to the importance of community in chapter 8, I will limit my comments here to a few thoughts on worship gatherings: specifically, the place of the Word and the sacraments as community means of grace.

Worship Gatherings

To worship is to express reverence or devotion.[17] Biblical terms for worship speak of both physical gestures and life orientation. One can also speak of worship as an event: a worship gathering where a community rehearses and renews its fundamental orientation toward God. Worship gatherings are for God and for the participants. In their doxological function (for God), worship gatherings are, as the Book of Common Prayer puts it, occasions to "set forth his praise."[18] We recite and sing statements of truth ("Great is thy faithfulness") whether or not we feel blessed. And yet there is also a formational function (for us) of worship gatherings. We gather to "hear his holy Word" and to "ask" in prayer.[19] We receive blessing even as we offer worship. Furthermore, Christian worship—an expression of devotion in the very presence of One who is not only supreme but also personal, loving, known, present, and active in our midst—ultimately transcends mere "for God" or "for us" categories, becoming a rich and mutual sharing of life together (God, individuals, community). Needless to say, worship gatherings are means of grace and ought to be consciously employed as such.

The very structure of a worship gathering—whether charismatic or liturgical, with music or without—forms us into Christ as it proceeds from our arrival, through our listening, and into our meeting with Christ. The very shape of Sunday worship, for instance, forms us into a people who expect to meet God and to leave different than when we came.[20] Receiving contributions from one another in worship gatherings also forms us, as one offers a song, another reads Scripture, and another brings a personal story or a testimony. This ministering one to another is offered as a means of bringing glory to God and edification (formation) to the body of Christ (1 Cor. 11–14). The Holy Spirit sovereignly participates in Christian gatherings for worship, stimulating thoughts, feelings, and actions that lift up Christ and shape members of the community, both individually and corporately, into Christ (Acts 4:31; 13:1–2; Eph. 5:18).

The Holy Spirit, as agent of formation, uses the gathered community to stimulate our formation in Christ. We make use of the gathered community as a means of formation when we expect to be formed through a gathering, when we prepare for this formational function of worship (through self-examination, reconciliation, and other practices), and when we participate in mutual formation by serving one another at our worship gatherings.

The Word

Many traditions speak of the Christian pastorate as a ministry of Word and sacrament. Proclaiming the Scriptures through preaching is an important means through which community functions as a vehicle of grace. Imagine a fourfold incarnation of the Word. The first incarnation is, of course, the birth of Jesus on earth, the eternal Word become flesh. The second incarnation of the Word is the inspired account of the gospel of Christ in the documents of the New Testament. In each of these two incarnations, faithfulness is expressed: faithfulness to a model and faithfulness to the expression of that model. Regarding the first, Jesus is a faithful manifestation of the Almighty; he is also a faithful expression in human form. Considering the second, the New Testament writings are a faithful representation of the gospel of Jesus; they are also a faithful witness to the early Christian churches.

A third incarnation of the Word takes place in the act of preaching. As the preacher is faithful to the text of Scripture and faithful to communicate authentically, the Word is again enfleshed. There is, finally, a fourth incarnation—namely, hearers' practicing the Word, the very mind and expression of God, in their lives. The Word is preached so that it might be obeyed through the power of the Spirit. Through our lives of obedience, we make the Word flesh once again.

We, therefore, are formed through the proclamation of the Word in our community. We are transformed through the hearing of the gospel in faith, a central element of the gathering community. We gather to hear this Word as a community of faith even as we are formed through the Word into a community of faith. The community is a means of grace for our formation that occurs during both the hearing and the living out of what was heard.

Sacraments

Some Christians take part in the sacraments more often than other believers do, and the number of sacraments observed differs by tradition too. The Roman Catholic Church has seven sacraments, whereas most Protestants have only two. Regardless of these variations, we acknowledge that all Christians expect the Holy Spirit to shape our lives through certain acts we perform together. Some find the Lord's Supper to be a special time of people remembering how Jesus died on our behalf. Others experience the very presence of Christ in the bread and wine. All understand the moment to be a means of grace. Your church may celebrate baby dedications and baptisms by immersion at adult conversion, along with marriages and funerals when appropriate, while your friend's performs infant baptism, confirmation, reconciliation, marriage or holy orders, healing, and last rites. Something happens in these moments, which the Christian church throughout the centuries has recognized as means of God's grace manifest in and through the community of Christ.

We make these moments into means of grace, just as we do with the worship gathering and with the proclamation of the Word. First, we expect God to show up, to be present, through these means. Just how we experience his showing up will, of course, look different at different times and for different people. Yet we ourselves are present in a special way when we expect God to show up. Part of our role in formation is to be open and attentive to the Spirit, and this is embodied through our sincere, expectant attitude toward the community means of grace. What are we looking forward to as we participate in a marriage ceremony? When we receive healing prayer? As we approach death? Second, we prepare for that ministry. This is why we fast and confess on Friday and Saturday in preparation for Eucharist on Sunday. This is why there are the seasons of intercessory prayer prior to the Communion service in a revival meeting. We expect and so we prepare. Finally, we participate. We participate by serving, perhaps setting tables or folding cloth. We also participate by committing to obey the invitations of the Spirit given us through the sacraments. Our participation may be affected by our season of life, when we find a sacrament particularly significant and want to give it special attention. Expecting, preparing, and participating make a community act into a means of grace.

The Trials of Everyday Life

Among the many means of grace are those we take on intentionally. We choose to fast. We elect to have a spiritual director or to meet with a small group. We pay special attention to our thoughts to recognize the movement of the Spirit in our mind. We can even choose to have the community of believers be not merely a context but also a means of formation—through our expectation, preparation, and participation. But there are other means that feel less intentional. We do not choose them. Instead, they choose us. On occasion, we feel powerless in the face of harsh situations in our life. We experience disappointment, loss, emptiness, conflict, abuse, and persecution, and we can't avoid the pain. How can we come to see these situations as—or work to turn them into—effective means of Christian spiritual formation?

One thing we can do is realize and remember that the trials of ordinary life can be our friends, our allies. They really can contribute to our growth in Christ. In the section on bearing the cross in his monumental *Institutes of the Christian Religion*, the Reformer John Calvin describes a number of ways in which sufferings "not only become blessed to us, but also help much in promoting our salvation"; that is, they lead us to trust in God, enable us to experience God's faithfulness, train us in patience and obedience, restrain our unhealthy indulgence, and correct our transgressions.[21] Similarly (and more recently), psychologist Elizabeth Lewis Hall has identified a few roles that the Holy Spirit performs amid our trials: enabling us to persevere, producing the fruit of the Spirit, shaping our longings through dependence on the Spirit, comforting us, and providing confidence in God's final outcomes.[22]

So, knowing the value of these trials in our spiritual formation, what attitudes can we adopt or actions may we undertake such that the trials of life become a conscious means of grace, an integrated part of intentional spiritual formation? First, life's trials become means of spiritual formation when we approach them with an *open heart*. "As wax cannot take the imprint of a seal unless it is warmed or softened thoroughly," writes Bishop Diadochus of

Photiki in the fifth century, "so a man cannot receive the seal of God's holiness unless he is tested by labors and weaknesses."[23] If we allow trials to soften, rather than harden, us, then we can begin to trust our life to God—lifting the container of our sufferings, to use an image from Dominican mystic Catherine of Siena, as a gift to be received by God and filled with the water of his grace.[24]

Second, these trials become means of spiritual formation when we approach them with a *clear mind*. By paying careful attention to the nature and character of our trials, we cultivate a discerning spiritual formation, which is appropriate to the real conditions of one's life. Coming to our trials with a clear mind also yields a determination to learn from our trials. In this work, a habit of self-examination, wherein we regularly account for the presence of God in daily joys and trials, is quite valuable.

Third, trials of life become means of spiritual formation when we approach them with a *strong will*. A strong will does not necessarily lead to a willfulness (*will*-full-ness) toward trials. It may instead produce a spirit of persevering willingness (*will*-ing-ness) to receive what trials have to offer. Indeed, perseverance, or what psychologists call *grit*, is characteristic of authentic Christian ongoing salvation.[25] Moses perseveres through the obstacle of the Red Sea, Hannah perseveres through her barrenness, Job perseveres through his complaint to God, and Paul perseveres with his thorn. When we persevere through trials, we let them have their full beneficial effect in our lives; and strengthened through willingness, we fully devote our heart to God.

But what about the times when trials (ours or others') are the result of injustice, spiritual or political oppressions, or a deeply ingrained pattern of sin? In these cases, facing our trials with a strong will requires a willfulness so we can gird up our loins and do battle with the enemy. Amma Syncletica, an influential fourth-century desert mother, summarizes the practices of the ascetical life by proclaiming that "this is the great asceticism: to control oneself in illness and to sing hymns of thanksgiving to God."[26] We cannot control illness. But in many cases we can control our responses to illness. We can sing when we suffer, as Paul did in prison. By controlling ourselves in the midst of trial, we make trials a positive means of grace for our formation in Christ.

Employing Means

Each community employs the means of grace in its own special way, from African American gospel music to Benedictine chant. Whether we are aware of it or not, we integrate skills of heart and mind, attitudes toward the forming process, habits of life and formation, and settled values into our own approaches. All this integration, accomplished within each of our contexts and with the help of the winds of God's Spirit, results in a personality or culture that I identified in chapter 4 as a charism: the divine giftedness that an individual, a community, or a tradition brings to its own formation. Thus the task of formation is to take the step of maturity using the means appropriate for the context, our charism, and so on.

In order to explore how we employ the various means of grace, particularly in light of our context and charism, I will present one more case study. This case study may initially seem like a digression on worship, but stay with me. You will get the point by the end. As you read, imagine that you are a worship leader starting your first church job.

Case 3: The Worship Leader

Suppose you have just been hired by the church you attend. The church, which is fairly new and not affiliated with any particular denomination, is interested in maintaining ties to Christian tradition while communicating a contemporary, creative edge. The senior pastor, to whom you report, has told you that your task is simply to lead this congregation in worship. Because the senior pastor and the congregation have known and loved you since the church's inception, you are given complete freedom to accomplish this task of forming the congregation into a worshiping community. What should you do? This, in turn, leads to a related question: What is worship? By defining worship, you will identify the aim of your formational task.

You could define worship as an activity: singing or reading the liturgy. Viewing worship as a liturgical *activity* puts your focus on accurately performing the activity. Essentially, this means your job is to make sure that the words are printed or displayed correctly and that the sanctuary is designed to facilitate the common prayer of the people. Then again, you might define worship as an *experience*, either contemplative or charismatic, which would lead you to ask: Does the congregation sense the presence of God? And how is the Spirit moving through the service? You will evaluate lighting (candles, colored spotlights), music style (contemplative, high energy), and congregational response (meditative Eucharist, ministry time) in view of how these foster an appropriate experience of God.

When taken to extremes, each of these perspectives misses the point and fails at bringing the congregation to worship. Viewing worship as activity can lead to a false formalism. Viewing worship as experience can lead to a false experientialism. Suspecting this, you, being a wise pastor, probe deeper to find out what worship truly is and how it is formed. You ponder what connects the aspects of worship presented in Scripture: posture, life orientation, and gathering. And the more you reflect on worship, the more you realize that worship is fundamentally a matter of the relationship between God and God's people. Worship is a mode of being before the Creator-Redeemer God that is lived within all of life, rehearsed and renewed in gatherings, and embodied in physical postures. After studying Scripture and reading widely, you conclude that worship can be summarized by the following seven phrases:

- obsessive admiration
- utmost respect or regard
- passionate interest
- absolute surrender
- willing service
- unconditional obedience
- embodied obeisance

It is one thing to admire some people, but when I get obsessive and just can't stop talking about their every characteristic, you look at me and say, "Friend, you don't just admire those people. You *worship* them." Again, it is one thing to have respect for someone, but when that respect is taken to the utmost, to the point that I am extremely careful not to give the least offense, then again you might look at me and say, "You don't just respect. You worship." When I offer an absolute surrender to their desires, which is more than just obeying without condition what is openly commanded, when no sacrifice is too great, when I cross the line from interest to absolute preoccupation, when I try to anticipate another's every wish, when I am willing to make myself totally vulnerable by posturing myself in total submission to one superior to me—insofar as these are present, you are going to accuse me of worship. This is what worship is all about.

If this is worship, then it cannot be understood simply as an activity or an experience. True worship includes aspects of all the phrases listed above—our submission is embodied in action, our admiration is experienced, our regard is practiced in life and in our gatherings—and so cannot be reduced to just one. The aim of worship formation is an "all things new" transformation wherein every aspect of our being is wholly oriented to the supreme deity. And for Christians, this is evident in our abandoned praise and service to the resurrected Christ through the ministry of the Holy Spirit in the communion of the body of Christ.

So then, now that we know something of what worship is, we must ask what it means to lead worship. Answering this will help you understand your charge as a congregation's worship leader and identify what you are to do.

You might begin by learning something of the culture and charism of this congregation. (Even if this has been your home congregation, you will want to carefully consider these.) It will do no good to introduce these seven phrases to your congregation and expect them to perform accordingly. Passionate interest, for example, cannot be manufactured, although when imposed it can be faked. What you must do is discover this congregation's natural understanding and practice of worship—however they understand it. Then, with this insight, you can take steps (with the Spirit's leading) to meet them where they are currently and form them over time toward an increasingly mature Christian worship.

As it turns out, this congregation thinks of worship either as the singing portion of a Sunday gathering or as a summary of what happens on Sunday at its "worship service." When pressed, many members would say worship is something that Christians do with their lives and even that it is something beyond personal devotions. Though they have read Bible passages about people bowing down and worshiping, thinking of worship as a posture is out of their experience. You decide it is best to start with the weekly gathering and work from there.

Being a relatively new congregation, members really have few habits in place. Valuing both tradition and contemporary creative expressions, they generally have a blend of musical styles in their worship services, so you intuit that trying to foster admiration of God through a heavy dose of Reformation hymns is not going to go over well. However, a couple of hymns here and there interspersed with God-centered praise choruses might help the congregation perceive God's beauty and stimulate interest and admiration.

One attitude this congregation embraces is risk taking. Since this is a recently formed congregation, currently unaffiliated with any particular denomination, members do not usually hold to particular ways of learning and changing. This openness is actually part of their charism, their gifted personality as a group. They think of themselves as pioneers who are trying to explore a creative way of life with God and one another. You decide to honor and make good use of this attitude in the way you lead them into worship. They are open, so you can experiment. To encourage in them an aspect of worship, you introduce various means of grace—altar calls and prayer ministry teams to encourage wholehearted surrender, response cards noting congregational needs that congregants can fill out during the service to encourage willing service, common physical postures used at various times of the service to encourage embodied obeisance—and later evaluate how well each worked and the fruit it bore.

One skill present in many members is creativity. This is a pretty artistic congregation. How can this charism be employed or developed to nurture their sense of authentic worship? How can you foster their skills of creativity alongside the skills of contemplative awareness that are so valuable in discerning the leading of God's Spirit toward paths of obedience?

Ultimately, you realize that perhaps the best thing you can do in this congregation to foster real worship is give them a sense of God's attractiveness. You decide to promote it by employing a couple of means of grace. First, you plan a pair of one-day retreats for the church that focus on the greatness of God. At the initial retreat, you talk about the book of Psalms and teach the participants to meditate on individual psalms, learning to praise God for who he is and for what he has done, and teaching them to write their own psalms. You recruit some of the people who attend this retreat to read the psalms on Sunday mornings. At the next retreat, you focus on Jesus by teaching the participants to read Gospel passages imaginatively and then to see—as if they were there themselves—just how wonderful Jesus is. Those who are excited by this practice become the people who read the Gospel lesson each week. Second, you institute a time of testimony in the Sunday worship service. You communicate a set of guidelines for giving testimonies in the service (covering length, appropriateness for all ages, plain language instead of Christian-ese, etc., so things do not get out of hand) and provide instruction on how members can share what God is doing in their lives.

By employing these small measures, these means of grace—meditation, journaling psalms, arts, imaginative Bible reading, training relationships, retreats, testimonies—you foster worship in a way that is appropriate to their own context, culture, and charism. A wise use of means is paying attention to an individual or community such that the means employed to foster maturity fit the people in our care.

This case study, in which a new pastor is charged with fostering worship in a congregation, is only a single illustration of the relationship between means and charism. Nevertheless, the point is clear: when the means of grace are divorced from careful attention, their application is likely to miss the mark. We must learn to appreciate who we are. What are your own habits of life? What values have characterized you over the years? What attitudes (assumptions, expectations, fears) do you bring to your own formation? What skills do you bring to the forming process? Answering these questions will help reveal your charism, your personality insofar as it affects your spiritual growth. God gifts and uses you right in the middle of your own mix of strengths and weaknesses. The task of formation is to nurture the appropriate next step of growth, so when we match the *intention* of formation (choosing to make use of the means of grace) with the *wisdom* of formation (selecting and applying means as they are appropriate to the contexts, culture, and charism of communities and individuals), we begin to learn the *art* of formation. In the chapters ahead we will see how this works in key areas of life.

Going Deeper

1. In this chapter, I've suggested that means of grace can be valuable for spiritual formation. But isn't there a danger in making too much of these means? Shouldn't we embrace the motto "let go and let God" and not try to manufacture our own sanctification through a program of disciplines, strategies, and relationships? Isn't God sovereign enough to manage our formation without our orchestrations? Just what are the advantages and disadvantages of making use of means of grace?

2. We have learned that the trials of life become means of grace when we appreciate the opportunities for transformation they can provide and when we nurture the virtues of perseverance: a soft heart, a clear mind, and a strong will. But where do we gain these virtues? How can we nurture a soft heart, a clear mind, and a strong will such that we find growth during our trials? Where do we find the grit to turn problems into possibilities?

3. We also considered the idea of nature as a means of grace. But as I mentioned, many Christians are just beginning to explore this phenomenon. What do you think? What are the connections between God's revelation through nature and our own formation through nature? What might be the concerns related to pursuing relationship with God through nature?

4. Perhaps the practice most clearly associated with means of grace is the practice of writing and living a rule of life, which ministry leader Stephen Macchia defines as "a holistic description of the Spirit-empowered rhythms and relationships that create, redeem, sustain, and transform the life God invites you to humbly fulfill for Christ's glory."[27] Indeed, the golden triangle of a rule of life, regular self-examination (in light of this rule), and nurturing relationships helps believers embody the gospel and grow in Christlikeness in the middle of real circumstances

and with the leading of the Holy Spirit. So how do you begin to write a rule of life? Simply put, follow these steps. (1) Pray and ask God to show you how you ought to live. (2) Take stock of how you are already living. (3) Dream of what a God-centered life in the context of your own particular circumstances might look like. (4) Try an experiment with one or two changes. (5) Review and revise.[28]

PART THREE

THE PRACTICE

7

···············

Formed into Prayer

Overview

In this chapter, we examine what the practice of spiritual formation looks like with regard to our relationship with God, particularly in the crucial matter of prayer. To answer the question of what prayer is, we will look at both the specific term and the broader concept surrounding the idea of communication with God. We also review a few important types of prayer: simple communication, intercession, and meditation. At that point, we'll consider how we pray and the roles that Scripture, imagination, distractions, and our bodies play in prayer. We will explore the human spirit in prayer and the Holy Spirit in prayer. We will consider answers, relationship, and union—the aims of prayer. Finally, we will apply our insights by asking what the task of formation—fostering the next appropriate step of growth—might look like as one matures in prayer.

···

Think about your prayer life for a moment. When you read the term *prayer life*, what came to mind? Did you think about something you do (or should do)? Do you picture yourself in church and praying with others? Does a vague sense of being in relationship pervade all your times of prayer? Just what is prayer to you, and what might it mean to be formed into prayer?

We have been introduced to the primary elements of Christian spiritual formation: aims, contexts, agents, transformation, task, means, and charism.

Now let's see how these parts work together as a whole, particularly with reference to the full, rich, and beautiful "all things new" promise that is the aim of Christian spiritual formation. My goal in this second half of the book is to show how Christian spiritual formation is practiced, particularly with regard to the elements among "all things" that are most commonly discussed in treatments of spiritual formation: prayer (relationship with God), community (relationship with others), intellectual and moral formation (relationship with ourselves), and mission (relationship with the world).

This chapter on prayer also marks the beginning of part 3, "The Practice," because it is the right place to start. If Christian spiritual formation addresses our spiritual life—our relationship with God—then it must begin with prayer. Prayer is by definition the relational meeting place of God and God's people. Even though our relationship with God extends into all kinds of other areas (in fact, it *must* spill over), it is centrally located in the midst of our prayerful communication with God. We must, therefore, first examine what it is like to be formed into relationship with God and into prayer.

We will explore our formation into prayer first by examining prayer itself and looking at the various ways that we, as Christians, pray. This will lead us to a discussion of what it means to pray in the Spirit and to pray with our spirit. In the end, we will see that the ultimate aim of prayer is an ever-increasing joining of persons: God and God's people. Finally, we will turn to the task of formation, keeping the idea of formation into prayer in mind. My goal is to equip you so you can help yourself and others recognize contexts, assess and attend to the spirit of their praying, make use of appropriate means and agents, and take appropriate steps for growing into harmonious communication with God.

What Is Prayer?

If we had lived in Britain decades ago, we might have encountered someone on a street corner and asked, "I pray, what is the o'clock?" The term *pray* as used here is a request, and some of the biblical words for prayer share this connotation. So is prayer merely petition? Not at all. First Timothy 2:1 recommends that "petitions, prayers, intercession, and thanksgiving be made for all people." Patristic theologians saw in this passage a reference to different types of prayer. The Lord's Prayer (Matt. 6:9–13; Luke 11:2–4), while being structured in a series of petitions, expresses adoration, confession, consecration, and more. Similarly, the Psalms have been understood from the earliest Christian centuries as an expansive resource for discovering and expressing "the stirrings and the equanimity of the soul appropriate to them."[1] Ultimately the term *prayer* has come to express both a specific meaning (petition) and a broader meaning (any expression of relationship with God).[2]

Generally speaking, Christian prayer is communication with God. It involves three central elements: speaking (using verbal communication as a model), listening, and what can be referred to as the space in between. We speak to God and God hears, or God speaks and we hear. The context—silence and relationship—gives shape to the speech and the hearing. Yet prayer is communication with God. So while prayer is mutual self-disclosure, it is not a conversation between equals. Prayer is communication between created and Creator, between saved and Savior. This distinction must always be retained lest, in the excitement of interpersonal communication, we fail to regard God as *God*. Our worship, our thanksgiving, and our meditation are all expressed before the Almighty One, who graces us with the very possibility of relationship.

Thus, the foundation of our prayer, the grounds of the very possibility of our praying as communities or individuals, is our God and the gospel itself. I like to summarize this by reciting the Gloria along with annotations that remind me of God's role in prayer:

> Glory be to the Father, *who has created and commanded prayer,*
> and to the Son, *who has modeled and mediated prayer,*
> and to the Holy Spirit, *who births and breathes prayer,*
> as it was in the beginning, *for God has always desired our prayer,*
> is now, *in me, my community, and the world*
> and ever shall be,
> world without end, *for our prayer will find its ultimate answer in the end of ends.*
> Amen.

Prayer, like human-to-human communication, can be looked at as an instance of communication, as an event, or as a state. We speak of saying particular prayers or of having a time of prayer. We can also speak of prayer as a state of somewhat continuous interpersonal relationship. Theophan the Recluse, a Russian Orthodox saint, writes regarding the latter, describing one whose prayer "continues within him in whatever he is doing, present when he talks and writes, speaking in his dreams, waking him up in the morning. Prayer in such a man is no longer a series of acts, but a state; and he has found the way to fulfill Paul's command, 'Pray without ceasing' (1 Thess. 5:17)."[3]

The history of Christian prayer is a long and fascinating story itself.[4] We hear of common prayer lifted to God from magnificent Catholic cathedrals and from quiet Quaker gatherings. We learn of conversational prayer expressed with meticulous care through the collects crafted by Anglican divines and expressed with abandoned spontaneity during American tent revivals. We discover the theologies of contemplative prayer reflected in North African sayings and Celtic Christian charms. The history of prayer is relevant because we need to recognize that Christian prayer often comes to us in a context, through a tradition or a "school" of spirituality. The way we picture God when we pray, the means we use to pray, and even the moods that govern our prayers are all shaped by the history of our Christian faith traditions.

Traditions exhibit both strengths and weaknesses. Lutheran confidence in our acceptance by God through Christ's death can, misapplied, become a shallow overconfidence in God's mercy. Pentecostal permission for exuberant praise can, when distorted, lead some to devalue the practice of quiet meditation. At the same time, the prescriptive atmosphere of some Baptist pleas for converts to come forward to an altar and pray the "sinner's prayer," while occasionally harmful, can be truly sanctified and lead to a sincere call that invites people to find new life in Christ. Our traditions are the birthplaces of the best and the worst of our prayers. The task of Christian spiritual formation is to discern how our contexts have influenced our praying and then to assess, in light of this, the resources, the realistic possibilities, and the challenges that face a community or individual as we seek an ever more Christlike relationship with God in prayer.

Types of Prayer

Often, when people think of prayer, they think of a particular type of prayer: the simple "Now I lay me down to sleep" prayer they said as a child, or requests that weigh heavy on their hearts, or times of silent contemplation. Many excellent books exploring the varieties of Christian prayer have already been written.[5] I will comment below on three kinds of prayer insofar as they illustrate our own formation into prayer.

First, there is simple prayer. The Lord's Prayer incorporates worship, surrender, confession, and more.[6] We might repeat a psalm or the Jesus Prayer ("Lord Jesus Christ, Son of God, have mercy on me, a sinner"), or pray in tongues quietly. African American work songs join laborer and Savior together through the hardships of the day. Ways of being present with God in prayer are myriad; forms of lifting up a brief expression of thanksgiving or a plea for help are endless. Essential to simple prayer is a simple attitude, for God welcomes us in our imperfection and invites us simply to "keep company."[7] Formation into simple prayer is just learning to be there, sincerely before God, presenting our bodies before God with a positive intention. Then we simply receive prayer when it is given, whether we are given something to say or something to hear. We notice it, flow with it, and, uninhibited, live with it, but we do not try to make more of it than what it is.

A second type of prayer is the prayer of petition or intercession, which is the communication to God where we offer up the needs of ourselves or another. We can lift a request to God through a simple prayer, but a practice of intercession takes some planning. Most mornings, I guide my time of intercession by following the prayers of the people in the Book of Common Prayer's morning prayer service. This set of prayers begins with the Lord's Prayer and provides suffrages, which are prayers that express common themes in word-for-word quotations from Scripture. Then I pray one or more collects—crafted prayers from the congregation to God that merge scriptural language, theological sensitivity, and a theme. Finally, I have an unscripted time of offering up my own varied concerns and thanksgivings for the day. This flow seems to fit my own movements, from the general to the particular, as I lift up intercession to God.

Another valuable model of intercession is the pattern used in the public prayer meetings of eighteenth- and nineteenth-century America and England. We arrive and begin with a song, a prayer, and a reading designed to inspire us to have confidence in prayer. Someone introduces a topic for our time together—for example, the success of God's kingdom in our neighborhood. Perhaps a couple of people are already prepared to offer testimonies of God's work in the neighborhood, and our faith is encouraged. We continue with simple prayer, making room for a song or a few words when appropriate. Then we plan the next meeting, if necessary, and close in prayer.[8] Whereas simple prayers can be offered to God in any situation of life, the ministry of intercession usually requires time (and often space) devoted to it.

To be formed into intercession is to be formed not only into a pattern but also into a way of thinking about God and God's interaction with the world. If God knows everything, why do we need to pray? If God is all-loving, why didn't he answer our prayer? Sooner or later, in order to grow into prayer, some people have to face these questions head-on. Some have little trouble finding a sense of God's presence even though they experience unanswered prayer. For others, unanswered prayer is a faith crisis. Formation into intercession may require not only a plan but also a perspective.

A third type of prayer is meditative or contemplative prayer.[9] This practice of being with and even communicating with God does not use many words. We may read a passage of Scripture slowly, taking time to quietly receive from the text, think about each phrase, listen for the Spirit's whisper, and offer a brief word of prayer when it arises. We may pose our bodies to express our feelings to God and to wait in God's presence, or we might just sit next to God the way we might sit on the porch quietly watching the sunset with a loved one. Sometimes words are not needed.

On the one hand, contemplative prayer may be the simplest prayer of all. It is the sigh we breathe even before we voice our thanks or our requests. But, on the other hand, many of us find it difficult to grow into meditative and contemplative prayer. Some never really feel comfortable in this milieu, just as some never seem to feel comfortable praying aloud in a meeting. And that's fine. For some people, within some stages of life—such as being new to the faith or having had little instruction—setting aside extended periods of meditative and contemplative prayer can be confusing. For others, however, contemplative forms of prayer serve as wonderful spaces for listening, speaking, or just being with God. Formation into prayer is a matter of wisdom: the right communication for the right people at the right time.

How We Pray

Think, for example, about common prayer—how we pray together. Some use a guidebook containing written prayers that we might say together or responsively. Others follow their own hearts. Some raise hands while others make a sign of the cross. Some kneel while others dance. Now think about conversational prayer or contemplative prayer. How do we then pray? Sometimes we read Scripture and think. Other times we pour out our feelings. Then there are those times when we just sit quietly with Jesus. Prayer is more than mere technique. Nevertheless, just as my communication with others can be improved by improving my communication skills, and just as the introduction of some new communication technique can, on occasion, stimulate a breakthrough in my person-to-person communication, so too our prayer life can be cultivated by consciously thinking about how we pray.

Certainly Scripture is central to our ways of praying. It is the Word of God. God communicates to us through the Scriptures, and Scripture gives voice to our own prayer. Many passages are themselves prayers. For example, through the words of the lament psalms, we can give voice to the sufferings of oppressed peoples everywhere. Even when passages are not themselves prayers, we can lift prayers fashioned from the meaning of the passages. For example, we might read Paul's proclamation of the unity of the body in Galatians 3:28, "There is neither Jew nor Gentile, neither slave nor free, nor is there male or female," and use this passage as a guide for our prayers of intercession: "Lord, I witness division in the church today. Races are still in tension. Rich and poor still do not welcome one another. Men and women are still at odds. Please, Lord, bring a time when there will truly be neither Jew nor gentile." Another approach to the prayerful reading of Scripture, as noted in chapter 6, is lectio divina, or sacred reading. Using lectio divina, we simply combine the acts of reading, meditating or reflecting, voicing prayer, being contemplatively present with God, and living out in action what has transpired. As you can see by just these few examples, Scripture can be variously and profitably employed as a means of prayer.[10]

We also use our imagination when we pray. We read the descriptions of heaven in Revelation and picture what it must be like. Or we read a Gospel story and imagine Jesus healing a leper. When we intercede, we picture what it might be like if our prayers were answered. When we give thanks, we remember the situation with gratitude in our heart. Imagination is a part of everything we do, and sometimes we can cultivate our communication with God by consciously engaging our imagination in prayer. Some like to picture themselves and Jesus together in a favorite place when they pray. Someone else may bring to mind a difficult memory and imagine Jesus present in that event. (Remember, Jesus *is* present. The active use of imagination in prayer can remind us of what is always true.) Yes, there are some concerns about using our imagination in prayer. We should ask: How do we represent the unrepresentable? Are we worshiping an image rather than the Almighty God? Are these imaginations just entertaining distractions that take us way from honest communication? Could we be led astray through these images? All of these misgivings must be addressed with care and wisdom. The God who made our minds and who commands us to love him with all our heart and soul and mind and strength (Mark 12:30) desires that the fullness of our experience, including the use of our imagination, be brought into ever-greater likeness to the mind of Christ. This is formation into prayer.

We also use our bodies when we pray. In contemporary Western culture, it is common to sit and pray with eyes closed, head down, and hands folded. Some of this can be traced to the submissive posture of a vassal before a king, but it has lost that expression. Today this posture simply communicates an approach to God that sees prayer as both private and interior. This is not necessarily bad, for prayer does indeed engage us in the most private and interior rooms of our hearts. Yet prayer is also more than that. And we can communicate this "more" with our bodies. Prayer is a celebration of the risen Christ, and I can communicate this with raised hands and a loud voice. Prayer is devotion to the Almighty, and I can communicate this through lying down flat on my face. Scripture tells us of people lifting hands and eyes, sitting, kneeling, standing, bowing, prostrating, dancing, and beating their breast, all in the act of prayer. Some like to walk and pray or to work and pray. While it may seem like a small thing to change our pose, for some people, just experimenting with different uses of our bodies for prayer can open up new vistas of communication.[11]

We can make use of all kinds of techniques to nourish our life with God through prayer. We make use of sight by placing a cross at the front of our church building or by gazing at a Christian icon when in prayer. We make use of sound by including song and music in our times of personal and community prayer. Repetition is a means of focusing ourselves on a single aspect of Christ or the gospel. We actively choose to think about (reason) or feel (emotion) what Christ might think or feel as we read Scripture or intercede or contemplatively wait with God. The possibilities are inexhaustible.

When we set aside time for prayer and employ means for prayer, we are beset by distractions. You try to pray but your mind jumps hither and thither. I remember a responsibility I forgot to put on my to-do list. A difficult conversation with a coworker pops into your head and you can't get rid of it. Sooner or later, most of us, as we are formed into prayer, end up having to learn how to deal with distractions. Sometimes I can simply make a note of that to-do item and return to prayer. It may help to spend a little time in reflective intercession, in which you hold up a difficult conversation before the Lord instead of trying to ignore it. Occasionally, a nagging thought or feeling becomes a topic for profound and prolonged self-examination with Christ. But distractions can also be a tactic our spiritual enemy uses to keep us from prayer, in which cases we recognize the strategy, rebuke the enemy, and return to prayer with greater vigor. But most importantly, as we mature into prayer, we learn not to make too big of a deal of our distractions. I like the way that author Simon Tugwell compares prayer to an ordinary conversation between humans, which is compatible with "quite a lot of distraction":

> When we talk to one another, there may be a hundred and one things popping in and out of our minds that are nothing whatsoever to do with our conversation, but they do not in any serious way impede conversation. . . . For practical purposes, we handle most distractions simply by not taking any notice of them, and just getting on with the conversation.[12]

When it comes to prayer, the process of Christian spiritual formation is a process of moving from where we are into an ever-closer relationship with God through Jesus Christ. We have considered how we pray. It is time to examine the spirit of prayer.

The Spirit of Prayer

Remember, prayer is not a matter of technique. It may be facilitated by the use of imagination or the repetition of Scripture, but prayer is communication—not the method of communication. Ultimately, this communication is the sharing of spirit and Spirit, so to be formed into prayer is to be formed into spirit/Spirit (as discussed in chap. 4). Speaking about spirit/Spirit, however, is not easy. I join these words together with a slash in order to indicate that the scriptural language for spirit/Spirit itself is ambiguous. The Hebrew and Greek words mean different things in different settings, so we need to investigate this as we learn how prayer is a joining of spirit and Spirit.

First, let us explore the place of spirit in prayer. Speaking prayer is itself an act of releasing air, spirit, breath—a breath given to us by God.[13] Quite often, the biblical words for spirit refer to the core of our personality, especially insofar as we are in relationship with God. Job simply has to speak, for, he says, "The spirit within me compels me" (Job 32:18). In 1 Corinthians, Paul makes a contrast between praying with our mind and praying with our spirit (1 Cor. 14:15), with the latter referring, it seems, to a part of us that communicates deeply in relationship with God, perhaps transcending certain rational processes. We are also commanded to pray "in spirit" or "in the Spirit" (*en pneumati*; Eph. 6:18; Jude 20). What does it mean to communicate with God from our spirit?

Picture a conversation between two people—yourself and a friend.[14] What is going on for you during this conversation? At one level, you are simply talking and listening. There is the forming of words, the hearing, and the making sense of the other's words. At the same time but at another level, you are navigating the conversation internally, with thoughts like these: *What does she think of me? Is that question for real, or is she just trying to get information out of me? She's looking at my shoulder. Do I have something on my shirt? I'm gonna have to go in a few minutes, but I want to introduce her to my friends before I leave.* And so on. If you pay careful attention to yourself during a conversation, you can actually be aware of what's happening on both levels at the same time.

But there is also a third level. Beneath the forming and hearing of words and beneath the questions and the posturing is you—you present to this person, and this person present to you. Can you feel it? All of the thoughts and words and such rest on top of the simple, fundamental presence you share with each other. In any conversation, this third level has its own character, just as the other two levels have their own character. When the other is a stranger, you are present in a different way than you are when the other is a close friend. For example, a second-level question like *What does she think of me?* feels different depending on whether you are present to a close friend or to a stranger. Your mood, the state of your relationship, and other factors influence the quality of this subtle presence to another at the third level. And if you are very attentive, you can actually be aware of all three levels of communication at the same time. Sometimes the richest moments of a relationship are when you are able to dwell in this third level.

Now let's change the scene. Instead of imagining yourself in a conversation with another person, imagine yourself reading the Scriptures. What is going on? Well, let's begin again at the first layer. You are reading the apostle Peter's writing, forming words and sentences in your mind or with your mouth (if you are reading aloud). At the same time but on the second level, you're navigating the text and thinking things such as *I've read this text before. That is a really strange comment. I never understood that phrase. I like the way the words flow from this verse to the next. Is that verse talking about me?*

But underneath the words, underneath the questions and responses, and silently grounding the very character of the experience of reading Scripture is your simple presence to God and God's presence to you. Even with your unconfessed sins, your spiritual hopes, your desire to be held in the midst of your pain, or the state of your relationship with God, this shared presence is there, right there, every time you open the Bible to read!

At times in our conversations, we correct another's communication because they are being inconsistent between these levels. Thus, you might say to me, "Come on, I can tell you're not really being honest with me. You are not talking to me." Or someone might say, "You're not listening to me!" In each of these cases, words are being spoken, and sounds are being heard. Nevertheless, you sense that I am not speaking or listening from the heart—or from the spirit. "You're talking to me as if we were business partners," you might say, or, "You're talking to me as if nothing ever happened." This is not a matter of failure to speak or to listen; rather, it is a failure to communicate the appropriate space in between. In these examples, there is a gap between the conversation and the quality of relational space that should be governing the conversation. To put it another way, if our words, tone, gestures, and presence don't match our spirit, then the conversation just isn't authentic.

And this, I think, is what it might be like to pray from our spirit—being as sincere with God as we are able. Understand this: you can have all the correct techniques, from the right words and meditation format to devotional gestures and deep emotional feelings. But if your spirit is not present, if there is a disconnect between the depth of your heart and the form of your prayer, it is not prayer. This is precisely what the Old Testament prophets cry out against (see Jer. 6:19–20; Hosea 8:13–14). "You make all the proper sacrifices," they warn, "but you are not offering them out of a place of sincere relationship with me!" Praying from the spirit happens when the words and the questions and the thoughts arise from an authentic relational presence with God. Sometimes this spirit-infused prayer may be the simplest thank-you or cry for help. At other times, this kind of speaking from our depths may transcend what we are able to communicate with our thoughts and words (hence Paul's comments in 1 Cor. 14:15; see also Rom. 8:26). Navigating communication with God at the deep level of our spirit involves being honest about our trust (or lack of trust) in God. It involves dealing with those times we feel we have been hurt by God, when our expectations were not met. It involves coming clean with God about our stealthy sins. It is with our relationship with God—spirit to Spirit—in mind that we are able to weed out the thoughts and such entering our experience from evil "spirits." And from our spirit issues gratitude and a sense of the beauty of God, overwhelming ordinary language such that silence (or, for some, speaking in tongues) seems to be the only form that can express what has to be expressed from our spirit.

Of course, our sensitivity to spirit and our ability to navigate from spirit will vary by person and by community. We have already discussed the various stages of growth in the Christian life. Just as young children mature in their own self-awareness and their ability to perceive and communicate within the nuances of ordinary relationships, so too we can grow more open in our presence toward God and more agile in our ability to perceive and communicate within the subtle ups and downs of our spiritual lives. To be formed into Christian prayer, then, is—in part—to be formed in spirit such that we communicate with God from the depths of our spirit.

But Christian prayer is not just communication from our spirit. It is more significantly a relationship with the Holy Spirit. Prayer is the joining of spirit and Spirit. We have already learned that the Spirit of God is the primary agent of our formation in Christ, and this is particularly true of our formation into prayer. The Holy Spirit characteristically introduces thoughts, feelings, images, and inclinations into our experience. A Christian congregation suffering persecution lifts itself to God in prayer and is filled with a sense of hope through the confidence of God's love for them (Rom. 5:5).

An anxious young woman reads—prayerfully musing on—the Sermon on the Mount, and Jesus's comments about worry speak to her heart in a way she has never before experienced. It feels as if Jesus himself were sitting next to her, comforting her in her fears (John 14:26). The activity of the Holy Spirit as agent of formation is particularly noticeable in the context of prayer.

First, the Spirit of God gives birth to prayer within the people of God. When the Spirit moves, prayer happens. The Spirit empowered Bezalel and Oholiab to design a place of prayer for the nation of Israel (Exod. 31:1–11). This same spirit/Spirit of God is promised to God's people in great fullness, as Zechariah proclaims: "I will pour out on the house of David and the inhabitants of Jerusalem a spirit of grace and supplication" (Zech. 12:10). Prayer is frequently mentioned following the filling or outpouring of God's Spirit (Acts 2:4, 42; 10:44–46; 19:6; see also Eph. 5:18–19). The Spirit gifts the gathered body of Christ with expressions of prayer (1 Cor. 12:10; 14:2). Interestingly, at the close of the Christian Scriptures, we find not only the bride and those who hear but also the Spirit, who is saying, "Come" (Rev. 22:17). New Testament scholar C. F. D. Moule writes,

> It is noteworthy that the Holy Spirit is, in a sense, the subject rather than the object of prayer. . . . We do not address the Spirit in prayer; rather the Holy Spirit enables us to address God. . . . The Spirit utters the words that Christians have to say: the Spirit enables their utterance to be in line with God's design.[15]

Second, the prayers of the people of God mediate the presence and activity of the Spirit. We read that the Spirit is communicated to people through the activity of the laying on of hands (Acts 9:17; 19:6; see also Luke 11:13). The Spirit of God visits us in the midst of our prayers as a gathered people or individually on "the Lord's Day" (Acts 13:2; Rev. 1:10). The Holy Spirit also responds to our prayers. Immediately following the prayers of Jesus's followers in Acts 4:31, we learn that they were all "filled with the Holy Spirit." It is also significant, I think, that some of the boldest promises of answered prayer in the Bible are found in the context of Jesus's discourse on his departure and the sending of the Holy Spirit (John 14–16). God's Spirit leads us to prayer and our prayer, in turn, opens doors to a still-more-expansive ministry of the Spirit.

This mutuality of interaction between our prayer and the Spirit's active presence can be understood, third and finally, in light of this: God's Spirit breathes prayer from within our spirit. This is, I believe, why translators have great difficulty trying to render the terms *spirit* and *Spirit* in passages that speak of prayer and worship (John 4:23–24; 1 Cor. 14:16; Eph. 6:18; Jude 20). When the core of our being is inadequate for prayer, we find the core of God's own being present, expressing that which is both our deepest desire and the will of God (Rom. 8:26–27). As the Dutch Reformed politician and theologian Abraham Kuyper states, in regard to our imperfect condition and the ministry of the Holy Spirit in the context of our praying, "the Holy Spirit comes to help our infirmities, *in* us to pray *for* us, as [though] *it were our own prayer*."[16]

Perhaps the paramount biblical passage in this regard is Romans 8:14–16. In what is perhaps the most important chapter in Christian Scripture on the Holy Spirit and spiritual formation, Paul writes,

> For those who are led by the Spirit of God are the children of God. The Spirit you received does not make you slaves, so that you live in fear again; rather, the Spirit you received brought about your adoption to sonship. And by him we cry, "*Abba*, Father." The Spirit himself testifies with our spirit that we are God's children.

"The Spirit himself testifies with our spirit." The essence of our relationship with God is an intimate sharing between our spirit and the Spirit of God. This communication of spirit and Spirit is the foundation of and the condition for the possibility of Christian prayer. And it is on the basis of what's described in verses 14–16 that Paul is able to speak of the ministry of the Spirit in and through our spirit in prayer in verses 26–27. If the term *spirit* is a way of speaking of who we are as a community or as individuals, and if prayer is essentially communication with God, and if God is characteristically present to us as Christians through the Holy Spirit, then we can begin to grasp how prayer most fundamentally is the mutual sharing of spirit and Spirit.

To be formed into prayer, then, involves not only the *how* but also the *who* of prayer: the who of the person in prayer and the Person to whom we pray (and our understanding and experience of that Person). On the one hand, in order to grow in prayer, we must develop a practical pattern of communication, just as one might schedule regular time to share with a loved one. We develop a sense of the ways we pray: using Scripture to stimulate our thoughts, using a prayer list to remember our requests, and so on. And we have to make this world of prayer our own. It must arise out of, and express, our personality. Some may need to write prayers in a journal. Others may need to pace about and cry aloud. In order to be formed into prayer, we will need to experiment and discover our own way of praying. Furthermore, we will fail to pray—or to take the necessary and sometimes difficult steps to grow into prayer—without adequate motivation. We must have some sense of the need or value of prayer—especially when prayer does not come easily. At times when we are stretched by God or by our own practices, we find that the enemy pummels us with all manner of thoughts and feelings to keep us from prayer. Only a clear motivation and the grace of God will keep us at it.

Being formed into prayer also involves developing our knowledge of God. Most basically, we grow into prayer when we have a view of God that fits the idea of prayer. If we think God is distant and uninterested in our lives, we are unlikely to pray. As I mentioned above, our theology of God and our practice of prayer are intimately connected. But our sense of the *who* of prayer is a matter of both theology and personal experience (or corporate experience if we are talking about the prayer life of a congregation or other community of faith). What is our experience of prayer? Have we recently encountered God in a powerful way? Have we had a long season of seemingly unanswered prayer? What do we know of the spirit and the Spirit of prayer? All of these—the *how*, the *who*, and the *Who*—play a part in our formation into Christian prayer, and we must be prepared to address each as it is appropriate.

Formation into prayer may be summarized as follows. It involves

- a sense of what prayer is about (What am I actually doing when I pray?)
- a growing view of God (To whom am I directing my prayer, really?)
- a plan to pray (What will I do practically when I pray? When do I do it?)
- a growing experience of God (How have I encountered God—and how might I encounter God?)
- a motivation for prayer (Why do I pray? What are my reasons for praying? What keeps me praying?)
- an openness to prayer (Am I OK with how this may or may not feel? What happens if I become uncomfortable?)
- a personal appropriation of prayer (How do I make all this authentically my own, an expression of who I am?)

The Aims of Prayer

Think about prayer again, only this time, think about *why* you pray. What are you trying to get out of it? What do you want when you pray? When we ponder these questions, we begin to explore the edges between the aims of prayer and the aims of formation.

At a basic level, the aim of prayer is answered prayer. Prayer is a kind of request, and the purpose of a request is to obtain an appropriate response—in this case, from God. With a petition, we look for a favor. With a confession, we look for assurance of reconciliation. With a prayer of deliverance, we look for freedom. Each kind of prayer seeks an appropriate response—as Christ taught in the Lord's Prayer. Even an expression of adoration seeks the glory of God to be made known. So formation into the prayer of Christ is formation into a life of prayer that regularly and dependently looks to our loving Father for daily needs, for forgiven acceptance, and for deliverance from those things that threaten to derail us from the rich life we were meant to embody.

At another level, the aim of prayer is an increasingly authentic presence before God. When we grow in our understanding of God, we see the God to whom we pray in new ways. When we are emotionally healed, we sense the love of God in prayer anew. When we give ourselves wholeheartedly or commit to the goal of making known the gospel of Christ's kingdom in evangelism, in community, and in justice, we find ourselves praying both within and for a world of need. Thus we are in a cycle where conversion transforms our prayer, and prayer leads to further conversion.

All of this, in the end, points toward a core end, an aim of Christian prayer perhaps at its deepest: mystical union with God. There is a vast amount of literature exploring the themes of mysticism and union as well as other themes such as contemplation.[17] For the sake of brevity, let me offer one Pauline reflection regarding our formation into mysticism and a few comments on our formation into prayerful union with God.

The apostle Paul's presentation of mystery was a subversion of both the Greek and Jewish ideas circulating in the ancient world. For the Greeks, the mysteries were religious schools or societies offering esoteric wisdom, healing, and salvation to those who carefully followed rules of initiation and rites of participation. The Jewish concept of mystery was rooted in God's revelation to Daniel (see Dan. 2:18–19, 27–30, 47; see also 1 Enoch 51:1–4; 2 Baruch 81:1–4; 4 Ezra 14:1–9; 1QH^a 7.26–27; 11.9–10; 1QHab 7.1–14). The Jewish apocalyptic culture present in the birthplace of Christianity saw God as One who revealed special things to special people. These special things were secrets—mysteries regarding God's plan that were communicated through special writings and then unlocked and interpreted by a chosen few to whom God imparted knowledge.

Paul, however, employed the language of mystery in order to subvert both the Greek and Hebrew perspectives. In Colossians 1:25–27, Paul describes his own calling:

> I have become its servant by the commission God gave me to present to you the word of God in its fullness—the mystery that has been kept hidden for ages and generations, but is now disclosed to the Lord's people. To them God has chosen to make known among the Gentiles the glorious riches of this mystery, which is Christ in you, the hope of glory.

Like both the Greeks and Hebrews, Paul affirms the existence of mysteries that have been "hidden for ages and generations," the knowledge of which provides "glorious riches." The meaning of these mysteries is now available—as Greek and Hebrew cultures also claimed—but access to the Christian mysteries, unlike that to the Greek mysteries, does not require special initiation rites. Furthermore, Christian mysteries were distinctive because their interpretation was not reserved for a special individual or chosen few but rather was "disclosed to the Lord's people" even "among the Gentiles."

But the most important aspect was the content of the mystery. The mystery hidden for ages but now revealed even to the gentiles was simply this: "Christ in you, the hope of glory." The meaning of meanings, which the Greeks sought within esoteric rites and the Hebrews anticipated in special revelations, Paul declared to all: "Christ in you, the hope of glory." God dwells within and is united to the people of God—this is the hope of glory, the beautiful vision of what is to come. It is a union made possible, as well as tangible, through the Holy Spirit, as we have already seen. The living presence of the Almighty God within the concrete experience of the Colossian church and church members, the life shared by God and humans, our own participation in the divine nature (2 Pet. 1:4)—these are facets of the mystery of the ages, the truth for which Paul was willing to suffer many afflictions (Col. 1:24).

Mysticism can not only be acceptably comprehended within a Christian perspective, but when properly understood it can even be seen as a primary aim of Christian prayer: "Christ in you, the hope of glory." This is what we seek in prayer: communication (comm-*uni*-cation) with God using speech directed to God that sincerely expresses the self to God and that comes from the most purified self possible; listening to the Spirit intentionally and receiving every invitation from the fullness of God within every area of our lives, both the natural and the supernatural; a connection with God that neither reduces God to some shallow, knowable image nor distances the self from an infinitely unknowable, transcendent God; a relationship with God that recognizes the place of both solitude and engagement. Authentic Christian prayer is, at its core, a simple sharing of spirit with Spirit. The more present our spirit is to God and the more present the Holy Spirit is to us, the more we are formed into Christian prayer.

Which brings us to a discussion of prayerful union with God. We must understand the theme of union from the perspective of its fundamental basis in Scripture. The God of Christian Scripture is a trinitarian unity, where we find each person of the Trinity sharing intimately with the others and all three sharing a single divine essence. This union of persons is most clearly manifest in the incarnation of Christ, who is for us not only a divine sacrifice on behalf of our sin, but also a living exemplar of human union with the Father. Though believers do not share the same ontological union with the Father as Christ does, it is clear from the Epistles that Christians share something similar in our own union with God through Christ and the Spirit, both individually and as a people of God (Rom. 6:1–11; 8:9–11; Eph. 1:3–14; 2:20–22).

Our union with Christ is, on the one hand, something that has already been accomplished—a truth profoundly emphasized by the Reformer John Calvin.[18] Our justification by Christ has brought us into a union with God through no work of our own. We have been adopted in Christ and now share in the benefits of the divine life: participation in the Spirit, membership in the family of God, and much more. And yet our union is also something yet to be fully realized. We must wait until Revelation 21 to hear, "God's dwelling place is now among the people" (Rev. 21:3). This is, of course, our Big Story. And in between the beginning and the end is our ever-growing union of every aspect of life with the life of Christ.

But what does this have to do with prayer and with our formation into prayer? Simply this: just as our intimate union with a loved one is experienced in our communication (shall I say, our intercourse?), so also our growing relationship with Christ is experienced in our communication. The analogy is absolutely clear in 1 Corinthians, where Paul warns his readers of sexual promiscuity with prostitutes: "Shall I then take the members of Christ and unite them with a prostitute? Never! Do you not know that he who unites himself with a prostitute is one with her in body? . . . But whoever is united with the Lord is one with him in Spirit" (1 Cor. 6:15–17). As your heart and mind and will and habits become ever more similar to those of God and as you invest yourself more deeply in prayer, there come those moments when you are simply one with God, and words do not express this union very well. The growth toward and experience of such union has been the focus of much Roman Catholic literature in the modern period. When we see union with God as part of the Big Story, we can understand the foundation, the development, and the final realization as different parts of the same mission. God desires that we join with him in union—a union of virtue, doctrine, and mystical and prayerful relationship. And that union is a worthy aim of formation.

The Task of Formation into Prayer

So then, what is our role in formation? How do we take appropriate steps to nurture ourselves or others into an ever-maturing life of prayer? In our previous chapter, we considered how the task of spiritual formation employs means to nurture a congregation in a life of worship. In that example, we saw how the task of formation, which involves discerning and implementing appropriate steps to nourish relationship with God, is employed with regard to a particular congregation in their life of worship. Let us in this chapter, then, consider two case studies of individuals being formed into prayer.

Case 1: Prakash

Prakash, a man from Nepal, grew up in a moderately devout Hindu home where his family maintained the family shrine with images of deities, candles, flower petals, and a few other decorations. Together, they would have devotions (puja) periodically, and Prakash himself would also privately kneel at the shrine and light incense, sing a hymn, and recognize one of the deities with offerings and washings. He believed in, and sincerely revered, God. Yet for Prakash, God was mostly a transcendent provider. As he told his friends, "Truly holy people might have some profound vision of a deity, but for most of us, it is a simple religion of devotion."

And then something changed. It all started when Prakash got sick with a serious illness that affected his breathing in particular. Prakash performed his rituals but experienced no relief. Being sick was beginning to affect his work, and he needed to work to help support the family. A friend told him of another friend who went to the Christian church and was healed of a serious illness. He was finding it harder and harder to breathe, so, in desperation, Prakash went to the Christians, despite the fact that relationship with Christians could cause division within his family. When he arrived at the home where a small group of Christians were having a Bible study, they welcomed him in, heard his story, and then prayed for him. He received their prayer and then went home. Nothing special had happened. That night, however, Prakash had a dream, and in this dream Jesus gently opened Prakash's mouth and blew into it. When he woke up the next morning, his breathing was completely normal. Not knowing what to do, he went back to the Christian home to offer thanks, bringing a small gift. They refused his gift, proclaiming that Christianity works the other way. The gift comes from God, through Jesus, to him, they instructed. He had no need either to earn merit or to appease anyone with gifts. God loves him, they explained, and offers life and healing as a gift of love. God only asks that he receive. Prakash's skepticism melted. A few weeks later, he became a Christian.

This, then, brings us to our question regarding formation into prayer. For now Prakash must learn how to pray. How does the Christian church—and Prakash himself—nurture Prakash's formation into prayer, into a life of sincere communication with the living Christian God? We can recount his experience using some of the tasks outlined in chapter 5.

A *vision* of prayer was implanted in Prakash's dream and healing and in the good news presented by the Christians. The Christian God is a God who welcomes us through grace. Jesus is to be revered as God, but he is also to be loved as a friend. This approach to relationship with God was both new and attractive to Prakash. And it was out of attraction to this God (in the context of a powerful healing experience) that Prakash expressed his *determination* to pursue Christianity through baptism, though he still had much to learn about the teachings about the Holy Spirit. To keep peace in the family, he brought a cross home from the church and added it to the family shrine, lighting incense and singing one of the Christian songs (*bhajans*) in his personal devotions.

He found *community support* for his growth in prayer in the Bible studies. The members would pray out loud, and Prakash would hear the others talking to God very informally. They would also mention something about hearing from the Holy Spirit, with whom Prakash was not familiar. They explained to him that the Holy Spirit of God sent the dream to him and that this same Spirit would bring thoughts and feelings to mind and that he could recognize them as a way of "hearing" God's voice. They encouraged Prakash to let them know when he thought he sensed something from the Spirit so together they could talk about it and learn together. This was the way all of the members in the Bible study learned—by sharing their experiences. They also gave Prakash a Bible, which he spent hours reading in the evenings. At times he would stop reading and meditate on a phrase. He had learned about meditation in his own Hindu practices, but now he was meditating on Scripture to bring him into a deeper personal interaction with Jesus Christ. Attendance at Bible studies, personal devotions, private Bible reading, and meditation were the means of grace *identified* as the most appropriate for Prakash for this season. He *implemented* these means with the guidance and empowerment of the Holy Spirit. Those times when Prakash would join his family at the house shrine became increasingly difficult because the other family members did not feel comfortable with a Christian cross at their shrine. This situation became something of a trial for Prakash, and he learned to bring his trials as well as his healings to the Lord. In the end, he created a second, tiny shrine next to the main family shrine with a cross, candles, a Bible, and a few other decorations. Everybody could live with this. He *experimented* and *revised* his practice and, over time, grew deeper and deeper into prayer.

Case 2: Martha

For Martha, things were different. Martha had been a Christian for many years. Indeed, she felt a little like what some jokingly call a professional Christian, having been a pastor's wife for nearly thirty years. She met Jake, her husband, in college, where they led small group Bible studies together. After she graduated from college, they married and he started studies at a conservative Protestant seminary. She worked at a day care center while her husband went to school. But through their dinner-table conversations, she became very interested in theology and took advantage of the opportunities the seminary offered to audit classes in evenings for free, though she didn't complete a degree. She loved learning, and her relationship with God grew in the process. Jake took a job as an associate pastor right out of seminary, and the next year Martha gave birth to their first son. Three more children followed in close succession, and for the next twenty-three years she devoted herself to raising their children and supporting her husband's work. She was approaching the point at which the two youngest children would leave home, and there would not be any grandchildren in the near future. Over the years, Jake had changed jobs twice. The first change took them to her hometown, where he was a senior pastor, but things didn't really work out there. After a season of searching, he took a senior pastor position three states away. The situation was satisfactory—he was appreciated, the climate of the congregation was warm—but the environment was static. It was pleasant but underwhelming.

Martha had been devoted to Christ all her life. She read her Bible either alone or with a child on her lap almost every morning. She listened to Christian music and sang along as she did her housework. And she prayed. She prayed through the ups and downs of church life. She prayed through the joys and sorrows of her family as her children grew up. When she could, she took time to listen to recorded sermons and, more recently, podcasts, cherishing the opportunities to nourish her relationship with God through the practice of study.

But slowly, in the space of a couple of years, something began to happen to her prayer life. It just didn't feel fruitful anymore. She picked up her Bible, tried to intercede for those she usually prayed for, and listened to Christian music, but she felt almost no life in these practices. What was wrong? Was it just that she needed a new routine? Or was it something else, something more directly related to her relationship with God?

Martha brought it up with Jake one night when their teenagers were gone for the evening. It was not really that she had put her spiritual life on hold all these years, she explained, but there had not been opportunities to invest in it. And as they talked, they each sensed something else. Perhaps this dryness was God's way of inviting her to something new. By the end of the conversation, she decided to explore spiritual practices, even though they anticipated that some of the members of their conservative evangelical congregation might be uncomfortable with it. After looking into a few options, Martha signed up for an extended retreat and about twelve sessions of weekly training at a Jesuit retreat center nearby, where she would learn about Ignatian prayer. It was all a bit unfamiliar at first, but in time she learned to employ Ignatian methods of prayer to usher her into special places where she listened to Jesus speak to her. But her formation was not just a matter of introducing a few new practices. As is often the case, there were inner matters involved. Through her retreat and her explorations, she began to realize that she had almost unconsciously been struggling with a lie. Martha knew she was good at running their household and she enjoyed being a mother, but deep inside there were voices telling her that she was really not worth very much. She also sometimes found herself reluctant to go to the retreat center for prayer training, worried that she was just being selfish or afraid that it would lead nowhere. And she could tell that at times Jake himself wondered about her spiritual life. Why did she need to go so far outside her tradition to grow in Christ?

So let's stop this case study right here. New practices, inner struggles, and family and church dynamics are all part of our formation into prayer. Learning to pray in a dark night of faith is different than learning to pray in the dawn. If you were Martha's close friend or her spiritual director, what factors would you examine? What might you advise?

The task of Christian spiritual formation is to facilitate the appropriate next step of growth. As you can tell, it is more than recommending or practicing a couple of new spiritual disciplines (means). We must also attend to context: church context, family context, personal history, and so on. Then there are the agents of formation, about which we ask, What is going on in Martha's own self-construction here? What is she trying to speak? What is she hearing? What is going on in between speaking and hearing? And what among all this novelty is the Holy Spirit's work? Is the darkness she's experiencing really God's invitation? And we ask the aim questions as well: Is this just about personal fulfillment through a change of life? Toward what might the gospel message be drawing Martha? The work of spiritual formation may involve not only clarifying her vision but also establishing community support, revising her identification of means, and celebrating the fruit of formation as her life in prayer matures. Asking these kinds of probing questions will help you form someone else into prayer.

In this chapter, we have explored what it means to pray, to communicate with the living God. We have seen that prayer can be complex: traditions, practices, culture, and personality shape the way we practice and experience prayer. And yet prayer is just sincere people (individuals or communities) being open before God and God opening up before us. In this chapter, we have learned something of how we are formed into prayer, into relationship with God. In the next three chapters, we will see how we are formed into relationship with others, with ourselves, and with the world.

Going Deeper

1. Just as you might reflect on the story of your faith generally (chap. 2) or you identify your current stage of transformation (chap. 5), so you might also recount your own personal history of prayer. I know I have had my own seasons of faithful prayer lists; of exciting, imaginative meditations with the Gospels; and of confused silence. Imagine the whole story of your prayer life, from beginning to the present, and describe what it looks like. Or summarize the prayer history of your local faith community with a few bullet points. You may find that you deepen your faith by recalling and naming those seasons.

2. One aspect of prayer that we barely covered is the history of prayer in the church. The history of Christian prayer—common, conversational, contemplative—is as interesting as it is important. Key issues regarding the nature of our relationship with God and the means by which we pursue and experience this relationship are among those debated in this history. The Messalian controversy in the fourth and fifth centuries, for example, was about the relative importance of sacraments and the tensions of Spirit and means, and the iconoclast controversy raised the legitimacy of using images to facilitate prayerful devotion. And these are just a few of so many perspectives. Take some time to read about a season of the church and the conversations believers were having about prayer at that time. As you read, see if you can identify some concerns still being discussed by Christians today.

3. One way of exploring the character of a community's formation is to examine the different types of prayer that have been used in the past and those that are important today. Can you list the different types of prayer that you have observed in this group? Do members pray aloud

at the same time (as is common in Asia)? Do they recite written prayers (as is common in liturgical congregations)? What aspects are common across prayer styles? What does an examination of prayer types reveal about the corporate spiritual life of this community?

4. One aspect of formation into prayer that deserves increasing depth is our attention to, and familiarity with, our spirit and the Spirit of prayer. What might you learn by taking a time of prayer and then reflecting back on that time to see what you notice of spirit or Spirit in the experience? You may learn something interesting by doing this for a couple of days. You will be changed forever if you do this for a year.

5. One prayer practice that people employ with great benefit is a relaxed use of a basic book of prayer. The most common of these is the Anglican or Episcopal Book of Common Prayer, which comes in various versions. The method balances the prayer book's structure and a relaxed approach. Pick a book that reflects the structure of Christian prayer as it has been prayed for many centuries—one that includes a wide range of the most important elements of and kinds of prayer. It will keep you from getting trapped in your own favorite or familiar prayers. It will, however, also give you the freedom of revisiting and ruminating on prayers if you feel the need to. Sometimes when we read a prayer, our mind is drawn to an issue, a person, or some aspect of our relationship with God, and we need to stay with it, regardless of whether the printed book anticipates otherwise. By using a prayer book in this relaxed way, we give ourselves permission to put the book down (regardless of whether we've finished the prayers in that service) and devote our prayerful reflection to what the Spirit has brought to our attention.

8

· · · · · · · · · · · · · · ·

Formed Together

Overview

This chapter will be divided into four parts. After some reflection on spirit/
Spirit and community, we will examine our formation together as households,
such as families and other small-scale dwelling communities.[1] Next, we will
explore congregational life, looking particularly at our experience of hospitality and "getting along." We will then entertain the idea of formation in
networks. What does it mean for a Christian to be not merely a member of a
local congregation of Christians but also a participant in a larger network of
believers? Finally, we will look at the potential for Christian spiritual formation
within the specific context of what has been known in Christian history as the
commitment to "religious life" and the new monastic expressions emerging
in the contemporary church worldwide. Our aim in each of these sections is
to gain a clear picture of what the attentive intention of Christian spiritual
formation—as a process and a task—is like in community. When we learn
to notice the unique dynamics of household formation, networking, or congregational reconciliation, we equip ourselves to better foster the maturity
of both individuals and communities in Christ.

As will be made clear by my returning to these topics, the present chapter
("Formed Together") and the following two chapters ("Formed in Thinking,
Feeling, and Acting" and "Formed into Mission") are deeply connected. The
formation of a Christ-centered community cannot be separated from the life
of Christian mission or the nature of Christian integrity. Biblical scholar Christopher Wright, for example, joins all three when he states, "The community

God seeks for the sake of his mission is to be a community shaped by his own ethical character, with specific attention to righteousness and justice in a world filled with oppression and injustice. Only such a community can be a blessing to the nations."[2]

Our formation as individuals and our formation as groups of people are deeply interwoven. Who we are is, to a large extent, who we are together. Two words speak of this idea strongly. The first is the term *ubuntu*, a Bantu word that spread beyond the Nguni peoples in southern Africa and became the symbol of an entire philosophical ideal. The word carries with it the idea of "humanness"—or perhaps "kindness" or "right conduct"—but embedded within is the idea of connection to others. *Ubuntu* communicates that my identity as an individual is dependent on our character as a people. The second term is *tsedeq*, a Hebrew word that means "justice" or "righteousness" and that really speaks of "right relationship." For the Hebrews, rightness is a matter not simply of individual performance but rather of being appropriately related to those around us (God, others, land, and so on). I am who we are. Consequently, Christian spiritual formation must be the formation of communities as well as individuals.

At times Christian spirituality and formation in Christ have been looked at from a simple "Jesus and me" perspective. While there is certainly benefit in plumbing the depths of personal intimacy with Christ, we must also acknowledge that this is only part of the story. Our life and our formation in Christ are corporate as well as individual endeavors. We are members of families, congregations, cities, and other groups. Who I am is who we are. Accordingly, we will devote this chapter to exploring the communal dimension of Christian spiritual formation.

Spirit, Community, and Formation

Christian spiritual formation is, indeed, *Spirit*-ual formation. Being conformed to Christ and the Christian gospel involves a growing sensitivity toward—and a welcoming openness to—the active presence of the Holy Spirit. This is true not only for individuals but for communities as well.

The first point to remember is that the Christian God is a community. There is a rich sharing of life among the persons of the Trinity (see John 14). Since the Christian God possesses a corporate dimension, it is only natural that we reflect the image of God as communities and that the ministry of God's

Spirit is extended *to* the life of communities. Ezekiel speaks to a collection of dry bones and to the breath/Spirit, and the bones come to life. Then God explains, "These bones are the people of Israel. . . . I will put my Spirit in you and you will live" (Ezek. 37:4–14). The promise of God's Spirit is made to the nation of Israel as a whole, not merely to individuals. We see the fulfillment of this promise in Acts 2, a communication of the Holy Spirit to the gathered community as a whole. It is not just that the Holy Spirit happens to appear to groups as well as individuals. No, more than that—the Spirit of our trinitarian God characteristically moves in the context of community.[3]

The Spirit of God also forms us *through* communities. This is the whole point of Paul's discussion of the gifts of the Spirit in 1 Corinthians 12–14, where he writes, "Now to each one the manifestation of the Spirit is given for the common good" (1 Cor. 12:7). As a congregation is worshiping and fasting, the Holy Spirit speaks—presumably through one of the prophets at this gathering—inviting Barnabas and Saul to a new work (Acts 13:2). Later, Paul notes that the Thessalonian church received his gospel "with the Holy Spirit and with deep conviction" (1 Thess. 1:5). This is body life.

Finally, Christian formation involves both our being formed *into* the Spirit and the Spirit's forming believers *into* harmonious communities. Paul envisions the Spirit dwelling in both individuals and communities of God's people (see, e.g., Rom. 8:10–11; Eph. 2:18–22). Is Paul urging the Philippians to stand together in one spirit or in the one Spirit (Phil. 1:27; see also Eph. 4:3–4; Jude 19)? We become a community as a consequence of the Spirit's work when we exhibit the fruit of the Spirit (Gal. 5:22–25). As we can see, the Holy Spirit of Christ is the agent of community transformation as well as personal transformation. The Spirit ministers *to*, *through*, and *into* community.

Can you remember a time when you experienced the Spirit in the context of community? Perhaps you experienced the healing of a strained relationship. Perhaps you were present at a gathering where something special happened. How would you describe the Spirit's influence? We are formed by the Spirit of God and we are formed together: in community, through community, into community. As we are mindful of the Spirit's invitation, we learn to shape our own intentions and join with the Spirit of God in our own maturation into the trinitarian God and the Christian gospel as communities of Christ.

Households

Family is our first community. And although the particular structures may vary from culture to culture, family remains the basic institution of human togetherness. Yet as we learned in chapter 4, our chapter on context, society is changing. Many people are choosing to marry later. Some Christians are choosing to live a single, celibate life, as the apostle Paul did. In China, the one-child policy has been phased out, and yet people there wonder about raising and supporting more children. Urbanization, employment of women outside the home, and migration of fathers searching for better wages and opportunities are changing the makeup of the world's families. Just as the apostle Paul chose to reside with friends (Priscilla and Aquila, for example) for short or lengthy seasons, today we find that some Christians are choosing to live in informal groups. It is not really adequate, then, to speak simply about our formation as families. Instead, in order to explore dwelling communities' unique potential for formation, I will speak here of our formation in households—such as nuclear families, extended families, or small-scale dwelling communities—and I will address intentional religious communities when we come to the section on formation into new monastic expressions.[4]

What do I mean when I speak of being formed as a household? I mean that the members mature in their relationship with Christ by means of the life of the family or dwelling community. Note also that when I speak of household formation, I'm referring to the formation of the group, though individual formation may be included. For example, Christian roommates may choose to establish weekly house meetings at which they divide up the chores for the week, discuss any topics that pertain to their common life, and spend a little time in prayer together. To be formed as a household is, then, to embody, in our common life together ("at home"), the fullness of the "all things made new" gospel. Our household facilitates our godly relationship with the earth by choosing to practice recycling and composting. We facilitate our common desire to introduce others to Christ by choosing to host occasional neighborhood celebrations and to invite those who might be sincere seekers into an inquirers' gathering. Every element of the rich, Christian gospel can be explored in the setting of living together.

Households offer a distinctive setting for Christian spiritual formation. First, members live in *proximity* to one another. We share washrooms, refrigerators, and garbage containers. We experience one another's ups and downs firsthand. When I fail to keep my devotional commitments or when I am especially impatient with another household member, everybody knows.

A household is also a place where we usually connect with *regularity*. Sometimes we eat together. At least we pass by one another as we get ready to leave for work. We can meet together for household worship with ease—no need to drive to a church meeting.[5]

Furthermore, households (and again, especially families where people mature together over many years) often are characterized by a high degree of *intimacy*. Our personalities and lives are connected by genetic, social, emotional, and economic bonds, so we are motivated to foster the formation of the other members of the household.

Finally, households often facilitate *time* together. We may share leisure time, whether resting after a hard day's work or taking a day off. Some elements of formation are best fostered within a relationship of leisure, and this is uniquely provided at home. We need a long time to get to know one another. For example, a sibling-parent combination can often live together for fifteen to twenty years or more, depending on cultural norms. You have time to hurt and to forgive. You have time to watch each other change.

Because a household offers such a unique advantage for the sake of spiritual formation, it is vital that we perceive our dwelling communities as particularly Christian households, relationships, and spaces given over to the kingdom of God. Paul makes this point in Ephesians when he instructs husbands and fathers. A husband is to love his wife as his own body, nourishing and cherishing her (Eph. 5:28). Likewise, fathers are to bring their children up "in the training and instruction of the Lord" (6:4). A formational purpose is embedded in each of these exhortations.[6] Christian writer Edith Schaeffer calls the family a "formation center for human relationships."[7] Family is not about economic advantage or social obligation. For Christians, family is about sharing life together in the Lord, which requires that we invest our lives and that we explore wholeheartedly the full story of the Christian gospel—including its implications in economic, social, and spiritual spheres.[8]

What might household formation look like in practice? Let me sketch out a possible scenario. It's late summer, and a family has just moved into the big city. Over the last few weeks, they've gotten most of their important stuff unpacked. Dad has settled into his new job at the university. Older brother (age fourteen) and sister (age twelve) have started school right away. Younger brother (age six) is homeschooling with Mom for the semester. They haven't homeschooled before, but it just seemed like the best thing to do in this situation. He is shy and had a difficult time in school last year, and the loud, large city school frightens him.

Things are not entirely settled. When Dad took this new job, he and Mom agreed that they wanted to live in the city where the university was located and where Grandma was, instead of moving to a suburb. They've found that this big city is, well, big—so many people, so many stores, and so much to do. It is fast and loud and frankly a bit unsettling compared to the small Midwestern town where they previously lived. Older brother and sister are noticing a lot of differences between these schools and their old ones and asking their parents questions about them—from different foods at lunch, to slang they don't understand, to evidence of poverty. Mom and Dad had not really anticipated how the transition from small schools with little turnover and very little diversity to large urban schools with an ethnically and economically diverse population might stimulate new discussions at home. Even choosing a church has been a daunting task.

This seems like a good opportunity to invest some time and effort into their spiritual life as a family. They've had devotions together before, but their practice was sporadic and not all that nourishing. Mom and Dad talk about the idea with the rest of the family and—after a little eye rolling by the eldest—they agree. In fact, the youngest suggests that they invite Grandma, who lives a few blocks away, to join them. Vision, determination, and community support are in place. But what will they do in this time?

After reviewing a few resources for family devotions, they decide to design their own. It starts with the children, who come up with a list of questions that they will explore together as a family. Then Dad, the scholar of the family, studies the questions and makes a list of Bible verses and other resources that might help them discuss these questions together. Then Mom (with help from Grandma) thinks up ways that each child can engage the question, the Scriptures, and the resources as appropriate for his or her age group—which requires a fair amount of prayerful attention to the needs of each child. Could they act out the Bible passage? How about drawing pictures of their question? What about practice assignments, where they each think of ways to respond to the questions and studies in real life? They decide to experiment with a variety of methods, to start each family service with a song, and to end with a time of open prayer. Now that they have identified and selected their family disciplines, they begin to implement them, making a two-month commitment to the project, after which they will have a conversation and revise their experiment.

It's now late fall, and in the first two months of family services, they've learned a great deal. First, they conclude that singing is not their strong suit. Second, they've learned that while they can usually meet together three evenings a week, it was unrealistic to expect more, given Grandma's commitments and the others' schoolwork. The children are engaged. They sincerely write their list of questions, and the adults are invested in preparing for their times together. Actually, they have fun working together. The quality of the family services, though, is mixed. Sometimes it seems like Mom and Dad are pulling teeth to get one or the other of the children to engage. But there are also those times when everyone knows that God is present with them, particularly when they review their assignments and when they (and especially Grandma) pray. They celebrate their growth together as a family in Christ, stimulated by their practice of family service.

Of course, this kind of creative investment in a family service curriculum may not be possible for some households, but there are many helpful and varied resources available to make this formation possible (see the resources listed in n. 5). The important point is that we can exercise some measure of responsibility for the formation of our households and that doing so can be an enriching adventure.

In fact, in the near future, I can imagine an increase in both formal and informal Christian households: communities including both families and singles. This may seem like a novel idea, because—even though God's people have usually honored both singleness and marriage (and, thus, families)—there was a moment when the church consciously decided to value singleness over marriage.[9] But then the Protestant Reformation came and turned all that around. Now I think the pendulum is swinging back toward center. Some are living a life of simplicity, fidelity, and humility in their ordinary married life.[10] Others are exploring the values of celibate life.[11] Will these be dwelling communities that take advantage of the opportunities for Christian spiritual formation? Only if the members so choose.

Congregations

While Christian households have significant formation potential, many households are mixed communities, with people of diverse faith commitments living in the same place. Sometimes it is simply not appropriate to press a household into spiritual formation commitments. Furthermore, while families are normally our first communities, the family—from the perspective of the Christian gospel—is actually not our primary faith community. That designation belongs to the church and the local congregation. Family was instituted by God, as described in the first chapters of Genesis, as a part of creation. The church, with its local expressions in congregations or churches, was founded by God as part of a Christian re-creation, as we read in the first chapters of Acts. At the juncture between the Gospels and the book of Acts, we find the resurrected Jesus transferring his ministry and mission to his followers. They are to carry on his work of proclaiming the kingdom of God and will now be accompanied by the powerful Holy Spirit. Scripture includes an account of humanity spreading throughout the world in the book of Genesis and an account of Christians spreading throughout the world in the book of Acts. And the primary social institution where Christians are gathered, formed, and sent to further spread the kingdom was then, and is today, the local church.[12]

What makes congregations distinctive, particularly with regard to Christian spiritual formation? First, the church is *voluntary* in its composition. Ties through blood, through economic advantage, or through mere friendship do not (or at least should not) determine the character of a church. The church is solely about Christ.

A second characteristic of congregations is that they are *gathered* communities. We do not meet simply because we happen to live together. We intentionally gather together. Our assembly comprises peculiar individuals from various locations for the purpose of affirming and nurturing our faith in Jesus Christ. You never know who may gather with you for worship, but you do know that whoever shows up will sing along to the same songs with you.

A third characteristic of church has to do with its role of *instruction and initiation*. As we have seen throughout this book, Christianity is both history—the way things are—and story—a narrative way of looking at things. If you don't get the story, you won't get the life. This story is communicated and received through Word and sacrament, and though these may be a part of some households or networks, they are not central in those communal settings the way they are within the church.

A fourth characteristic of the church is the environment of *fellowship*, a deep and sincere sense of mutuality among members, many of whom are willing to offer others financial help, a listening ear, or a word of correction. The people gathering for church bring a wide range of gifts to offer the formation of the body. Within the setting of congregational life, we see modeled a wide range of virtues and ways of living out the gospel. All ages, all maturity levels are on exhibit in a congregation. We are formed through sharing, in love, ourselves in all our difference.

The breadth and depth of our formation are nourished in the environment of a congregation. We are formed *in* the congregation as we allow the ordinary life of this community—with its quirks and questions—to guide our own maturity in the gifts of the Spirit. We are formed *by* the congregation as a member gives us encouragement in our acts of evangelism or service or as a common prayer is accompanied by the touch of the Spirit. We are formed *into* a congregation as we practice sincere common worship, loving fellowship, and missional life together.

We have already seen something of the place of formation in the context of worship gatherings.[13] Here I will simply reflect on two further arenas of Christian spiritual formation within the context of congregational life: the ministry of hospitality and the work of reconciliation. Each of these highlights a distinctive aspect of formation together as a congregation.

Hospitality: Formed through Welcoming

I have been increasingly struck by Jesus's welcoming personality in my reading of the Gospels over the past few years. Young children find a home on his lap (Matt. 19:14). The woman caught in adultery receives no condemnation from Jesus (John 8:1–11). Another questionable woman bathes his feet with her tears, and he praises her when others would have sent her away (Luke 7:36–49). His critics accused him of being "a friend of tax collectors and sinners" (Matt. 11:19; Luke 7:34). In the end, Jesus died with his arms open wide, forgiving our sins and providing a way for all to be welcome in the presence of God.

Yet Jesus is also the guest, a stranger who requests our welcome. Jesus invites himself over to Zacchaeus's house to share a meal (Luke 19:1–10). The one who welcomes strangers also welcomes Jesus (Matt. 25:31–46). He made the world, yet the world did not know him. But to those who welcomed him he gave the power to become children of God (John 1:12). Jesus is both the host who welcomes us with open arms and the stranger waiting to be welcomed by us. It follows that the practice of hospitality is not some minor, extracurricular activity of congregations. No, it is the gospel itself. To be formed into hospitality is to be formed into the character and mission of Christ at the root of things.

If the worship service is the element of congregational life that centrally embodies our common vertical relationship with God (incorporating and symbolizing many things in one gathering), perhaps it is the church potluck meal that centrally embodies our horizontal relationships with one another—symbolizing relationships with our congregation, strangers, and God in one common practice. A search of the New Testament reveals that common meals are mentioned almost as often as worship services. (In addition to the many instances found in the Gospels, see, e.g., Acts 2:42, which may be a Eucharist, a meal, or both; 11:2–3; 16:34; Rom. 14:2–3; 1 Cor. 8:9–13; 10:23–33; 11:20–22; Gal. 2:11–14; Rev. 3:20; 19:9.) Indeed, it is interesting how a meal—the *agapē* (Greek, "love") meal—used to be intimately connected with these early worship services. It appears that the worship service and the meal both embodied their common faith and formed them into a holy congregation.

What I find most striking about hospitality is that the basic elements needed for a good common meal are the same as those needed for healthy prayer, spiritual direction, and outreach. Furthermore, these elements are suspiciously similar to the structure of a worship service: gathering, sharing of the Word, receiving, responding, and leaving. First, we create a welcoming place by preparing the food and arranging the tables. The next step is conversation, for a welcoming ear is just as important as a welcoming place.[14] There is some risk involved—who knows whom you might end up talking with?—but this risk is necessary.[15] We meet another and open ourselves to hear whatever this other might bring, allowing him or her to tell their story.

When the time is right, we share something too, perhaps something carefully considered from our own story or perhaps a piece of the Big Story. Hospitality is not about prying out details of a stranger's life. It is an open and fresh conversation between two (or more) people. And who knows, we may find ourselves entertaining angels (Heb. 13:2).

All of this is done in an atmosphere of care and love. Professors Jualynne Dodson and Cheryl Townsend Gilkes describe this element in their discussion of hospitality in the context of African American church meals:

> It is this hospitality, this love, that is symbolized in the preparation and giving of food. The love ethic that pervades the ideology of African American churches is constantly underscored and reaffirmed in the exchanges of food and the celebration of church events with grand meals. This love and this hospitality remind the congregation that they are pilgrims and strangers and that as they feed somebody one day, they may stand in need on another.[16]

A welcoming space, a welcoming ear as we meet, a shared conversation conducted in an atmosphere of love and care—again, this scenario is not far removed from the basic structure of Christian worship: approach, meet, share, change, and depart.[17] Because all relationships, whether with God or with others, possess common elements, to be formed in worship is to learn something about hospitality and vice versa.

Hospitality is part skill, part practice. We learn how to set the table correctly and how to listen carefully. But forming a community of hospitality is a matter of skill and culture.[18] Good "potluck" culture associates practices with meaning, such as welcoming with valuing others. In time, not merely practices but also feelings, values, and more are formed. Scholar and pastor Richard Valantasis recounts the transformation his congregation underwent through a coffee-hour ministry, writing, "Once members of the parish were hosts for a Sunday, they became regular ministers of hospitality throughout the year so that not only was the coffee hour transformed, but so that the entire parish culture was changed from exclusivity to hospitality."[19] Coffee hours and potlucks are not the only way for a congregation to experiment with hospitality.[20] Nevertheless, we see in this example how a congregation can be formed through exploring the simple practice of hospitality. Vision, intention, community support, choosing actions, experimentation, and so on all play their role in forming a congregation closer to the fullness of the gospel.[21]

Getting Along: Reconciliation

Life together serves as an important crucible for refining our love of both God and neighbor. We are formed through interpersonal interaction. Fourth-century bishop Basil of Caesarea emphasized this point in his "Long Responses" (in which he answered questions from his followers), arguing that "community life offers more blessings than can be fully and easily enumerated" and is valuable "both for preserving the goods bestowed on us by God and for warding off the external attacks of the Enemy."[22] Even the desert elders, who withdrew into solitude, had sufficient occasion for interaction such that community life among fellow nuns or monks served as ascetical training in the Christian life.[23] "As iron sharpens iron," the proverb goes, "so one person sharpens another" (Prov. 27:17). It is striking that 1 Corinthians 13, the famous "love chapter," is positioned in the middle of a discussion about worship-gathering disagreements. We need to bring patience and kindness to the ordinary disputes about how we live (and worship) together as a community of faith, and leave behind self-seeking and anger. We are formed into greater likeness to Christ through our loving treatment of one another in the contexts of everyday conflicts.

The Bible—and more particularly the Epistles, which address church life directly—speaks about common worship and about hospitality. But it speaks ever so much more about getting along. Our list of the so-called seven deadly sins consists of vices such as gluttony, lust, anger, and pride. These are *personal* sins, though they have social implications. While Paul's lists of deadly sins include these, he also mentions things like "discord, jealousy, fits of rage, selfish ambition, dissensions, factions" (Gal. 5:20; see Eph. 4:31–32). These are *social* sins, and sins like these lie behind the writing of virtually every epistle in the Bible: tensions between Jewish and gentile segments of congregations are addressed in Romans, tensions between those with some spiritual gifts and those with others are detailed in 1 Corinthians, and tensions among those who practice the Jewish law differently are brought up in Galatians. The Epistles are a virtual guidebook for getting along. Isn't it interesting that in the one instance where Paul uses the word *formed* (Gal. 4:19), he is speaking about problems the Galatian believers were having with other people?[24]

It's clear, then, that when we think of the spiritual formation of congregations, we must think beyond adult education classes and worship structures. We must focus attention and intention on facilitating Christlike maturity in the very character of our relationships with one another. Our work is not to develop creative programs; it is to create a culture. We are to instill habits in groups and individuals such that, as in Tertullian's day, unbelievers might look on the church and proclaim, "See how they love one another."[25]

But how is this done? Let's say you are the pastor of formation in a congregation and you want to facilitate members' maturity in navigating conflicts. First, prepare the congregation and yourself for conflict. You must let members know that conflict is normal. Most conflict is not to be avoided or quickly resolved to avoid discomfort but rather to be celebrated. We are many and one! You must also get to know your church. What stage of development is your congregation in? Has the makeup of church membership changed much recently? Is the congregation generally focused inward or outward? What is your congregation's theology, and how broad a range of theology is "permitted" in the community? How strong is your common sense of vision?[26] Conflicts can involve a number of factors, each of which must be addressed when the time comes. Best to prayerfully consider these before you face them head-on.

Part of this preparation is to establish within a congregation a set of best practices, habits of thinking and relating that acknowledge the probability of conflict, and to choose a healthy path of reconciliation. For example, a church leadership team might craft statements like these:

- We understand the difference between uniformity and unity. Unity is a work of the Spirit. Uniformity is a counterfeit.
- We tolerate and actually encourage dissent. We create a safe place for all to be heard.
- We encourage (to a point) task conflict, but we keep a tight rein on relational conflict. Task conflict leads to better decisions. Relational conflict leads to fights.
- We have good decision-making practices. Our need for a sense of group cohesion will not override the value of adequately evaluating options.
- We nurture a constant presence of low-level change so the group becomes adept at living with change.[27]

Formation into these habits of thought and relationship is a spiritual discipline. You are training yourselves as a congregation, through small actions, to recognize the difference between unity and uniformity, say, or to improve your skills in task conflict. This formation is also a work of the Spirit of Christ. Members perceive that their hearts are softening to one another. They sense that the group is coming together or that several members are understanding the concern of one member. Spirit, community, trial, discipline—all function together as you are formed together.

Second, when you can, actively prevent unhealthy conflict. Rather than focusing attention on what divides us, we can nurture what is common among us. Cultivate Christian virtues. All the time. There is nothing like a dose of humility, or courage, or compassion to help a group avoid unhealthy conflict. Contemporary Orthodox monk Cosmas Shartz writes about this with regard to life in a monastery:

> They say that in any average monastery nine out of ten who come to try the life end up leaving. It's all about handling the pressure of interpersonal relationships. Either you give up and go away or you stay and make it work. Ultimately there is only one way to make the monastic life work—by demonstrating the willingness to resolve conflict by forgiving others, asking their forgiveness, reconciling with them, and by humbling yourself even when you think you are right.[28]

Third and finally, form practices of peacemaking and conflict resolution when these are necessary.[29] Train members of the congregation to take the log out of their own eye (Matt. 7:5) and admit their unhealthy contribution to a given conflict or their having overlooked an offense of theirs that should have been acknowledged. You can train members how to gently restore relationships by making room for crucial conversations, speaking the truth in love, taking another along when appropriate, or even bringing a matter before the church.[30] We teach them through example, through classes, and through real situations how to be reconciled—learning to forgive, learning to overcome evil with good.[31]

Formation into harmony will require every step of the task of formation we explored in chapter 5. We must see a *clear vision* of what a church is like that is "one as we are one" (John 17:22). We must exercise a *strong determination* to see our congregation move forward in this area. We must develop *support* for unity both inside and outside the congregation. We must *identify* those specific elements that are in most need of attention, and then we must *select* those habits of thought, feeling, and practice that must be cultivated. Then, *paying attention* to the dynamics as they play themselves out, we prepare to *implement, revise,* and *experiment* as the congregation develops in their growth in unity and reconciliation.

Networks

I have a friend here in my Colorado town whom I will call Lucy. She is a devout Christian and active in pursuing spiritual formation and living out the gospel. If you were to ask her where she goes to church, she would say that her family attends the same church as I do, but . . . she does not regularly attend the adult education class. She is currently taking an online course from a Christian university. She does not attend any of the usual women's gatherings, but she has been a part of a small home study and accountability group for years. She volunteers regularly at a local shelter. Her family helps out with music at church. She meets one-on-one with a spiritual director in a nearby town. She also provides spiritual direction for people both inside and outside our congregation. What is Lucy's community of formation? Perhaps all of these groups.

Lucy's situation is a good example of a phenomenon that is increasingly common, especially in the West. I call this "networking spirituality."[32] I mentioned this idea in chapter 4 when discussing the "schools" of formation, but I will develop the idea of networking spirituality here because it is directly related to our approach to being formed together.

Networking is not all that novel, really. If we could travel back to the Great Awakening, we would recognize people's tendency to float between meetings in different churches and homes. Going back further, to the late thirteenth century, for example, we would witness the rise of Beguinages, bands of Humiliati, and local chapters of the Secular Franciscans—religious orders that influenced one another through loose bonds of connectedness, not unlike spiritual movements today. We might also think of churches we know nearby that are too small to have a viable youth group and outsource, so to speak, their youth ministry to the local Young Life club. I wonder how the apostle Paul would have responded if someone had asked him what church he went to. I think he might say something like "the Christian church anywhere and everywhere." I think Paul's Christian identity was developed through the broad network of relationships that supported and received from him.

Networking our formation is becoming more and more prevalent today. This is not a minor church trend. We are seeing the transformation of human society globally, and one of the fundamental characteristics of the emerging structure is networking. Whereas in modernity we thought of ourselves as members of organizations, in postmodernity we are beginning to think of ourselves as more or less connected to various networks. Networking is changing nearly every aspect of our lives, and we need to understand that it will change church—and spiritual formation—as well.[33]

Think of how medicine is practiced now in contrast to the way it was sixty years ago. I remember as a child having my doctor come to my house for a visit when I was sick. Very rarely did we see a specialist. Today the world of medicine consists of a network of physicians, machines, internet self-diagnosis guides, and alternative health organizations. Some components involved in our care (the database used to compare our blood sample information, for example) link millions of cases together.

Nowadays I think about my classroom. Once upon a time, I stood in front of a group of people and we discussed topics face-to-face. Now I have an online classroom and the students "attending" my classes are from around the world—though they don't even leave home to get to class. In one small group I "met" with last year, students from nearly every continent gathered virtually to discuss the study questions for the week. Education today draws on students' connections to local employment relationships, temporary social media groups, globally connected learning management systems, ordinary textbooks, web-conferencing platforms, interactive video lectures, and more; these are only a few examples of how networking is changing the way we live.

We must be prepared to see Christian spiritual formation—and even the corporate dimension of Christian spiritual formation—in terms broad enough to include an individual embedded in a single congregational environment as well as individuals and groups and resources of every kind mutually influencing one another through multiple links, both strong and weak.[34] If you are discipling a single member of your congregation, for example, remember that this person is probably also being formed actively through a number of other sources and that this same person could have a number of friends who are being touched through your discipleship of this one person, even though none of this may involve any formal program. Furthermore, it is not enough to remember these circumstances; we must also understand that the effectiveness of our leadership will depend on whether or not we are threatened by them.

Christian spiritual formation happens *in* networks. It is in the midst of networks like concrete Bible studies that God touches me and I come to know God more. Formation also happens *as* a network. As relationships between individuals and groups are strengthened—remember Paul's appeal for a collection for the saints in Jerusalem?—the whole church matures. And as the church grows, this, in turn, influences individual maturity. Formation also happens *by* or *through* a network. Networks, then, are both agents and means of formation. An individual can champion a cause and gather through her own networks all kinds of support for a worthy cause. Finally, we are ultimately forming Christians *into* a network, into a vast, wonderful, harmonious body of Christ in which every tribe and every tongue will sing, together, praise to our Lord. This is the aim of formation in Christ. Spiritual directors, pastors, and others engaged in the task of formation for groups and individuals in this networking society will have to pay attention to the links connecting individuals and groups to one another for the sake of the gospel. Where, we need to ask, is clear vision expressed and communicated? With which connection will a statement of intention find the best fit? How do we draw community support for a particular appropriate step for formation when that community seems to be so scattered? Often, identifying appropriate disciplines or relationships is a matter of discovering which connections will serve our needs best. This is all a part of spiritual formation in a networked society.

I see both advantages and dangers in a networked spiritual formation. One of the advantages is the opportunity for making use of those we could regard as specialists. As I noted above, the field of medicine has changed; the country doctor making home visits just simply did not have the knowledge or the equipment available to provide adequate diagnoses and treatments. Similarly, the small-church pastor may not have the resources in the church to develop a high-level adult education program, but that online class from the Christian university might be just the thing for Lucy. The strength of parachurch organizations and other institutions is that they can recruit and deploy a sufficient cohort of people with a high commitment level and common interest toward a single worthy cause.

Another advantage to networked spiritual formation is the value of informal relationships, which offer perspectives and models of relationship with God close at hand.[35] We have at our disposal, through our networks, a wealth of new ideas, creative practices, and interesting possibilities for our own formation. Furthermore, these relationships come to us through our own networks—channels that we manage rather than those being imposed on us. Our closest relationships invite us outside of ourselves, such that we end up bringing something new into ourselves. This is true of experimenting with food. (Ever tried a new dish at a restaurant at a friend's encouragement?) It is also true of our spiritual lives.

I have already hinted at the third advantage: networked spiritual formation is generally more self-directed than is the case otherwise. We learned in chapter 4 that an important agent in our formation is ourselves. The Spirit of Christ is the primary agent, but we must also take responsibility for our own formation. When an individual or a group draws its resources for formation (and its expressions of formation) from a variety of sources, that individual or group is obligated to navigate the relationships among these sources for themselves. This kind of self-constructing spiritual formation strengthens the self as agent.

I also see a few dangers associated with networked spiritual formation. One of them is the potential for shallow community. A community's depth or intimacy is nurtured when we share many different things over long periods of time with the same people. When we piece our formation together through a string of short-term relationships—each of which may be focused on a different, single aspect—we may not develop deep relationships, the kind where we really learn who we are and then can care for one another well when we need it most.[36]

Another danger stems from the very strength of a self-directed formation that draws on informal relationships—namely, choosing who adjudicates our formation. Our breadth of understanding will only be as wide as our own perspective and the spectrum of those whom we allow to affect us. There are weaknesses with having authorities over our lives. But there are strengths as well.

Along with the self-direction question is the issue of the fullness of spiritual formation. Throughout this book, I have been advocating for making growth in the fullness of Christian human experience—"all things new"—the aim of Christian spiritual formation. Our formation in Christ comprises worship, education, community, mission, relationships with the land and efforts for social justice, freedom in the Holy Spirit, and much more, because we seek the fullness of church for the sake of the fullness of the gospel. So here is the question: Is this growth in fullness found by remaining solidly within a single congregation and participating in every aspect of that congregation's life? Or is it found by networking aspects of this fullness that are underrepresented in a given congregation?

Just as we are formed together through households and congregations, we are also formed through our networks. Indeed, we are even formed into a global network of the body of Christ. Some individuals have given up on congregations and pursue their formation in Christ and their service to Christ solely through networking.[37] Still others remain happily immersed in a single congregation. I think an increasing number will mix a bit here and there. While some endure, others will explore and invent. Welcome to formation in our changing, network age.

New Monastic Expressions

For decades now, I have been a friend of a specific group of Christian servants: InnerChange, a Christian order among the poor. "We send teams to live and work in marginalized neighborhoods around the world—places most people want to avoid or ignore," its website states. "We seek to live out the good news of Jesus among the poor, both with words and deeds." The group identifies itself as a collection of communities whose members "seek to exemplify a style of community life befitting an order, placing the well-being of people and the quality of their relationships before programs."[38] Communities, religious orders, living among the poor—this does not sound like your ordinary household. But it is not a congregation either, for it is too specialized. It could be seen as a parachurch mission organization, yet members choose to live in communities and use the word *order*. Just what kind of group is this, and what does spiritual formation together look like in such a setting?

InnerChange is one of a number of new expressions of religious life: groups of people who consecrate themselves together to live lives fully devoted to Christ and the gospel, usually with a few particular emphases.[39] (For Inner-Change, the emphasis is on serving and living among people suffering from poverty.) *Monasticism* is another word people have used to describe groups like this. I briefly mentioned new monastic expressions in chapter 4 when I was discussing countermovements. Let me develop this idea further here.

We read about what appears to be a special religious order in Numbers 6, which discusses the Nazirites, a group of individuals who offered themselves in complete consecration to God. As part of this life, Nazirites abstained from wine, kept their hair long, and stayed clear of dead bodies (which were unclean). We also see hints of something similar in the description of the Rechabites in Jeremiah 35. Nearer the time of Jesus, a community of Jews often called the Essenes lived a special, consecrated way of life together. One of the Essenes' extant documents describes the ideals of the community, a ceremony of initiation, general wisdom regarding their central values, and particular regulations regarding relationships, ministries, property, and their life together.

When Jesus sent his followers out to minister in the surrounding villages, he gave them an outline of their way of life (see Matt. 10; Mark 6:6–13; Luke 9–10). He identified their mission—to heal, deliver, and proclaim—and gave them instructions regarding possessions, relationships, and ministry activities. The people surrounding Jesus and his followers would have seen them as a unique, special, consecrated community that followed God through their leader, Jesus. This was an early form of a Christian missionary order. Recall that in Acts 13, the Holy Spirit asks the church at Antioch to "set apart" Paul, Barnabas, and others for apostolic ministry. And when we read the Epistles, we discover that the apostolic communities seemed to guide their traveling ministries in a manner similar to that outlined by Jesus in the Gospels. Finally, I think it is also fair to see—in the comments in 1 Timothy 5 regarding a widow who "continues night and day to pray"—at least a seed of the order of widows that developed more formally in succeeding centuries.

Scripture does not give specifications for consecrated groups' organizational structure or character any more than it gives precise directions for the structure of local congregations. But in Scripture we do find the barest outlines of—and permission to create—a common life that intentionally distances itself from dependency on family and occupation and that is intentionally devoted to God. The Bible does not assert that these groups of Christians are somehow better than other Christians, for whether monks or mothers, all of us can invent ways of being better or worse; it is simply that each of us receives a unique vocation from God.[40]

When considered alongside other corporate environments for spiritual formation, a community of religious life can be understood as a household on steroids. Nearly all of the features we discussed above with regard to households are relevant for intentional Christian communities. Religious (when used as a noun, *religious* refers to a person or people living a consecrated life) usually live with or near one another. They encounter one another regularly amid life's most ordinary tasks. They develop an intimacy, though not necessarily the same kind of intimacy that develops in a family. And because one does not usually join a religious community for a short spell, members of the community develop their relationships and are formed together over a long time.

There is more. Unlike a family or a household (but like a congregation, though still more intense), a religious community allows its common values and commitments to dictate the agenda for the life that members share together and to create an atmosphere of formation. Indeed, often a good deal of formation is required by the entry process into religious life; and a wholehearted, ongoing, formative pursuit of God and the gospel is often described as the aim of religious life. Often, members of religious communities discuss and then identify, in dialogue with other members, key agents who will serve as guides for each member's formation. A community will sometimes network with other communities or recommend particular networked resources for members, but even these cases involve much more corporate oversight of one another's formation than we might find in a strictly self-networked spiritual formation.

When lived out well, a religious community is a spiritual formation greenhouse. The orchestration of time, intensity, designated relationships, resources, and such is designed to facilitate the members' growth in gospel life, whether this be a life of silent prayer or one of active ministry among the poor. Furthermore, partly because they do not have strong ties to economic necessity (they usually require fewer living expenses) or family (sometimes members commit themselves to a life of celibacy), religious communities have a great deal of freedom to experiment with ways of living the gospel and have been especially adept at exploring and pioneering fresh expressions of gospel life in times of great change. Egyptian sketes, Celtic monastic settlements, Franciscan mission teams, women's Beguinages, Jesuit houses, Anabaptist homesteads, missionary brotherhoods—all of these helped shape the character of the Christian church.[41]

I think the time is ripe to reappropriate religious life and to reinstitute new monastic communities as means of forming segments of the body of Christ. This kind of recovery will require our investment in a few key tasks. First, we will need to review the foundational documents (rules of life, constitutions, biographies and autobiographies of founders, council decisions, and such) of religious communities, both past and present. In these documents, we discover what forms of religious life might best serve as models for communities today, what strengths and weaknesses might attend the establishment of various expressions, what theological or cultural issues underlie the development of new monastic communities, and what resources (in text and in person) might be available to mentor us in our attempts.[42]

Second, we must also give ourselves the freedom to develop simple experiments with life together. Christians of all kinds—Pentecostals, Methodists, Roman Catholics, unaffiliated evangelicals—are exploring and starting many new monastic experiments.[43] A healthy atmosphere of mutual resourcing and networking pervades the scene as one group shares its discoveries with others. I admire the courage of the families and individuals who have given themselves permission to explore (and to fail at) these arrangements for the sake of embodying new forms of life together.

Third, we must also train people who will serve as formation directors in this kind of context, because intentionally forming a religious community requires a special kind of training, particularly in the milieu of contemporary society. The interest the church has had in caring for, forming, and nourishing those who serve with mission organizations must also be cultivated and directed toward those pioneering new forms of religious life. As I mentioned above, both initial and ongoing formation are at the center of traditional monastic life, and we will need to reappropriate this priority within the contexts of—and for the sake of—the new environments of monastic expressions today.

Finally, an authentic reappropriation of religious life will require fresh and deep theological reflection that is informed by history and rooted in a careful examination of Scripture and theological analysis. It is important to determine the meaning of vows, of celibacy, of voluntary poverty, and of community and fellowship, all of which are embedded in religious life. Does God call a few to follow in a more "consecrated" way than others? By encouraging the development of new monastic expressions, are we promoting an unhealthy elitism in the Christian church? What is the relationship between our doctrine of salvation and our sense of monastic pursuit? These and many other questions must be addressed if we are to see a successful recovery of monasticism.

New monastic expressions are simply not reasonable choices for most people. While I think monastic expressions are important—and will increasingly be so—I recognize that only a few of us can or will choose to pursue this way of being "formed together." And yet I want to encourage those few whom God might call into this life. With a combination of wild experiments, close connections with historic traditions, theological reflection, and loving commitment to work things out as we go, there is significant formation potential for new religious communities today. To develop this any further will require another book.

░░░

Christian spiritual formation is not merely the formation of individuals in their interior life of prayer. Private prayer is important, but it is not the whole story. Christian spiritual formation is also the formation of a people. We are a people of God: visible in households, congregations, networks, and monastic expressions. Figure 8.1 (p. 172) summarizes the features of each of these in a single chart.

Missionary theologian Lesslie Newbigin writes, "The Church is an entity which has outlasted many states, nations, and empires, and it will outlast those that exist today. The Church is nothing other than that movement launched into the public life of the world by its sovereign Lord to continue that which he came to do until it is finished in his return in glory."[44] The final portraits in Scripture of God's forming work are those of a bride and a city—illustrations of personal relationship and of a transformed corporate identity.

Going Deeper

1. One way to deepen your understanding of community is to take some field trips to different communities. When I teach classes on worship, I assign students fieldwork exercises in which they visit a worship service that they have never encountered and participate as if they were

Figure 8.1
Formed Together: Various Forms and Features

Membership	Proximity	Regularity of Meeting	Diversity of People
Household blood ties, friendship	same house or neighborhood	very regular, often daily	less diverse, household
Congregation volunteer, gathered	scattered dwellings, common meeting place	often regular, but seldom daily	"fellowship" of diverse ages, maturity, and such within one tradition
Network varies from loose to tight	very scattered, even globally	depends on particular connection(s)	highest possible range
Religious Life commitment	very close, house, neighborhood	most regularity, often multiple times per day	often narrow range (tradition, gender, no children, mature)

Diversity of Activity	Time Together	Intimacy or Depth	Instruction/ Initiation	Direction
Household widest range, all of life	personal leisure over long periods of time	usually high	little here, just join and live	who leads a home? (family, friendship)
Congregation church life and perhaps a bit more	church time and perhaps a bit more		variety depending on centrality of Word and sacrament	varies by tradition
Network varied depending on choice of networks	fragmented	wide variety	variety, specialists and resources	self-directed
Religious Life all of life, yet perhaps narrower than household	much time together over long periods of time (yet usually not childhood)	intimacy through time and commitment	formation is central	direction specified by community

regular attenders or congregation members. They are also expected to observe the service as an anthropologist might. This is not about having students search for a new church to join (in fact, these trips usually confirm students' preference for their regular worship home), but rather it serves to give them a broader sense of what Christian worship is all about in its essence and variety. What might happen if you were to try this kind of exercise as a way of developing your sense of community formation? Visit, conduct interviews, observe. What do you see? What do you learn?

2. This chapter introduced the idea of networked formation. It might be interesting to reflect on your own networks and see just where you are formed. For example, what podcasts do you listen to, and why? Do you frequent any blogs? What small groups do you participate in, and for what purposes? Where and from what relationships do you draw spiritual nourishment? You might want to create a network chart (like those found when you search online for *network* and *diagram*) to display the configuration of your own spiritual connections.

3. One thing not discussed in great depth in this chapter is the formal doctrine of the church, known as ecclesiology. Our sense of the forms of community available to us and our sense of practicing Christian spiritual formation within these forms are intimately tied to our understanding of church. Is church primarily a fellowship of believers, a communion of saints, an apostolic institution, or something else? The way we prioritize Spirit, Word, or sacrament is influenced by our theology of the universal church and the local church. Carefully consider your beliefs about church and how they influence your approach to Christian spiritual formation.

4. As mentioned in the section on congregation, perhaps one of the key practices of congregational formation is the practice of hospitality. Where is your congregation expressing hospitality currently? When have you seen signs in your congregation of the steps of welcoming? What might your congregation experiment with in order to take further steps of growth in the virtue and practice of hospitality?

9

Formed in Thinking,
Feeling, and Acting

Overview

We were introduced to the fullness of human experience in chapter 3 in order to see that the "all things new" gospel really is about all things: transforming every aspect of human experience into an increasing likeness to the person and message of Jesus Christ. In chapters 7 and 8, we discussed what formation might look like with regard to our relationship with God (through prayer) and our relationships together with others (households, congregations, networks, religious communities). Now we will consider what formation might look like with regard to our relationship with ourselves: intellect (thinking), emotions (feeling), and will (acting). My intention is not to develop any specific account of the human faculties or even a full integrative account of the Christian formation of human experience. A number of works on spiritual formation already cover this ground quite thoroughly.[1] Rather, my aim is to illustrate the nature of Christian spiritual formation with regard to our relationship with ourselves by offering a few reflections on formation relating to the broad categories of thinking, feeling, and acting.

It seems to me that theological formation—formation of our intellect in Christ and the truth of the gospel—has not received the attention it deserves in works on spiritual formation, and so I will explore formation in truth. Then we will attend to feeling, considering what it is like for our emotions to be formed in Christ, and examine choice and action, particularly human habits—and I'll outline the steps to change a habit. As a final example of this interweaving, we will look at one final aspect of the formation of human experience: the work of spiritual warfare. Spiritual warfare, a topic that appears throughout the history of Christian spiritual writings, is worthy of consideration in a text on spiritual formation today.

One note: whereas in the previous chapter our attention was aimed at the corporate dimension of Christian life, in this chapter I will place greater attention on the individual. This is not because congregations do not have "minds" or deal with spiritual warfare (they certainly do) but simply because the concepts are more easily presented with reference to individuals.

It was a matter of theology, more particularly about *pneumatology*—the doctrine of the Holy Spirit—that Reverend Ineda Adesanya was dealing with. She writes, in an article recounting her journey as an African American spiritual director, "In March of 2010, God and I had a conversation about pneumatology."[2] This was also a matter of life choices: her life and others'. "God called me to help others toward a life of joy and abundance," she writes, "by recognizing and yielding to the Holy Spirit."[3] But then again, it was about being attuned to her feelings as she opened up to her spiritual director, "Kay," about the death of her grandmother, Mamanenda. Adesanya shares, "I felt the comfort of the Holy Spirit in me particularly when Kay's responses triggered me to reflect on the good times prior to Mamanenda's being struck with Alzheimer's."[4]

But this practice, this relationship, this discipline of spiritual direction, within which she opened herself and learned to receive the openings of others, was somewhat new. I say "somewhat" because the ministry of compassionate listening and wise counsel has been present throughout the history of the African American religious experience.[5] Nonetheless, Adesanya concluded that there was something in the practice of spiritual direction—complete with training and supervision—worthy to be learned and then employed in her cultural setting. She recounts how her growth in contemplation (a term that she had to reassess in light of her own, more expressive background) has influenced her personal experience, her family life, and her ministry of spiritual direction as minister of spiritual life in an African American Baptist church. Her story of formation involved not just learning about theology but learning to live into it, a learning that would ultimately involve every aspect of her personality and all of her relationships. Formation is a formation of every part of human experience.

Every part. Theologians and non-theologians use different terms for the parts of human experience. For example, some use the word *heart* to refer to the central core of a human person (synonymous with *mind* or *spirit*), while others use it to refer to the emotions. Similarly, some use the term *mind* to refer to this same core or center, while others use it as a synonym for intellect. In different centuries, people have used these words in different ways. Following what I introduced in chapter 3, I will speak of *intellect* (and thinking), *emotions* (and feeling) and *will* (and choosing/acting).

That thinking, feeling, and acting are entwined in our formation is not surprising. Indeed, I understand the apostle Paul's story as a continual interweaving formation of these. Paul, a devout Jew, is confronted on the way to Damascus by a vision of the resurrected Christ. This experience certainly affected both his body, blinding him, and his feelings. The passage does not state this specifically, but I think it is safe to say that Paul would have felt overwhelmed. Whatever Paul did in Arabia (see Gal. 1:17), we can be sure that he did some rethinking (see his early sermons in Acts 13:16–47; 14:8–18). To be confronted with the risen Christ was to discover that Jesus was really the Messiah. And if Jesus was the Messiah, then Paul needed to rethink his entire understanding of salvation. Now he was not just waiting for the promise; he was living in its fulfillment. The law did not mean what he had previously thought it meant (see, e.g., Acts 22:3; 26:4–5; Gal. 1:14; Phil. 3:5–6). Paul's own formation was a Spirit-led, interweaving transformation of his thoughts, his emotions, and his choices.

The transformation of human experience is a complex dance. The enlightenment of our intellect triggers a new sense of beauty. This tugs at our emotions. Transformed emotions motivate our will, and actions follow. New actions lead to new experiences, which in turn inform our thinking and feeling. And on and on it goes.

Thinking and the Intellect

In Ephesians 3:14–21, Paul continues a prayer he had begun in 1:15–23. The two passages are a single prayer for the formation of his readers. He prays that "the glorious Father, may give you the Spirit of wisdom and revelation, so that you may know him better" (Eph. 1:17). He prays "that the eyes of your heart may be enlightened in order that you may know the hope to which he has called you, the riches of his glorious inheritance in his holy people, and his incomparably great power for us who believe" (1:18–19) and that they, "rooted and established in love, may have power together with all the Lord's holy people, to grasp how wide and long and high and deep is the love of Christ, and to know this love that surpasses knowledge" (3:17–19). Wisdom, revelation, enlightenment, grasping the fullness of a knowledge that surpasses knowledge—clearly the apostle Paul is burdened before the Lord with the prayer that Ephesian believers grow in their understanding and heartfelt knowledge of God and the gospel.

Paul's fundamental understanding of Christian formation is that it is a formation into the gospel of Christ and, consequently, a deeply theological formation. This is the common way we understand the division of many of Paul's Letters: the doctrinal part and the practical part. For instance, one can review Romans 1–11 (doctrine) and 12–16 (practical); Galatians 1–4 (doctrinal) and 5–6 (practical); Ephesians 1–3 (doctrinal) and 4–6 (practical); and so on. In our previous chapter, regarding congregational reconciliation, I mentioned that the one time Paul uses the term *formed* (Gal. 4:19) is in the context of congregational conflicts. Let me also point out that this situation is not merely *social* but also *doctrinal*. Paul understands the Galatians' formation to be a process of growing in their understanding of the gospel of freedom such that they are not moved by the talk of false zealots. Paul's desire is that we might be saved "through the sanctifying work of the Spirit and through belief in the truth" (2 Thess. 2:13).

Peter expresses similar sentiments in the closing sentences of his second epistle: "Therefore, dear friends, since you have been forewarned, be on your guard so that you may not be carried away by the error of the lawless and fall from your secure position. But grow in the grace and knowledge of our Lord and Savior Jesus Christ" (2 Pet. 3:17–18). Growing in grace and knowledge and learning to avoid error are among the encouragements we find throughout the Christian Scriptures. To the writers of the New Testament, our formation as Christians is both rooted in and deepened through our increasing growth in knowledge of God and the Christian gospel. We distort the Christian faith when we approach our spiritual life as simply a matter of felt intimacy with the Spirit in prayer or character development. I'll explain why in the following five points. First, our formation as Christians is a formation into Christian truth: there is a necessary doctrinal component to our formation. Truth is the way things really are. For example, God really is the Creator of the universe, so Paul explains that those who worship the creation rather than the Creator have "exchanged the truth about God for a lie" (Rom. 1:25). And because Jesus Christ really rose from the dead, one who doesn't believe in resurrection has a useless Christian faith (1 Cor. 15:14). Coming to Christ is coming to "a knowledge of the truth" (1 Tim. 2:4; 2 Tim. 3:7). This is the whole point of the Christian catechetical enterprise.[6]

Second, we must realize that the truth claimed by Christianity is not simply a principle or a proposition but, ultimately, a person. First John acknowledges that "the Son of God has come and has given us understanding, so that we may know him who is true. And we are in him who is true by being in his Son Jesus Christ. He is the true God and eternal life" (1 John 5:20). Jesus himself declares, "I am the way and the truth and the life" (John 14:6). So truth is not the result of an equation; it is the state of a living mind.[7] Only in Christ—Infinite Mind—is found the fullness of truth. As we grow into Christ, we are increasingly formed into truth. When I get to appreciate someone I know, I begin to share that person's way of looking at things. I am, it could be said, formed into his or her mind. Likewise, to live in a loving relationship with Christ through the Spirit is to have "the mind of Christ" (1 Cor. 2:16).

Third, the formation of our thinking is led by the Holy Spirit. The Spirit who inspired Scripture (2 Pet. 1:21), who lies behind our very affirmation of Christian faith (1 Cor. 12:3), and who instructs us as we grow deeper in the truth of our relationship with God (John 14:26) is a Spirit of truth (14:17; 15:26). The Spirit of Christ confirms the gospel of Christ through inner confirmations and outward demonstrations (Rom. 8:16; 1 Cor. 2:4–5) and aids in the preservation of the gospel (2 Tim. 1:14). The Spirit stimulates thoughts, perspectives, and attitudes that reflect those of Christ and the Christian gospel.[8]

Fourth, our Spirit-led formation into truth is confirmed communally. The classic biblical text on this is Acts 15:1–29. This passage recounts a disagreement regarding the necessity of circumcision for gentiles. The only way through this disagreement was to gather, listen to testimony from all sides, have sincere discussion with reference to Scripture, and see how the Spirit might guide. At the end of what seemed to be a difficult conference, they were able to proclaim, "It seemed good to the Holy Spirit and to us" (Acts 15:28). As I mentioned above, truth is a person, Infinite Mind. Our individual minds are finite. Yet the community's mind is larger than the individual mind, particularly when the community is humbly surrendered to Scripture, the Spirit, and one another. This raises the issue of the relationship between authority and ecclesial structure, which the Christian church has debated throughout its history. One mechanism, the council, has brought the body of Christ in all major traditions toward a unity of Spirit. If the church is to be formed as a people into the thought and mind of Christ, councils are, I believe, the best means of authentic progress.

Finally, as I mentioned at the start of this chapter, the intellectual, emotional, volitional, and relational components of being formed in our minds cannot be easily separated. Truth is not something you simply believe. It is something you *experience* and act on. It involves feelings and actions along with ideas and concepts. Take another look at Paul's prayers for the Ephesians. He prays that the "eyes of your *heart* may be enlightened" (Eph. 1:18, italics added). The content of the enlightenment he prays for is God's "*love* that surpasses knowledge" (Eph. 3:19, italics added). True, there is a doctrinal component, but this doctrine is intimately connected with our rich experience of reality, of the way things are: God's forgiveness, the power of the resurrected Christ, the unity of Jew and gentile, and much more. Formation into Christian truth is a formation into loving wonder of the beautiful One who both reveals himself to us and is beyond all knowledge. In this way, our formation into doctrine (through, for example, the practice of common liturgy) is a formation of *desire* as much as a formation of concept.[9] Truth is also something that is *done*, that is lived. Thus, 1 John pronounces that "if we claim to have fellowship with him and yet walk in the darkness, we lie and do not live out the truth" (1 John 1:6). When we are formed into the One who is Truth, truth is understood, felt, lived.

One consequence of this way of looking at the formation of our thinking is seeing the discipline of study as an important spiritual practice. Prayerful, careful, meditative, self-evaluating study is a vital means of forming ourselves ever closer to the truth. Christian doctrine has a vitally important "pastoral function," to use the phrase of theologian Ellen Charry.[10] Works we might think of as theological texts, like Augustine's *On the Trinity*, were guides for meditation as much as theological treatises. Conversely, works we know of as manuals of meditation, like *The Practice of Piety* by Puritan bishop Lewis Bayly, read like theological treatises. God's presence—and sources of theological reflection—is to be found in a wide range of places.[11] Perhaps it is time we recover the medieval, pre-university, monastic practice of meditative study.[12]

An intellect formed in the gospel—through sincere, communal, prayerful study accompanied by a commitment to live the truth—meets the postmodern world with a framework for Spirit-led dialogue. Our intellectual formation is necessarily missional, for Christ's thought is at odds with and therefore must confront views of the world. But thinking formed as I have described above does not come to the world with mere facts and arguments in favor of the Christian faith. Rather, we present a paradigm, a basic belief, a plausibility structure or research program that has been thoughtfully considered and personally experienced and that can be discussed intelligently by believers and unbelievers alike. A church formed in welcoming hospitality, wholehearted theology, and the power of the Spirit brings much to the "all things new" expression of God in the world (as we'll discuss further in chap. 10).

Feeling and the Emotions

Christian spiritual formation is not only a matter of thinking. It is also a matter of feeling. Our moods, emotions, and feelings (known in the past as *affections*) are—like our thoughts, beliefs, and concepts—part of the "all things" transformed by the Spirit of God into ever-greater likeness to Christ and the gospel. Just as God means for us to believe the things God wants us to believe, so too God also wants us to feel about things the way God feels. God desires that we cry about the kinds of things God would cry about. God desires that we would share in divine joys. God desires that we would know and experience ourselves as much as possible as God experiences us.

Our feelings are not unnecessary accessories in our Christian life. They are vital to our faith. "True religion," Puritan pastor and theologian Jonathan Edwards writes, "in great part, consists in holy affections."[13] He defends this claim amply with text after text of Scripture, demonstrating how God urges us to be "fervent." Edwards shows how Scriptures identify emotions such as fear, hope, love, hatred, desire, sorrow, gratitude, compassion, and zeal as important elements of our faith. Regarding sorrow, for example, we read, "Blessed are those who mourn, for they will be comforted" (Matt. 5:4) and "The LORD is close to the brokenhearted and saves those who are crushed in spirit" (Ps. 34:18). The Lord Jesus sincerely expressed zeal (John 2:17), anger (Mark 3:5), pity (Luke 13:34; 19:41–42), and desire (Luke 22:15). Sin is described as a hardness of heart, a statement that certainly has an emotional component (see Ezek. 3:7; Mark 3:5). There are many, many passages that proclaim how God desires that our affections (the term Edwards uses) be transformed in a godly manner. Each fruit of the Spirit (Gal. 5:22–23), for example, expresses some emotional component. Certainly, then, the task of spiritual formation requires that we discover appropriate means of nurturing "holy affections": patterns of emotion that are of increasing conformity with those of Christ and the gospel. This is the formation of the heart.

But human feeling is not always easy to understand. Emotions are notoriously difficult to define and describe.[14] I mentioned in chapter 3 that emotions tend to inform us about the meaning of our person-environment relationship, using the examples of meeting up with a snake and having a beloved child rescued. Our emotional experiences reveal how we evaluate and respond to our world as each event of life unfolds. The problem with defining emotions is that psychologists, who might be best qualified to define emotions, tend to emphasize one or another of the various components that together make up emotional experience. Some draw attention to physical components, such as facial expressions, physiological changes in heart rate and hormones, and particular brain activity. Yet our emotions have a vital cognitive component. As I mentioned above, emotions are statements about how we evaluate our world-self relationship and its meaning. Even if, for some reason, we may have little physiological expression, we can still feel grief deeply as it declares to us the meaning of a loss in our lives. Still other psychologists emphasize the role that "action tendencies" play in emotional experience; for instance, when we are delighted, we tend to be energetic and want to literally jump for joy. Clearly, emotions are actually complex processes that synthesize a number of various components and do so differently for different people.

Emotions are central to human experience. Furthermore, it appears that some of our basic emotions are expressed and recognized throughout the world: anger/disgust, sadness, happiness, fear/surprise, and so on. Most of our emotional experience, however, is a blend of emotions or is best described as some feeling not easily identified with any basic emotion. Consider, for example, the emotional experience of your first day of work as a caregiver (the first job you have landed in your desired field) in an environment where the previous employee was removed for reasons of abuse. You are excited, full of anticipation, and perhaps a little anxious. You feel joy for getting the job. You have anger toward the previous employee and compassion for those you will be working with. You experience all of these emotions together as you leave in the morning for work.

Emotions can be lingering or fleeting. Some feelings are very brief, like a slight sense of pleasure when you glance at a handcrafted chair in a room. You appreciate the style and shape of this chair, but the emotion is so brief and so slight that you would only notice it if you were paying careful attention. Other emotions endure, like my regret for a poorly chosen phrase in a social situation. Still other emotions, whether painful or peaceful, evolve into moods or habits of feeling that govern our entire way of being. Medical conditions such as depression and anxiety have long-term, life-shaping emotional aspects.

Furthermore, our heart tends ultimately to be led by our *emotional orientations*. Some concerns are minor, such that we experience only a mild dissatisfaction when the dish we ordered at a restaurant is overcooked. Other situations touch on our concerns for basic livelihood, so we respond with stronger emotion, such as when you learn that the organization where you've happily worked for many years is reorganizing and your position is being discontinued. While many emotions are *self-oriented*, we can also respond out of an *other-directed orientation*, such as how we sincerely feel joy when a loved one has received good news even though this news may cause us suffering. Aesthetic emotions—where we are caught up in the excellence of an object in itself, no matter what its significance is for us personally—are of a similar type. And, of course, the highest of our relational, aesthetic, other-oriented emotions are *religious* emotions, where our feelings are triggered by a sincere and deep connection to the Ultimate Concern. When we share the heart of God, our emotional framework is, one could say, tuned to the same frequency as God's, and we begin to experience emotion within the influence of the Holy Spirit.

This, in turn, brings us to distinctly Christian emotions. When we have transferred our concerns from self to God and when we have the body of Christ as our community frame of reference, then new feelings become possible—feelings born from relationship with God through Christ. We learn what it means to feel awe or thanksgiving, to experience heartfelt repentance, to cry out in intercession, to lament before the presence of God. In all of these examples, we respond to an appraisal of a situation informed by our Christian orientation and worldview, tending to act in certain ways (lifting hands in praise) or experience inner changes (praying with sighs too deep for words) in light of our relationship with God. The goal of the formation of our feelings, then, is to facilitate changes in our emotional experience so we increasingly interact affectively with God and the world in view of our relationship with God.

Efforts to bring about changes in the habits of our emotional experience are generally described in secular culture as *therapy*, but perhaps *facilitated formation of feeling* is a better term. Models of therapy, like definitions of emotion, tend to emphasize one or another of the components that contribute to emotional experience and expression, including cognitive appraisal, personal history, social environment, body chemistry, and present awareness.

The point of *Christian spiritual* formation of our emotional experience is to discern the leading of the Spirit (What is God touching in me? What might God want to touch?) and then to actively cooperate with what we've discerned. For example, one young mother may realize how a misplaced concern governs her frustrations with her children: she has a need to see herself as a successful Christian parent, yet God simply asks that she love as best she can. So she decides to open herself up to a new, godly concern by flooding her heart and imagination with a view of what parenthood free of duty and full of freedom might accomplish for her children and for herself. Attracted to and pursuing this vision, she finds a greater contentment with sincere love, and she avoids being crushed by the weight of a false parental ideal. Thus, by these kinds of exercises, she trains the eyes of her heart. Or a husband might realize through an unfortunate event at home that he actually has little control over his emotions. Yes, some of this might have to do with his basic sense of identity, but it also might help if he were to learn some simple self-regulation skills (counting to ten, deep breathing, and so on). Or perhaps his self-control problem is that he generally expresses no emotion at all. If this is the case, then he must learn, by the leading of the Spirit, to recognize and follow those inclinations of heart and body that speak of joy, sorrow, and other emotions long hidden.

Some of the work needed on our emotions likely involves reeducating ourselves about the truth of Christ and the gospel. For example, the re-formation of my social anxiety might be best facilitated by allowing the gospel message of one's unconditional acceptance by God to permeate my being and perhaps accompanying this with disciplines of self-examination or spiritual direction. By receiving the truth of God's plan for humanity into the depths of my heart, I facilitate hope and trust—countering the emotional patterns of an inappropriate fear or sadness. I live out God's forgiveness and care through my own acts of forgiveness and care for others, acts that embody the truth of God's heart and serve as a healing salve for my soul. Through the fellowship of a caring small group, I might share my troubled history and discover the misguided interpretations I have ascribed to that history over the decades.[15]

Another feature of the Christian spiritual formation of our emotional experience is the simple rehabituation of patterns of thought, feeling, and action. Regarding thought habits, for example, I may find myself tempted by inappropriate sexual preoccupations, so I simply avoid the environments where those kinds of thoughts might be triggered. As you address feelings, you might recognize anew the connection between mind and body and choose to pray in a posture that reflects confident trust in God, rather than promote passivity by praying with your shoulders hunched over and hands folded. Your prayer partner, looking to adjust his habits of action, could choose to set aside time each night to reflect on the day, writing down a few items for which he is grateful.[16] As you experiment with relationships, with times of prayer, and with eating and sleeping habits, pay attention to how these influence various aspects of your emotional experience. These examples reveal the significant link between spiritual disciplines and emotional formation.

Finally, we simply place ourselves in the presence of God. We cannot heal our own wounds. We cannot transform the patterns of our feelings all by ourselves. This work belongs to the Spirit, though the Spirit works through our own actions. We pray and silently wait. We receive prayer from a few friends. And, as best we can, we learn to grow in the core Christian emotions of faith, hope, and love. Sometimes the Spirit does a marvelous work and a piece of our heart is rewired in an instant. Sometimes it takes many years and much struggle to see our feelings formed into Christ. Our formation may simply be a matter of acquiring a new skill, or we may find that the Spirit needs to take us deep—deeper into our selves than we have ever been—which requires a relationship or community of healing to assist in the realigning of our feelings.[17] We may be frightened and not recognize our feelings. It may feel as if our affection for God has disappeared. The ways of the Spirit and heart are mysterious. Christian spiritual formation is not a formula but a journey of discovery.

Choosing, Acting, and the Will

The formation of one's self also involves the changing of one's actions and habits: the will. Mind, heart, life, morals, character, habit, intellect, emotion, will, doctrine, relationships—these are all engaged as we pursue authentic relationship with God. Consequently, as you have already seen above, these divisions can be somewhat artificial. Nevertheless, it can help to look at these categories separately, even though sometimes we do lean toward one dimension or another. One person focuses on a very private "Jesus and me" relationship with God, apparently unaware that a relationship with God has implications for moral life in society. Another person lives a passionately activist life in evangelical mission and advocacy for justice, apparently unaware that she is on the verge of burnout because her personal relationship with God has little depth. Perhaps we discover, to use the language of Scripture, we are not "living the truth" (see, e.g., Gal. 2:14). To my mind, when we believe a truth but do not live it in habits and morals, we have both a formational and a theological problem. Christopher Wright identifies the significance of walking in Christ-likeness for the sake of Christian mission when he writes,

> If God's people abandon their ethical distinctiveness by forgetfulness, idolatry or disobedience, then not only do they jeopardize their own well-being . . . , they also frustrate the broader purposes of the God who brought them into existence by his electing love and brought them out of bondage by his redeeming power.[18]

There is a vital connection between Christian theology, Christian ethics, and Christian spiritual formation, and it is broader than we might think. Is formation merely the practical task of getting us to the point where we do the ethical act? No, formation in Christ also shapes us so that we make ethical evaluations in the Spirit and mind of Christ. Let us examine this aspect of formation by considering a slightly altered true story and then outlining the steps one might take to change a habit.

I met once (and only once, during a conference) with a man I will call Hank, who asked me if I could help him change a habit. He was concerned that this habit might be damaging his life. The habit? Wasting time watching television. Hank was retired, and while he had other interests, he simply found himself ignoring them in order to watch his favorite shows. Hank was concerned because he had watched his father turn into a television zombie in the final years of his life. Hank's dad would spend most of the day gazing at the TV set, not engaging with the people or activities that he once loved. Hank described his father's final passing as a tragic death: he was a Christian man who at the end just seemed to want to escape from life. And now Hank was beginning to see signs of the same tendencies in his own life. Hank had prayed that God would simply "take it all away," but nothing had changed. He felt conviction—and perhaps even a leading of the Spirit—to address this situation. But what was he to do?

Once Hank demonstrated to me that he was not making a false association between his own habits and his father's situation and that his desire to change this habit was something he really did perceive from the Spirit (I had wondered whether I should advise him to lighten up and enjoy a few television shows in his retirement), we began to talk about change. This was the only time I would see him, so my approach was much more directive than I would generally have used in other situations. Through the course of our conversation, I presented him with a number of steps. As I was making this presentation, I realized that I was giving an outline of the task of formation with regard to a single habit. Of course, no one will take all of these steps, but the steps together illustrate what formation of life habits might look like.

One step is to gain a new vision for your life. I suggested that Hank might want to employ his memories of his father for the sake of this godly desire to change. Trying to place his father in his mind—perhaps by periodically, intentionally, prayerfully remembering Dad's problem—Hank would cultivate a desire for a life lived differently. Perhaps Hank might even want to spend some time imagining what a different kind of life might look like for him. What activities, what relationships, what feelings might be present as his dependence on television wanes?

Another suggestion I had was simple: move the TV. If his wife would comply for the sake of Hank's spiritual life (assuming she didn't already want their television to be less intrusive), perhaps they could keep the television in a less accessible or desirable location. Or perhaps they could create an initial goal together to watch less television each week. When we distance ourselves from the triggers to our unwanted habits, they are easier to change.

Hank also needed some community support for his formation. I asked if he was a part of any small group or had a close friend. Hank explained that he and a couple of other men had gotten together for breakfast and prayer once a week for many years. "Bingo!" I cried. "Just let these men know that you want to change this habit, and ask them to ask you how you are doing each week." I inquired if they were avid TV watchers. Hank told me that no, they weren't. In fact, one of the men himself had in recent years tried to curb his own television news consumption—a conviction that contributed to Hank's own efforts. I explained that this was wonderful, because hanging around a community with common values would provide a strong support for Hank's own formation.

I asked Hank about times during the day when he was more likely to watch television. Were there situations, body rhythms, or moods that made him more susceptible? He explained that he did tend to feel lazy after lunch these days and that when he and his wife had a disagreement, he would want to just turn on the TV and escape. I encouraged him to pay attention to what was happening at those times. Perhaps he could reflect on these situations and moods at the end of each day in a brief time of prayerful self-examination. What does he sense God is encouraging him to do in these moments?

Of course, I knew—and perhaps Hank did as well—that there were deeper issues involved: his own sense of identity, his rediscovery of meaning and life after retirement, things I might call issues of healing. But this one, short encounter was not the time to bring up all of that. These were issues he could bring up with his friends or his pastor back at home. What I could provide in this meeting was some formational wisdom for the moment.

And in those situations when he actually sensed the struggle, he could cry out for divine help. I encouraged Hank to notice the moments when he was most tempted and to simply cry out to God. We looked at a few phrases from the Psalms that might help him give voice to his cry for help. I encouraged Hank to find alternative activities, even very brief ones, that might be used to take the desire for television and redirect it. Could he take a walk? Could he listen to music or read a book or write a letter to a friend?

I reminded Hank of the maxim that goes something like this: when you fall off your horse, get right back on—and take a moment to reflect on why you fell. Hank actually had a ranching background and knew this principle well. He needs to pay attention and notice where and how the Spirit of God is present as he discovers a new life for himself.

When we were finished with the conversation, Hank confessed to me that he had hoped, and expected, I would have very little to say. He had grown up in a "pray that it goes away" type of Christianity and had not pictured so many options, particularly ones that fit well with the Christian faith. Now (*shucks!*) he would have to go home and do something. But Hank knew that he was not alone. It was the Spirit who led him to be concerned in the first place, and he felt that our conversation was part of the Spirit's guidance. The God who began a good work would be faithful to bring it to completion (Phil. 1:6).

Figure 9.1
How to Change a Habit: A Few Factors in the Formation of Our Will

- Gain a new vision for life: imagine what might be if you broke this habit or made a new one.
- Remove triggers: rid yourself of (or at least avoid as best you can) those things, places, people, and situations that reinforce the habit.
- Enlist community support: meet with others, tell them what is going on, and let them hold you to account.
- Address deeper issues: together with God or a trusted friend, look into the factors that perpetuate this habit and make it hard to change.
- Cry out: when the heat is on, call out to God for help.
- Develop alternative activities: establish new habits that meet similar needs.
- Pay attention and persevere: examine yourself and your setting and then try again, and again, and again.

Spiritual Warfare

By using the ominous word *tempted*, we have already stepped into the realm of spiritual warfare. Hank, his friends and family, and the Holy Spirit are not the only players on the field. The Christian tradition makes it clear that there are counteragents—an accuser and tempter, demons—who wish to do us harm.[19] "Your adversary, the devil, prowls around like a roaring lion looking for someone to devour" (1 Pet. 5:8). We are to expect conflict in the Christian life, including spiritual conflict. Spiritual formation is not a process whereby we grow past the experience of conflict. Rather, as we mature in Christ, we become increasingly able to navigate conflicts, living more and more victoriously in the midst of them—whether the conflicts are with others or within ourselves or with our spiritual enemies.

Satan and his forces wield their influence on every aspect of human experience they can touch. Satan causes tragedy in the circumstances that surround Job's life (Job 1:1–19). The devil is "a liar and the father of lies" (John 8:44, targeting intellect), attacking the thoughts in our minds. We are warned to resolve our anger quickly, lest we "give the devil a foothold" (Eph. 4:27, targeting emotions). Demons are known to cause people to be unable to speak and to attempt harm to themselves (Matt. 17:15–18; Mark 5:1–5; Luke 11:14, all targeting actions). In 2 Corinthians, Paul encourages the Corinthian believers to forgive and reaffirm their love for a man from whom they had previously distanced themselves. Paul explains that one reason for this restoration was that "Satan might not outwit us" (2 Cor. 2:10–11). The implication is that Satan can inflict division within the relationships we have in congregational life.

The devil tempted Jesus with promises of provision, protection, and power (Matt. 4:1–11). In Ephesians, Paul speaks of principalities and powers (Eph. 6:12 KJV), which influence not only individual minds but also the structures and systems of thought and power of society.[20] We can be sure that we will encounter conflicts with our spiritual enemy. Again, spiritual formation intends to strengthen our relationship with God so that we, like Jesus, are able to withstand the onslaughts of the devil ourselves and to help release others from their own captivities, not to find some space of tranquility where we do not experience conflict.

The devil is the enemy of Christ and Christ's gospel, so it follows that the devil will try to prevent our formation into ever-greater intimacy with Christ and the gospel at any and every point. The accuser will stab us with false condemnation to keep us from ever stepping forward. The forces and powers of oppression will keep us down so that we have little freedom to explore transformation. The devil will cause suspicions among those who might serve as agents of formation for one another. When we experiment with a means of grace and do not experience the instant transformation we hoped for, the enemy will bombard us with discouragement, telling us that it will be much easier if we simply give up all hope of change. We will be filled with thoughts of pride such that we think that we have no need of formation (or at least not this kind of formation). The enemy of Christ is the enemy of our formation into Christ, both individually and as communities.

Our task as believers in formation amid conflict is to stand (Eph. 6:13), to resist (James 4:7), and to conquer with the authority of the name of Jesus (Acts 16:18). We learn to acknowledge the devilish lies of the society within which we dwell, for example, by openly disagreeing with the advertisements we see or hear. We flee tempting situations (1 Cor. 6:18; 10:14; 1 Tim. 6:11; 2 Tim. 2:22), moving our television into the basement. We learn to talk back when we perceive the devil's suggestions using brief passages of Scripture—like Jesus did when he responded to the enemy's temptations by speaking truth (Luke 4:5–12). Then, when compassion and the Spirit lead, we command unclean spirits to depart (4:33–35).

The task of spiritual formation—formation of our thinking, feeling, and choosing or acting—requires wisdom as we learn which means are best suited to which people and which situations. Spiritual formation also requires courage. There is a battle to be fought and won. We cannot avoid it. Instead we must step in and, by the power of the resurrected Christ, win.

True Religion and Spiritual Formation

Christian spiritual formation touches every aspect of our experience. If it does not, at least to some extent, it is not part of true religion. *True religion* and similar phrases (such as *authentic religion, true faith, real Christianity*) are common in evangelical Christianity. Evangelicals of the eighteenth and nineteenth centuries frequently distinguished "true" or "real" Christianity from a number of counterfeits. Scottish theologian Henry Scougal, for example, introduced his influential *The Life of God in the Soul of Man* with a discussion of common "mistakes about religion." The errors he enumerates include viewing religion as merely "orthodox notions and opinions," considering the faith to be a matter of "external duties," and thinking of it primarily "in the affections, in rapturous heats and ecstatic devotion." Scougal argues that all these have a "resemblance of piety and at the best are but means of obtaining it, or particular exercises of it." "But certainly religion is quite another thing," he proclaims. True religion is, as he puts it, a "union of the soul with God, a real participation of the divine nature, the very image of God drawn upon the soul; or, in the Apostle's phrase, *it is Christ formed within us.* Briefly, I know not how the nature of religion can be more fully expressed, than by calling it *a divine life.*"[21]

True religion sees what relationship with God—and consequently spiritual formation—is not and what it is. Authentic relationship with God is not merely the restatement of correct words (intellectualism) or the observance of proper forms (sacerdotalism); it is not merely respectable morals (legalism) or emotional experience (enthusiasm). It involves the transformation of all of these yet can be reduced to none of them. To be formed into Christ is to be formed into a union, a relationship with the living God. The danger of spiritual formation is that we become consumed with the self-improvement of it all: healing emotions, developing character, battling demons, broadening our minds. It is a delicate line to walk, learning to express the fullness of the gospel and remembering all the while that it is really a sincere relationship and not some kind of product we are trying to create out of ourselves. On the one hand, our formation in Christ demands every part of our being both as individuals and as communities. This is very, very complex. On the other hand, Christian spiritual formation is just taking the next step in an honest relationship with God. It's that simple.

Going Deeper

1. Thinking, feeling, acting—which comes most naturally to you? What have been your predispositions? How have your own tendencies in your

patterns of thinking, feeling, and choosing or acting shaped your relationship with God? Are you different in groups than alone? How have you experienced conversion of your thinking, conversion of your emotional experience, conversion of your habits and actions? Where do you sense your current need for formation will take you next?

2. In chapter 6, we discussed different means of grace: the Spirit, disciplines, the community of faith, and the trials of everyday life. In this chapter, we learned about the formation of different parts of our experience: intellect, emotions, and will. Are some means more suited to dealing with one area than with another? What disciplines, community relationships, or sorts of trials might be especially beneficial with regard to the early formation of Christian thinking? Which of these might be most fruitful with regard to re-forming habits or with regard to forming mature feelings in prayer, for instance?

3. One aspect of the formation of human experience that we have left undeveloped is the area of the healing of emotions or, as the church has called it, the cure of souls. We discuss this ministry under a variety of names, including therapy, counseling, prayer ministry, spiritual direction, and spiritual warfare. A healing component can also be found in the ministries of mentoring, coaching, teaching, and discipleship, however these are construed, and a number of models of care are associated with each of these. How might one explore the relationship between spiritual formation and the re-formation pursued by these healing ministries?

4. The relationships between doctrine, worship, and formation are also ripe for investigation. Our worship services (whether liturgical or charismatic or somewhere in between) are structured to express beliefs and to form individuals (or a people). How does each of these elements—doctrine, worship, formation—influence the development of the others? How can each be best employed to foster growth in Christ and for the greatest glory of God?

5. The practice that I call "talking back" is especially useful for changing a habit. When Jesus was confronted by the enemy, he responded with a Scripture passage that directly addressed each attack (Luke 4:1–13). Why not reflect on those places where you regularly come under attack? Why not replay in your mind the lies the enemy uses to attack you and then consider what Scriptures might be appropriate to quote back at him? With such preparation, you will be prepared to fight victoriously, just as Jesus did.

10

....

Formed into Mission

Overview

We have explored formation with reference to our relationship with God (chap. 7), with our community of faith (chap. 8), and with ourselves (chap. 9). In this chapter, we will discuss our formation as Christians with reference to our relationship with the world. After introducing a case study that will serve as a backdrop to the issues discussed in this chapter, we will survey what I am calling the "new missions consensus." For many, our view of missions has changed. We now see missions not merely as something that *we* do but primarily as something that *God* does. We see the mission of the church as inextricably part of the fabric of the Christian gospel story. We operate from the assumption that the work of missions involves more than changing beliefs, making disciples, providing services, or planting churches. We are realizing, finally, that missions should not be seen simply as something we do "over there"; our understanding of missions includes what is all around us locally and, in part, defines us as church.

Having examined the basic components of the new missions consensus, we will look at the Holy Spirit and the relationship of Spirit and mission: inspiring the church, orchestrating our participation, empowering the work of missions, and producing the fruit of mission growth. Then we will focus our attention specifically on the task of Christian spiritual formation with regard to mission, considering the issue of our identity as Christians—missional Christians—in a pluralistic world. We will look at a few important missional skills; discover the value of a vibrant, well-formed Christian life for the sake of mission; and reflect on our formation in the power of the Holy Spirit and our formation in the development of missional relationships with others. We'll also explore the meaning of forming a culture of mission within a community of faith.

Finally, we will look briefly at the who, the how, and the why of missional formation, because mission—which is more than just a program run by a congregation—can be integrated (formed) into the life of households, networks, new monastic expressions, and any other form of Christian living. We will be reminded that our participation in mission and formation into mission is shaped by our own diverse gifts within the body of Christ and reflect on the powerful relationships between liturgy and mission. In closing, we see how our sense of the end, our eschatological vision, directs our practice of mission just as our aim of formation guides our practice of formation. And, indeed, they are the same end.

One note as I begin this chapter on formation into mission. Some recommend that we eliminate the term *mission* from our vocabulary entirely.[1] *Mission*, for these people, is too tightly connected to the West's history of subjugation and exploitation and to the patronizing attitudes that accompany it. I have considered this objection, sharing the critics' sense that the church needs to repent for the horrible actions performed in the name of Christian mission. At other places in this book, I have chosen to employ terms such as *plan*, *purpose*, and *vocation* and have even spoken of God's *desires*. And yet I have retained the term *mission*. To my thinking, *mission* is fundamentally a theological term that describes the sending of the Son from the Father and describing the trajectory of the Big Story of the gospel. Perhaps in using the term, we can find cause for both repentance and reappropriation—a cause that, I also sense, lies behind much of the new missions consensus today.

St. Cuthbert's Church (our imaginary case study for this chapter) was on the edge of something very new—but St. Cuthbert's was anything but edgy. It was founded centuries ago near the center of one of the largest cities in England. It was not the cathedral, that honor being reserved for a larger, older church that sat in the heart of the city's financial district. St. Cuthbert's was located near the center in a neighborhood that prospered in the eighteenth century and became a steel-manufacturing and shipbuilding hub in the nineteenth and early twentieth centuries. St. Cuthbert's survived bombings during World War II, though some of the manufacturing plants did not. In time, the steel-manufacturing industry struggled. Scores of workers were laid off.

Many moved away, hoping to find work elsewhere. Rows of three-story brick flats were left empty for decades. Others were bought by the government as foreclosures became more common. Some had begun to crumble.

The people of St. Cuthbert's were always a hearty bunch. They were active in propagating the Christian message during the nineteenth century. Many missionaries in previous generations had left from St. Cuthbert's to travel to India, Africa, and China with the good news of Christ. As times got hard, the congregation drew closer together. Though some members had left the city to seek employment elsewhere, there was still a core group of strong, committed believers. It was now, however, a smaller and grayer congregation than it used to be.

But now times were not just hard. They were different. The culture or, I should say, the cultures around the aging congregation were different. Rents were dropping in the old flats, and people were moving back. The old factory workers were not returning, though, for they had long ago settled elsewhere. Other kinds people were moving in: young people looking for affordable housing and new venues, who liked the retro feel of the neighborhood, and many, many refugees, initially from Bangladesh and Vietnam and later from central Africa and the Middle East. The government flats were just waiting to be occupied and now there was need of them, so this was good for all. And yet the city was now very different than it had been—different clothing, different smells, different languages, different viewpoints. One member of St. Cuthbert's said he felt lost on his own block.

The variety of non-Christian viewpoints seemed to surprise the people of St. Cuthbert's the most. And it really wasn't the religious beliefs of the refugees that surprised them, since they sort of expected that. It was the beliefs of the new generation of Brits, who were not Christian in the least—not even interested. If anything, they were anti-Christian. Many of them thought that Christianity was a scourge on the earth, that it had served its purpose in history (for better and worse), and that it was time Christianity went the way of the honey wagon—a cart that used to ride through back alleys collecting human waste from apartment buildings and outhouses. And they were glad to be done with it.

It came down to this: the people of St. Cuthbert's, who had been sending missionaries to foreign lands for over a century, now felt like they themselves were in the middle of a foreign land. Frankly, they were unprepared. The congregation was good at raising money to give to the mission society, but members did not know the first thing about initiating authentic welcoming relationships with people whose faiths were so different from their own. Once upon a time long ago, they used to go out canvassing—knocking on doors and telling people about their faith. But back then, everybody knew what terms like *God* and *saved* meant. Everything was different now.

Not only were they unprepared, but there were some in St. Cuthbert's—and, to be honest, many of these were the younger people in the congregation who actually had the skills and energy to start something—who had questions about the whole "missionary thing." They had watched missionaries leave and return burned out, barely hanging on to their faith. They had read stories of missionary history that left them wondering just how beneficial the Western church's missionary enterprise really was.

The members of St. Cuthbert's knew they couldn't just sit still in their fortress. (The church building was large and stone and actually resembled something that could have once been used for protection.) They had to do something. Not doing anything would mean the congregation's slow death, and it just didn't seem Christian to settle for a content but isolated existence. What St. Cuthbert's needed was a new mission perspective, a new mission spirit, and a new mission practice. What the congregation needed—and wanted, if they could have articulated it—was to be re-formed into Christian mission.

St. Cuthbert's was not alone in its struggle to rethink formation and mission. Theologian Lesslie Newbigin, who had been a missionary for decades and had returned to England to discover that his home country was itself a mission field, opened his landmark book, *The Gospel in a Pluralist Society*, with these words: "It has become a commonplace to say that we live in a pluralist society—not merely a society which is in fact plural in the variety of cultures, religions, and life-styles which it embraces, but pluralist in the sense that this plurality is celebrated as things to be approved and cherished."[2] His book is an attempt to reexamine what it means to communicate the Christian message in just such an environment. Missiologist David Bosch speaks of what he calls the "crisis" of mission in his comprehensive book *Transforming Mission*. Advances in science and technology, the dechristianization of the West, the integration of religious cultures once separated by oceans, the history of abuses associated with Christian missions, global divisions of rich and poor, the growing autonomy of indigenous Christian churches in various cultures—these and other factors contribute to a situation that Bosch considers a crisis. He points out that the Japanese character for *crisis* is a combination of the characters for *danger* and *opportunity*. This, Bosch suggests, is precisely where the Christian church finds itself today: in a place of danger and opportunity, in a crisis.[3]

And what concerns us here is that this crisis of mission has deep formational implications for churches and Christians. Seminary professor Darrell Guder and several of his colleagues (collaborating under the name The Gospel in

Our Culture Network) mince no words as they speak to the church in North America.

> Changes associated with the move from a modern to an increasingly postmodern condition have created a cultural crisis. But the churches face a crisis of their own. They manifest an increasing disease with their heritage of a functional Christendom and forms of church life shaped by modern notions of voluntary association and rational organization. This is a time for a dramatically new vision.[4]

The people of God must be formed anew into the mission of God for our time. And the missionaries and missional communities of Christ must be formed anew into depth of relationship with God and with the Spirit of Christ. This is being formed into mission. But how is this accomplished? How do we facilitate the maturing of people into the mission of God in this moment of crisis?

As I mentioned above, St. Cuthbert's is not alone in considering these issues. Others have not only raised new questions but also suggested new answers. By summarizing and applying the wisdom of the new missions consensus, particularly with relationship to Christian spiritual formation, we will reflect—as we have throughout this book—on the ministry of the Holy Spirit, the Spirit of mission. Then we will consider more directly what it might look like to be formed into Christian mission.

The New Missions Consensus

Christian leaders who think carefully about these things have, in the past few decades, arrived at some shared convictions about Christian mission—convictions that now shape the way that many in the Christian church are pursuing mission, church life, and even Christian spiritual formation. I will summarize four of those convictions.

Mission Is Primarily God's Work

The first and perhaps most important conviction that has emerged from the conversations among mission-minded people recently is that mission is less about us and more about God. Though yielding to current understanding, the widely held belief has been (and for many still is) that missions are our actions on behalf of someone else—namely, those people out there. People we sent to do that were called *missionaries*, and *missions* was the name we ascribed to the endeavor by Christians to reach the lost or provide hospital care or accomplish some other good, faith-driven intent.

Now we talk less about missions and missionaries and more about mission and being missional. These words may differ by only a few letters, but these changes mean a lot. Mission (Latin *missio*, "send") is most fundamentally an act of God. Thus, Newbigin proclaims, "It seems to me of great importance to insist that mission is not first of all an action of ours. It is an action of God."[5] The Gospel in Our Culture Network echoes this, stating, "'Mission' is not something the church does, a part of its total program. No, the church's essence is missional, for the calling and sending action of God forms its identity."[6] Biblical scholar Christopher Wright, in his magisterial *Mission of God*, concurs, saying,

> *Mission is not ours; mission is God's.* Certainly the mission of God is the prior reality out of which flows any mission that we get involved in. Or, as has been nicely put, it is not so much the case that God has a mission for his church in the world but that God has a church for his mission in the world. Mission was not made for the church; the church was made for mission—God's mission.[7]

The term *mission* was used originally in Christian theology to speak of God's sending the Son and the Spirit. God sent himself in order to accomplish God's mission. This *missio Dei* (Latin, "mission of God") is the foundation of all Christian missions today.

Mission Is Connected to the Gospel Story

This follows directly from the first conviction. If Christian mission is something God is doing, then our sense of mission as a church must originate in an understanding of the gospel of God through Jesus Christ. And this comes from considering the Big Story of the Christian faith presented in Scripture. The Christian Scripture was written as God's people—inspired by God's Spirit—reflected on the work of God in the midst of mission. Our belief in one God (Christian monotheism) is missional, for it is this very God and no other who created the world, who restores it to wholeness, and who desires to be known as an intrinsic part of this restoration. The gospel tells the story of a God who entrusts the fulfillment of God's mission to people, offering them the chance to be lights to the world and agents of the kingdom of God.

I have tried to display the vast and beautiful plan of God throughout this book, particularly in chapter 2. Our task as we pursue formation into mission is to learn to see the world with the "all things new" vision of God. We must see ourselves as partners with God in a formative, cooperative process of restoring creation to wholeness and holiness. In his article "Living into the Big Story: The Missional Trajectory of Scripture in Congregational Life," pastor Allen Hilton describes how formation into the missional gospel story might be cultivated.[8] His suggestions, which we'll explore later in this chapter, stretch us to practice Bible interpretation in the context of missional relationship with others.

Mission Involves More Than It Used To

"The whole church taking the whole gospel to the whole world!" was the cry of the International Congress on World Evangelization in Lausanne, Switzerland, in 1974. It was a cry that both reflected and stimulated the formation of evangelicals' thinking about mission. The Lausanne Covenant, an influential document crafted by the participants, expresses their "penitence" for "having sometimes regarded evangelism and social concern as mutually exclusive" and affirms that "both are necessary expressions of our doctrines of God and man, our love for our neighbor and our obedience to Jesus Christ."[9] Wright—seen as heir to the mantle of influential cleric and prolific author John Stott, one of the primary organizers of the Lausanne Conference—speaks of "God's comprehensive redemption," a work of God that addresses personal devotion, doctrine, social structures, ecological health, and more. Wright argues, in the context of a discussion of God's redemption of Israel in the exodus, that "our commitment to mission must demonstrate the same broad totality of concern for human need that God demonstrated in what he did for Israel."[10]

This is where mission meets the fullness of formation. This is where mission meets the formation of mind, heart, and life. The consistency of our walk with God speaks God to the world. The truth of Christ, incarnated in the flesh, expressed in Scripture, and sent in the proclamation of the church, is finally incarnated, expressed, and sent through the transformed practice of our lives in all its fullness. So the very act of our "all things new" formation as individuals and communities is a "light to the nations." The Salvation Army knew this, for founders William and Catherine Booth sought to bring salvation and relief to the destitute of their own time and place (nineteenth-century London). They blended high esteem for evangelistic proclamation, holy living, compassionate service to the least, and courageous confrontation of social evils as a way of intentionally expressing the fullness of the gospel to meet the wide-ranging needs of the people they met and loved.[11] Mission is not a matter of just being good and keeping silent for the sake of not bothering those who might be put off by your Christian beliefs. No, it is rather a radical commitment to Christ and Christ's life made with our whole being, a dangerous pursuit of authenticity in all of life's dimensions that risks following the Spirit and Scripture to places that shallow religion and worldly interests would avoid.

Conversion of belief is important, but we must remember Jesus's rebuke of those who "travel over land and sea to make a single convert, and when you have succeeded, you make them twice as much a child of hell as you are" (Matt. 23:15). Right conduct is important, but we must remember that Christ spoke most harshly with those who "clean the outside of the cup and dish, but inside they are full of greed and self-indulgence" (Matt. 23:25). Making disciples is essential to Christian mission. Indeed, this is the primary verb in Jesus's Great Commission (Matt. 28:19). But making disciples is not the whole of Christian mission, though it may be especially valuable among those who are seekers or do not know much about the faith. Our missional aim includes "teaching them to obey everything I have commanded you" (Matt. 28:20), forming people into an "obedience that comes from faith" (Rom. 1:5; 16:26).[12] Community and church planting are valuable, but if the communities we form are full of division, vice, or lies, we may find ourselves planting "the synagogue of Satan" (Rev. 3:9). Our aim, therefore, in both formation and mission is to display to the world an attractive and challenging "true religion," for it and the divine "all things new" life (described at the end of chap. 9) are also the beacon of mission.

Mission Is Done Here Too

As St. Cuthbert's was learning, the church's mission field is not simply overseas; it must now include our next-door neighbors. Globalization—the international integration arising from the exchange of worldviews, products, ideas, and other aspects of culture—means that we are in contact with one another more than ever. My online "classrooms" are now "attended" by students all over the world. Similarly, cities and even countries all over the world are experiencing significant demographic shifts. Walls around the world, both real and imagined, have been torn down, and new walls are being constructed elsewhere. The population of non-Western peoples in Western countries is growing quickly. Pluralism is here to stay. And in addition to globalism and pluralism is secularism—or at least a post-Christian religious mind-set.[13] Believers are finding that in parts of the Western world, Christianity is neither respected nor understood any longer. What does all this mean? It means that at this moment, the whole world, virtually every region of the globe, can be seen as both home and mission.[14]

We have trained our missionaries to go (somewhere away from here) and do cross-cultural ministry. We have taught them the cultural sensitivities required to adapt to other cultures. This kind of Christian cultural formation develops the framework possible for the Christian gospel to be heard for what it truly is. But many of us are unprepared for this kind of ministry ourselves, since we think we have not been called to be missionaries. We imagine missionaries need language instruction (and this can help), but it's also important to learn how to be present with people of another culture, how to practice hospitality. We too must form ourselves into these sensibilities. And furthermore, as we have seen, I suspect our openness to cross-cultural formation will require that we stretch our ideas about the practices and relationships of formation itself. It is one thing for us to do evangelism or service for others. It is another to welcome these same others into our congregations as equal participants. Spiritual direction might look different for a Korean woman than for an African American woman. A life of prayer might look different for an American widower than for a Nepali convert.[15]

But embracing mission at home also means learning to be a cross-cultural community, because we rub shoulders with folks from other cultures more often than ever before. What might it mean to share church together? What music would we sing? How would we make decisions? A multicultural missional church must rethink the term *we*. Missional formation, then, is a matter of contextualizing communication. It is also a matter of community identity.[16] Those articulating the new missions consensus are convinced of this.

Let's review the four convictions. Mission is primarily God's work. Our participation in God's mission is guided by our own assimilation of the gospel story. Mission requires that the people of God participate in the full restoration of the world in every area of life. And mission is something that we do right here and right now. This is the consensus (or at least some of it). Perhaps you can already see the implications of this new view of mission. Our identity as Christians, at least Christians in the West, is not gained through our heritage as part of a centuries-old Christian culture. Rather, our identity as a church and as individuals in Christ must be rediscovered in the midst of interacting with people and groups who may be very different from us. For those of us whose home is not the Christian West, there are other missional challenges; multiple religions and cultures, even those that have interacted in the past, are relating to each other in novel ways. As Newbigin puts it, "The fulfillment of the mission of the Church thus requires that the Church itself be changed and learn new things."[17] To see mission as integral to formation and formation as integral to mission—this is the challenge before us.

The Spirit of Mission

Learning to reposition ourselves so we are moving toward others in light of a clearer understanding of contemporary mission is not easy. It is a challenging formation. But we need not despair, because the Spirit of the risen Christ is the chief agent of our formation. The Spirit who equipped the church for the mission of God at the start equips the church today. The Acts of the Holy Spirit (we usually call it the Acts of the Apostles, or just the book of Acts) presents a paradigmatic account of how the Spirit forms the Christian church into mission. Let's take a look.

First, the Holy Spirit inspires the church into mission. In the beginning, believers could hardly help themselves. There was a rushing wind in the room. Filled with the Holy Spirit, they opened their mouths and spoke. And the crowd that gathered heard them "declaring the wonders of God" in their own tongues (Acts 2:1–12). Elsewhere in Acts, we read that the Holy Spirit speaks to a gathered congregation and calls Paul and Barnabas to a life of traveling mission (13:2). In different ways with different individuals or groups, the Spirit gets the ball rolling, so to speak, stimulating the people of God to cooperate with God's mission in a given time and place. Sometimes the Spirit births in someone a heart for a neighbor, a need, or intercession. At other times, when circumstances are pressing, someone gets—from somewhere—an idea for relief. And then there are those outpourings, and the room is filled, and people just leave speaking boldly (4:31).

The Spirit also orchestrates our participation in the mission of God. The Spirit commands Philip to hang out with the Ethiopian eunuch (Acts 8:26–40). The Lord (through the Spirit, we assume) arranges for Paul to meet Ananias and receive his initiation into the Christian church (9:10–19). Similarly, Peter is guided to the gentile Cornelius, and as a result, the gift of the Holy Spirit was poured out on the gentiles (Acts 10). God's Spirit arranges appointments and births strategies through which the restoring work of Christ is spread both inside (Acts 15) and outside the church.

The Spirit of Christ also empowers the mission of Christ. This is what Christ promised before his ascension: "You will receive power when the Holy Spirit comes on you" (Acts 1:8; see also Isa. 61:1–2; Luke 4:16–21). And sure enough, as we read the account of the church in Acts, we find it exhibiting the power of Christ: healing, casting out demons, teaching with authority, raising the dead. The church performs the wonders of Jesus and even greater acts in the course of its empowered ministry (John 14:12; see Acts 4:33; 6:8; 9:22).

And finally, the Spirit produces the fruit of the mission of God. True, there were three thousand added to the church on the day of Pentecost. But

there is more. Listen to the conclusion of Luke's account of Pentecost in
Acts 2:42–47:

> They devoted themselves to the apostles' teaching and to fellowship, to the
> breaking of bread and to prayer. Everyone was filled with awe at the many
> wonders and signs performed by the apostles. All the believers were together
> and had everything in common. They sold property and possessions to give to
> anyone who had need. Every day they continued to meet together in the temple
> courts. They broke bread in their homes and ate together with glad and sincere
> hearts, praising God and enjoying the favor of all the people. And the Lord
> added to their number daily those who were being saved.

We often read this passage and see everything up to the last sentence as a
summary of the transformation of the people into a functioning and model
church. Then we read 2:47b—"And the Lord added to their number daily
those who were being saved"—as a statement of how this transformation
empowered the church's mission. But this is not correct. Rather, Luke presents this final summary as a way of demonstrating how God has fulfilled
his mission fully. It is not the last sentence that describes the fulfillment of
God's mission but rather the entire paragraph. Luke, who in his Gospel mentions economic disparity, the authority of the gospel message, the miraculous work of the Spirit, and the sharing of meals, now shows that when the
Spirit falls, all things are made new. The communities of the Spirit are both
a means of God's mission and the very fulfillment of that mission.[18] Things
we once labeled formational goals are revealed to be part of God's mission.
Things we once labeled missional aims are also part of our formation. This
complete restoration is the mission of God accomplished by the work of the
Spirit.[19]

Formation into Mission

We must return to the congregation at St. Cuthbert's. Now that we have
learned about the new missions consensus and have gained a sense for how
the Spirit might lead, we need to explore the task of formation into mission.
What does our active cultivation of appropriate Christian transformation
look like with regard to our participation in the mission of God? How do
we nurture the agents, means, and so on given the widely diverse contexts
that surround the missional church today? What steps can the members of
St. Cuthbert's take to become an authentic Christian presence in their own
neighborhood?

First, they will have to rediscover their own *identity* in this neighborhood in light of the Christian gospel. More than getting inspired for a new program, they need to see themselves as a church—and as individual members of this church—differently. This kind of change does not usually happen quickly, but it can be facilitated. The broad vision is effectively communicated through sermons, but I suspect that the best means of transmitting the gospel to the rank and file may be through small-group Bible studies. The members of St. Cuthbert's are simply not capable of tracking with a yearlong adult education class that works painstakingly through a theological tome like Wright's *The Mission of God*. Instead, it might be more appropriate to select key Scripture passages that together summarize the mission narrative as it develops through the Bible and then teach them in an eight-week class that has lots of room for prayerful reflection, honest questions, and one-on-one appointments after each class. The point is to enable the congregation to hear and reconsider the gospel for their situation (and their lives).[20]

A second step is nurturing appropriate missional *skills*. In the past, St. Cuthbert's had sent their missionaries to a training program where they'd learn skills like language, culture, and communication. Now church members need to be trained too. They might not all need to learn a new language (though it might be good for a few to make that commitment), but learning a few words of the languages being spoken in their city is always nice. Perhaps one or two members who have close neighborhood friends with backgrounds unlike those of the members could invite them to small, safe, living-room gatherings where they have the freedom to talk about their culture and their stories. I suspect that even one or two of the atheists about town (who may identify themselves as "nones," those who would reply *none* when asked about which religion they practice, or "dones," those who once practiced religion but no longer do) might be interested in sharing their stories in the context of a friendly dinner. One necessary skill for mission is listening, which we can develop as we practice listening to one another. I have found that some of the training materials for spiritual direction are also helpful for fostering this kind of missional listening.[21]

A third step in formation into mission is the ordinary formation into a vibrant, virtuous Christian *life*. As Bosch emphasizes, "*Evangelism is only possible when the community that evangelizes—the church—is a radiant manifestation of the Christian faith and exhibits an attractive lifestyle.*"[22] I've addressed this elsewhere in this text, but it is worth mentioning again. People are currently leaving the church because they find Christians to be unchristian. As we are formed into a radically Christian life, we become a lovely fragrance for some, even though others might see us as a scourge. The attraction of the desert mothers and fathers, of Francis of Assisi and the Franciscans, and of the Welsh revivals and other movements was at least in part an interest among those nearby in the character and lifestyle of those movements' followers. Wright, in discussing this aspect of Israel's missional life, summarizes the logic of the relationship between holiness and mission in the following three points:

- Holiness and cleanness were the preconditions of the *presence of God*.
- And the presence of God was the mark of Israel's *distinctiveness from the nations*.
- And Israel's distinctiveness from the nations was an essential component of *God's mission* for them in the world.[23]

Sometimes actions speak louder than words. St. Cuthbert's can facilitate the formation of its own distinctive holiness simply by encouraging members in the practice of self-examination.

Fourth, as we develop virtue, we grow in sensitivity to and ministry in the power of the *Holy Spirit*. Paul is clear that his ministry was not grounded in his own clever persuasion but in the power of the Holy Spirit (see, e.g., Rom. 15:19; 1 Cor. 2:4). We saw above that the Spirit of God accompanies the message of God with demonstrations of the power of God: healing souls and bodies, delivering captives from the power of the enemy, and drawing people into a transformative relationship with Christ. The Spirit's powerful ministry has been present in innumerable missional movements throughout history. But how do we grow in the ministry of the Spirit? I offered a few tips earlier in this text, such as paying attention to thoughts, feelings, and inclinations. But I have also seen that interaction with others who are more experienced in the ministry of the Spirit can be helpful. Members of the body of Christ, in all its rich variety, have something to offer one another. Perhaps St. Cuthbert's might benefit from having some of their members attend a conference on the power of the Holy Spirit, where they can encounter the Spirit through experienced mission-minded believers firsthand.

A fifth step toward missional formation is the development of missional *relationships*. One of the best ways of learning how to fit in with a new culture is simply hanging out with people from that culture—which is what missionaries abroad do all the time. Identify the coffee shops that the young atheists frequent, and become a regular customer. Learn which parks are frequented by Vietnamese families, and go there to walk your dog or have a picnic. Natural opportunities for conversation will present themselves. We develop interest in others when we pray for them and when we have brief (or longer) conversations passing each other on the street. Our formation in humility and listening will come in handy as we discover (through trial and error) what may or may not be appropriate for conversation. One of my students was a chaplain in the Canadian military and described the "cultural training" they received when traveling to other countries: learning, for example, the proper expressions of greeting, whether it is normal for men to hold hands, and how close to stand near someone when in conversation. Missional relationships, which also involve a bit of cultural training, are largely nurtured. Members of St. Cuthbert's could take something like informal field trips to places their neighbors congregate. They can also pray that they might each be able to develop one friend and read about their neighbors' cultures.

Finally, now that they have gained a sense of identity and a few new skills, now that they are growing in the virtues relevant to missional living and in the power of the Spirit, and now that they are taking first steps into authentic relationships, members of St. Cuthbert's are ready to form a missional *culture* as a community. Certainly hospitality will play a significant role in this missional culture, but it will have to be an expression of hospitality that is appropriate for the neighbors. Some mothers might not feel comfortable if members of St. Cuthbert's were to start children's programs where they are separated from their child, for instance. Missional culture involves sharing faith (and listening to others share) in an atmosphere where neighbors are best able to give and receive in those relationships. A missional relationship with young atheists who feel hurt by their previous experiences with Christianity may look quite different from one with cultural Muslims from the Middle East who know very little about Christianity. In the end, these practices become steps for discerning vocation as a congregation. In the end, some congregations similar to St. Cuthbert's in size and history may simply decide (and honorably and rightly so!) that not all congregations are meant to live forever and that it is most reasonable for them to sell the building to a younger group wanting to start something new. The change required to reframe their idea of church life and mission may be simply too much. But then again, St. Cuthbert's may decide that it is ready to engage in one more big step of formation into mission.

I think that our formation into mission is both risky and powerful. In fact, it has the potential to address the current crisis of mission by offering a means of growth into a new missional perspective, a new missional power, and a new missional practice. Figures 10.1–3 (p. 207) summarize and illustrate this potential.

Figure 10.1
Forming the Church into a New Perspective

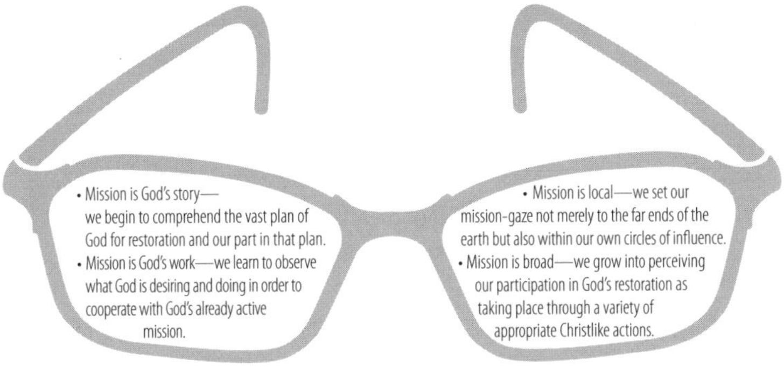

- Mission is God's story—we begin to comprehend the vast plan of God for restoration and our part in that plan.
- Mission is God's work—we learn to observe what God is desiring and doing in order to cooperate with God's already active mission.

- Mission is local—we set our mission-gaze not merely to the far ends of the earth but also within our own circles of influence.
- Mission is broad—we grow into perceiving our participation in God's restoration as taking place through a variety of appropriate Christlike actions.

Figure 10.2
Forming the Church into a New Power

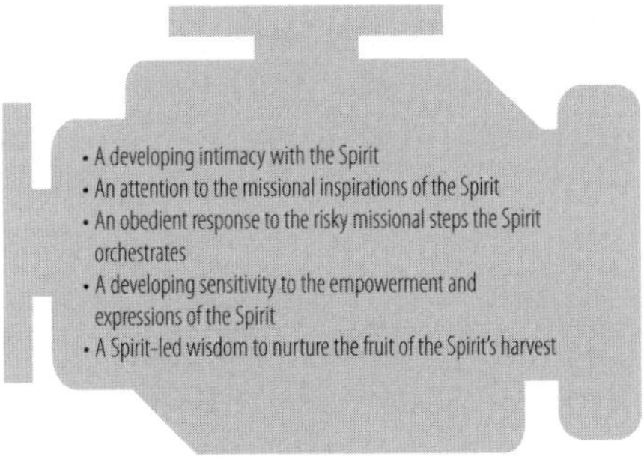

- A developing intimacy with the Spirit
- An attention to the missional inspirations of the Spirit
- An obedient response to the risky missional steps the Spirit orchestrates
- A developing sensitivity to the empowerment and expressions of the Spirit
- A Spirit-led wisdom to nurture the fruit of the Spirit's harvest

Figure 10.3
Forming the Church into a New Practice

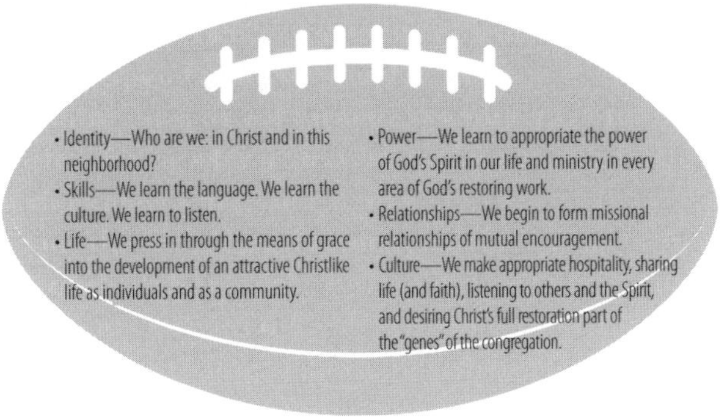

- Identity—Who are we: in Christ and in this neighborhood?
- Skills—We learn the language. We learn the culture. We learn to listen.
- Life—We press in through the means of grace into the development of an attractive Christlike life as individuals and as a community.

- Power—We learn to appropriate the power of God's Spirit in our life and ministry in every area of God's restoring work.
- Relationships—We begin to form missional relationships of mutual encouragement.
- Culture—We make appropriate hospitality, sharing life (and faith), listening to others and the Spirit, and desiring Christ's full restoration part of the "genes" of the congregation.

The Who, How, and Why of Missional Formation

With all of this in mind, there are a few other matters to consider—matters that are important to the integration of formation and mission but that do not fit neatly into any of the categories above. I think of these matters as addressing the who, how, and why of missional formation.

To start, regarding the *who* of missional formation, we can take a broader view of community and missions. I have been approaching this topic from the perspective of a congregation (St. Cuthbert's). But, of course, all of this can be viewed from any perspective. Households can explore hospitality. Individuals can learn to listen to others who are different from themselves. Intentional new monastic communities can, like nuns and monks in previous centuries, give themselves to contemplative prayer in private, liturgical prayer in community, and Holy Spirit–empowered interactions with others. My dream is that God would raise up a massive supportive network among Christian individuals and groups such that, working together, we can accomplish far more than our current isolated missionary programs.[24]

Also in regard to the *who* is the reminder that individuals and groups cooperate in missional formation as members of the body of Christ. Some believers are evangelists, and some groups are more gifted at evangelism. Others are prophets or apostles or healers or administrators or those who offer encouragement. Each missional monastic order (the Dominicans, the Franciscans, the Jesuits, and so on) expressed its own unique charism or gift throughout history, and we see this today among various missional groups (like the Salvation Army or the 24-7 Prayer Boiler Rooms in Great Britain). We need not feel inadequate if we find ourselves weak in power ministry or in defending our faith, in ecological restoration or in vulnerable listening. I think all of these are important, but ultimately it is the whole body of Christ that is the agent of the kingdom of God. I'm not saying that we can let ourselves off easy and not pursue formation into mission by simply saying, "Not my cup of tea." I am saying that we must be realistic. Rather than assuming we can and should be able to do everything well, we can join with others as we are all formed according to our gifts and callings. The task of formation is the next appropriate step forward. We simply do the best we can and bring others along who do what we can't.

Then there is the *how* of missional formation. Let's start by recognizing the important connection between mission and liturgy and sacrament. We approach God through our gathering: we meet, we hear, we are changed, we leave. We experience God's mission through worship, and we express God's mission in our daily life. And yet God's mission is also encountered and transmitted through liturgy. We are touched when someone lays a hand on us and offers a prayer of healing as we kneel to receive Communion. A song of confession speaks the words our heart has been feeling but couldn't quite express. We join others in the praise dance and are lifted above our troubles. We are formed into baptism, which has been a central sacrament since the foundation of the church, through catechism. Our formation starts with baptism and continues throughout our life, renewing our baptismal vows every Easter and every time we receive the body and blood of Christ at the Lord's Supper—what a supreme model of missional life! Just as the bread is taken, blessed, broken, and given for the benefit of those who receive it, so we as individuals and as the body of Christ are taken by the Spirit, blessed, broken in the trials of life, and then offered for the benefit of others. Eucharistic living is missional living. We are formed through the eucharistic sacrament for eucharistic living. We are formed through sacramental living for an ever-deeper eucharistic receiving.[25] Gathered and sent, sent and gathered—both mission and formation are present in each.[26]

Finally, we should be reminded of the *why* of missional formation through a word about eschatology, which expresses the final aim of the gospel message. Where we are headed is where we should be heading. Our eschatology determines every step of our formation and informs the character of our mission, as some who have reflected on the new missions consensus are keenly aware.[27] Our own sense of the nature of salvation and of its ultimate ambition will drive our own formation into the mission of God. I have argued throughout this book that God sees the final end of things as an "all things new" redemption, encompassing both heaven and earth. This eschatological vision inspires us to enter into a formation that can be experienced here and now but that will only be completed in the new heaven and the new earth. The task of formation, then, presses us to find and follow the element of this "all things new" vision that seems appropriate to explore here and now—a work that requires discernment, the topic of our next chapter.

Going Deeper

1. I've suggested reflection and journaling exercises in earlier chapters, and it might also be helpful here, as a way of going deeper, to make a survey of your own personal missions experience. If you were to write a personal mission history, what might it include? How were you formed into ideas and practices of missions in your earliest Christian life? What relationships were crucial in the development of your own sense of

missional living? What is your current understanding of mission, and how did you arrive at it?

2. The way the church looks at missions is really shifting. The development of a new missions consensus is an interesting and important piece of recent Christian history. Significant books, gatherings, and figures have played key parts in the development of this consensus, and yet it is much broader than simply a few ideas from a few people. Read the resources cited in this chapter's notes to learn about how this common agreement emerged and how it reached this level of what we call a consensus. Can you see a similar reorientation of the idea of mission in your faith community? What aspects of the new consensus do you find most challenging?

3. The spiritual formation movement (if I can call it that) has at times been accused of being overly private, of being interested in personal spiritual development but largely divorced from missional activity. Conversely, members of the missional community have been chastised for overactivity at the cost of their own spiritual health and, ultimately, the success of their own mission plans. This tension between the contemplative life and the active life has been present for centuries. (Remember the account of Mary and Martha in Luke 10:38–42?) How do we reconcile these? What do the classics of spirituality have to offer our pursuit of a workable reconciliation? What wisdom regarding this tension does the history of missions have to offer? What fresh new ideas might we discover in our own listening to the Spirit of Christ?

4. If I had to assign one practice to help form an individual or community into mission, it would be the practice of local ethnographic observation—choosing to hang around people different from us and pay attention to who they are. What do they wear? What do they talk about? What activities are they interested in? How do they relate to one another? What issues are important to them? Such questions are as endless as your curiosity. When you have observed long enough and carefully enough, begin to ask follow-up questions. Why are they interested in these events? Why is this community concerned with these issues? Try to see the factors that make this person or this group of people the way they are. And then prayerfully ask, "If I am going to share my life and my faith with this person, with this group of people, what approach would make the most sense to them? What might make them uncomfortable?"

11

Discerning Formation

Overview

The structure of this chapter is simple. After exploring just what discernment is, we will consider two aspects of discernment. First, we will look at what it means to be *formed into discernment*—namely, what practices, virtues, and principles best form us into people who are good at discerning. We will also consider how we can gain these virtues for ourselves. Then we will turn the terms around and ask about our *discernment of formation*: how we, as maturing Christians or as ones who might serve others in their spiritual development, can ascertain wise and appropriate strategies for fostering Christian maturity in the varied contexts in which communities and individuals find ourselves.[1]

Let's begin by listening in on a conversation held by a committee of three people—Amy, Hans, and Eva—who are trying to discern whether to hire a particular candidate as the new pastor of their congregation.

Amy: So my question is this: we all think the answers on the application are fine, we all like the sermon, and it was a great visit we had with the family. But have we heard from God here?

Hans: So what were you hoping for, Amy? Handwriting on the wall?

Amy: Well, I think we should be open to a little more than "We like this" and "We like that." This is a church of God, not a retail store. Listen, I have seen the Spirit of God fall on a congregation, bringing them to tears as they sought God in prayer and fasting and giving them a supernatural unity around a particular decision. Another time I saw God raise up a woman who gave a word of prophecy that was exactly what that congregation needed right at the moment. It's not that all that other stuff isn't helpful. It is. It's just that we don't have any real divine confirmation of God's will. Eva?

Eva: You know, Hans [turning to Hans], that I have been a little uneasy about this candidate from the start. In spite of all the formal stuff. Yes, we gave this application a higher score than all the rest. Yes, the sermon was good. But I still feel unsettled. Mind you though, Amy, I do not need some supernatural confirmation. I know that God could send some big sign to us, but couldn't the Spirit of God also lead us through our own hearts? And besides, I'm not real excited about someone standing up in church and telling us that "God said" we should choose this or that person to be our next pastor. Self-appointed prophets can be deceived, you know.

Hans: But we have done all this homework. We reviewed ten different applications. We listened to six different sermons. We have interviewed four people, and we have had two come visit here. Chris is clearly on the top of the pile. Are we going to throw all this away while waiting for some inner peace or a miraculous sign? Can't the Spirit of God lead us through the nuts and bolts of ordinary business? Why did we do all this work in the first place?

Amy: But then how will we know that it's really God leading us and not just our own self-interest?

Hans: That is a good question, Amy. Just how does the Spirit guide ordinary folks like the people in this church?

So what is going on here? Well, the committee seems to have a problem. Each of its members identifies God's will or the Spirit's leading for the congregation with different signs. Amy is looking for charismatic or supernatural phenomena to confirm their direction. Hans defends the typical management approach to things, in which God leads the committee through simple interviews and rational analysis. Eva seems to be searching for a more personal, intuitive sense of the Spirit's guidance. How do we reconcile these differences?

The problem really is that these three have been assigned a task for which they have not been properly prepared. They have been asked to co-discern the guidance of God's Spirit, but from what we can see, they have not been formed into discernment. They lack the breadth of knowledge, the skills, and the virtues and sensibilities to discern together, and consequently each operates out of his or her own experience, background, and personality. Sometimes, we simply make do with what we have and trust that God will guide us. But still, it would be nice if they could be better formed for this task.

Now let's consider another story, this one from fourth-century Egypt. Abba Moses is telling a story that illustrates failures of discernment (here called *discretion*):

> What shall I say of those two brothers who, when they were living beyond that desert of the Thebaid where the blessed Antony had once dwelt, were not sufficiently motivated by prudent discretion and, while traveling across the immense vastness of the desert, decided to eat no food at all except what the Lord himself would offer them? When the Mazices (a people more inhuman and cruel than almost any barbarian nation, for they are driven to bloodshed by a ferocious temperament alone rather than by a desire for booty, as other nations are) sighted them afar wandering in the desert and nearly dead from hunger, they approached them with bread, contrary to their own savage nature. One of them, with the aid of discretion, received with joy and thanksgiving what was offered to him as if it came from the Lord. He considered that the food was divinely ministered to him and that it was God's doing that these men, who always delighted in human blood, should have given life-saving sustenance to persons who were on the point of expiring and perishing. But the other, refusing the food as having been offered him by a human being, was carried off by starvation. Although the two men started out with a blameworthy idea, nonetheless one of them, with the aid of discretion, corrected what he had thoughtlessly and foolishly begun. The other, however, held out in his foolish presumption and was totally ignorant of discretion. Thus he brought upon himself the death which the Lord desired to keep him from by not believing that it was by divine inspiration that cruel barbarians, forgetting their own savagery, had offered them bread instead of the sword.[2]

As you can see, there is a problem here as well—indeed a couple of them. The most important problem, though, was the choice to set out on this journey eating only what the Lord would offer. Abba Moses calls that decision "blameworthy," "thoughtless," and "foolish." Clearly, this was an example of poor discernment. But I want you to see what the discernment in this story was about. This was not discernment about a calling in life. These men were not trying to discern whether some experience was from God or not. They were simply navigating their personal ascetical commitments, trying to select a particular spiritual discipline (fasting) that was appropriate to their situation—and this is where they failed. They failed to discern the appropriate application of the means of grace for their own lives. True, the Lord provided for them in a special way anyway, in spite of their foolishness. (God does that sometimes!) But Abba Moses still pronounces them blameworthy. They failed to discern their formation.

The commonly encountered issues of discernment and formation—being formed into discernment and discerning our formation—are discussed in this chapter. You have likely heard or asked yourself questions like these: How can I mature so that I can better discover God's will for my life? What kind of application should I make at the close of my sermon this week so that church members will step into their own destiny like they know they should? I want to be fully devoted to God, like some of the people I read about in my devotional classics. Perhaps I should try getting up in the middle of the night to pray. But how long and for how many days should I persist in prayer? I had a vivid dream where I was crying about people who are hurting and who need the Lord. Does this mean I am called to be an evangelist?

All kinds of Christians, in all kinds of situations, need discernment. We need to learn how to be formed into discernment. We need to learn how to discern our own formation as communities and individuals.

We have been heading toward this point all through our survey of Christian spiritual formation. As *Christian*, spiritual formation is rooted in a universal and normative story, the "all things new" story of the gospel. Furthermore, because this is *Spiritual* formation, we can be sure of the leading of the Holy Spirit. We are not alone in our formation, playing some game of religious self-improvement. No, Christian spiritual formation is, from one perspective, simply our active response to the invitations of the Spirit of the living God. Our formation must be guided by this clear vision. And yet as *spiritual* formation and as *formation*, this process leads us to balance our normative vision with a sensitive wisdom about the contexts and the charisms as well as the stages and the breadth of our lives. We must exercise both vision and wisdom with a frank confession of our own weaknesses in finding and following God. Given that this is the case, our proximate aim in Christian spiritual formation is not perfection; it is simply increase. Our task is the active cultivation of appropriate Christian transformation. And right there, with the word *appropriate*, is where we find discernment. For as we have learned, formation is an art, an adventure, not a formula.

What Is Discernment?

Discernment at its roots is a kind of knowing. Take our stories above. The first story was about a committee trying to "know" who to hire. The second story was about the failure of a couple of monks to adequately "know" how to design their ascetical practice. In the latter account, one man failed to realize (know) that God was providing food through the barbarians, but more important was the monks' failure to know how to manage their spiritual formation. Yet discernment is not simply a knowledge *that*; that is, discernment is more than just knowing *that* you should pick this person or eat this food. Discernment is more profoundly a knowledge *of*—a knowledge of God. Discernment is our lived knowledge of God in the midst of the ambiguities of life.

God wants to be known and to be involved in our lives. This is the first principle of Christian discernment, as we've been reminded in our exploration of Christian spiritual formation. The Christian gospel begins with God, who is creating, delivering, and inviting us into relationship and transformation. God reveals himself through creation, through Christ, through Scripture, through the Spirit.[3] God's wanting to be known, intimately known, is a divine desire, and thus we find the fulfillment of our covenant relationship with God in this eschatological proclamation in Revelation 21:3: "Look! God's dwelling place is now among the people, and he will dwell with them. They will be his people, and God himself will be with them and be their God."

How are intimacy and discernment connected? Let me offer an analogy. Over more than forty years, I have developed an intimate relationship with Cheri, my wife. Because of my respect and love for her, my knowledge of Cheri influences my sense of where I am going and what I choose to do, even in very practical ways. I have developed a sense of how she might feel about things. I listen to her advice. I don't always anticipate her concerns perfectly, and I don't always hear her advice clearly, but I do try to take my knowledge of Cheri's will into consideration as I make my way through life. I think that a discerning knowledge of God functions somewhat similarly. And yet, as we learned in chapter 7, our relationship with God is not a simple relationship of equals. Christ is our Lord. Christian Scripture offers not only a declaration of our acceptance by God but also a pattern of life in God. Likewise, to live in the Spirit of Christ is more than encountering the love of God poured in our hearts; it is also submitting to the leading of the Spirit.

Our knowledge of God and God's lordship is carried out amid life's uncertainties, as is made explicit in Scripture. Jesus warns us of the influence of false prophets (Matt. 7:15). Leaders in the early church could not reconcile their viewpoints and had to call a council to discern what seemed "good to the

Holy Spirit and to us" (Acts 15:28).[4] Paul warns the Roman church about those who use smooth talk but deceive (Rom. 16:17–18). We are warned that "Satan himself masquerades as an angel of light" (2 Cor. 11:14).[5] Even our conduct in common meals is treated in Scripture as a matter for discernment (1 Cor. 8–11).[6] When we experience what appears to be a touch from God or we hear some word inside our head, we ask, Is this the Spirit of God?[7] When we are confronted with the latest religious trend in theology or liturgy, we wonder, Is God present in this, or is it just our own worldly notion?[8] When we sense a desire to press further into spiritual disciplines, we ask, Is this foolishness?

In light of both the active presence of the Spirit and the ambiguities of life, we are compelled to evaluate and determine, as best we can, the presence and leading of God. Rather than being conformed to the world, we are urged to "be transformed by the renewing of your mind" and "to test and approve"—with godly discernment—the will of God (Rom. 12:2). Similarly, John encourages his readers to "test the spirits" to see what is from God (1 John 4:1; see also 1 Thess. 5:21).[9] At times, this testing requires a process of community evaluation, as described in Acts 15. Or God may grace someone with a special ability to distinguish between spirits (1 Cor. 12:10). Each situation is unique, necessitating a creative blend of gift and skill as we endeavor to ascertain the presence or will of God in the midst of life's confounding situations.

With this background, we are now prepared to venture a definition of discernment. I understand discernment to be *the evaluation of inner and outer stuff in light of our relationship with God with a view to a response.*[10] Discernment looks at *stuff*: experiences, trends, ascetical strategies, decisions, and so on. As we have seen, discernment is some kind of *evaluation*. We are trying, in discernment, to know something. But discernment is not mere rational analysis. It is evaluation *in light of a relationship with God*, drawing from Scripture, church, and Spirit. Finally, we discern not simply out of academic interest, but rather *with a view to a response*. Our congregation wants to know God's will because it intends on following it. I desire to discern the best spiritual disciplines because I intend on employing them in my own formation.

Having learned something of what discernment is, we are ready to examine what it means to be formed into discernment and how we might discern formation.

Being Formed into Discernment

Let's return to our pastoral search committee. What are Amy, Eva, and Hans going to need in order to discern well? How can I, perhaps as a spiritually respected member of the congregation and friend of these folks, help form them toward discernment? Of course, each individual needs their own encouragement and pastoral care, but if I were to help the group—as a group—be prepared for discernment, I might invest in a few areas. Let me add that it is useful to nurture these same areas in the life of any individual who desires to be formed into a better practice of discerning God's will for his or her own personal life.

Perhaps I would begin by acquainting committee members with the primary elements of discernment so they can see where problems and possibilities might lie: (1) a discerner or discerners (2) dwelling in a set of contexts (3) engages in a process of evaluation (4) by paying attention to different signs (5) and looking for indications of God's presence or action. These elements, which are based on my definition of discernment above, provide a sense of perspective as the members navigate their relationships in the context of group discernment. Furthermore, these elements identify an outline for my own role as a formation guide.

My next task, then, might be to encourage the formation of the discerners themselves. Discernment is less a product of a good discernment process and more a product of good discerning people. I must help my three friends

Figure 11.1
The Elements of Discernment

(1) A discerner

(3) engages in a process of evaluation

(4) paying attention to various signs of discernment

(a) The focus—
   what the discernment is about
(b) The sources—
   that to which we look in order to resolve the discernment
(c) The criteria—
   particular patterns or configurations of sources, which serve to indicate
(d) The meaning—
   the spiritual significance of the situation

(2) dwelling within a set of contexts

(5) pointing the discerner toward the end or goal of discernment (e.g., God's will, next step)

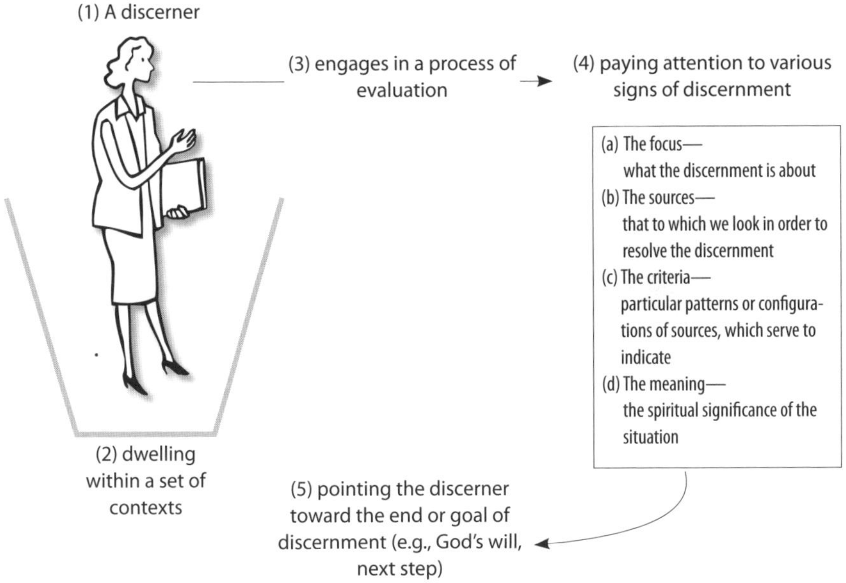

develop the important virtues of discernment—freedom in faith, obedience, sharing God's heart, listening, humility, prayer, wisdom, and love—by facilitating activities designed for that purpose. I would invite them to encourage one another with stories of when they have felt free to step out in faith. I would lead them in times of guided prayer in which I use Scripture to fill them with a sense of God's unconditional love for the congregation and for them individually. I would introduce the group to listening prayer, a practice in which they wait on the Lord and then share what they sense in their mind and feelings. I would encourage them to soak themselves in Scripture, particularly with regard to issues of leadership and community (given their task), so that they might grow in sharing God's heart for church life. I might also have them each do a little self-examination exercise each week that focuses on a predetermined virtue, after which they would record their progress in what I call a discernment virtues journal. It is not just a matter of wishing—or even praying—that the committee members would do their job well. Virtues can be fostered, and as one tasked with forming them into discernment, I would consider helping them gain these essential virtues as part of my task.

Reminding them that they are discerners dwelling in a set of contexts would be part of my early work in their formation. It is important that they hear one another's stories early, so that misunderstandings do not arise later and get in the way of good, discerning dialogue. Amy needs to tell her stories of God's powerful work and be heard and respected by Hans and Eva, just as it is important that she and Eva hear and respect Hans and his sense of seeing God work through practical procedures. Sometimes men and women discern differently—as do introverts and extroverts, as well as people from different generations—so they'll need to welcome such variations.[11] These differences can be proactively acknowledged if people have a chance to share early. This listening and being listened to is part of forming discerners.

In addition, forming a people for discernment often involves formation into very particular discernment situations. This is true in convents, in discerning what to do after graduate school, and in a pastoral selection committee, the latter of which dwells in the context of hiring protocol. Just what is expected of them? Are they recommending someone who will be voted on by the congregation, or are they selecting the pastor themselves? Will there be another process with a denomination or even a bishop? As you imagine these scenarios, you will see that each endgame is slightly different, and each puts a different burden on the group. Helping to clarify your goal in light of your situational context is an important early step of discernment.

If I were forming this group in discernment, I would also make sure that none of them is caught up in any of what I regard as discernment myths.

People get stuck in discernment, sabotaged by thoughts like these: God won't speak to me because I'm not spiritual enough. I can only trust guidance from God that comes through supernatural means. I must do this exactly right or else I will miss God's will and my life will be ruined.[12]

In order to form Amy, Eva, and Hans in discernment, we might review a few case studies together (as we did for the story of Abba Moses at the beginning of this chapter). I would ask them to identify what myth is being assumed, a better way of thinking about this situation, and how a better way of thinking would affect their discernment practice. We are often formed through our own analysis of case studies, but when a group does the analysis together, it forms common perspectives and potential practices for the future.

Christian discernment is rooted in our practice of paying attention to the Holy Spirit. Throughout this book, we have seen that the Holy Spirit reveals God to us by initiating thoughts, feelings, inclinations, and such within our experience. Training the group to pay attention to the Spirit through their experience (individually and corporately) will be an important part of forming them into discernment. I would foster this by assigning them a God Hunt, which I learned about from "Chapel of the Air," a radio show led by Karen Mains and her husband, David, that I used to enjoy long ago.[13] On her blog, where she periodically recounts God "sightings," Mains writes, "A God Hunt begins when you teach yourself to look for God's hand at work in the everyday occurrences of your life." I would instruct the committee members to take five minutes each day (or as best they can) to review their day. This exercise is usually done at night, just before bed, but a few people find that they can do it better at some other time. I would have them ask this one question as they watch the day play out in their minds: Where did I notice God today? This is not a self-examination exercise, where you would rummage for God by reviewing your feelings; it is a more general review of any signs of the presence or activity of God. It involves your feelings, yes, but perhaps those found in nature, or with another person, or in a passage of Scripture—anywhere. I would tell my directees to look back over the day and identify anywhere that they can say, "That was God." Then they would briefly record that in a journal. I would talk with the group members about their God Hunt journals, first meeting one-on-one and then later together.

Not surprisingly, each of us seems to recognize the Spirit more in one area of life than another, and in forming this group into discernment, I would help them discover where each usually notices God and where each tends not to notice. Some are naturally drawn to find God in nature, whereas others find God in Scripture reading, or in contemplative prayer, or in dreams, or in ordinary conversation, among other ways. Reviewing relevant chapters of *The Way of Discernment* by spiritual-life professor Elizabeth Liebert and *Hippo in the Garden* by pastor James Ryle together might be an excellent way of getting in touch with their own unique sources of discernment and their distinct sense of the Spirit's work.[14] Again, when this is done in a group setting, it increases the possibility of mutually broadening each other's sense of the Spirit and respect for one another and, importantly, creates common ground for discernment practice. A journal for recording where and how they perceive the Spirit's activity over a given period might come in handy here too.

Sooner or later, however, discerners will have to be formed in evaluating what they've learned to notice. They will need to learn how to examine the *content* of an impression for its harmony with Scripture and the character of God. They will need to learn how to assess the *spirit* of an impression for a sense of conviction and spiritual tone. They will also need to learn to recognize the *fruit* of the Spirit in the midst of discerning impressions. Through this they will learn to distinguish instances when that evaluation reflects their own agendas (or the voice of the enemy) from instances that appear more likely to reflect the character of God, and they must be formed to do this both on their own and together. A good technique for helping form people in this aspect of discernment is to use their own previous discernments and evaluate them according to criteria of discernment found in Scripture and tradition.

At some point, I would introduce this pastoral search committee to Ignatius of Loyola's "Three Times of Making an Election," because it is so helpful and because eventually they (like all of us) will have to make a decision (or, as Ignatius calls it, an election).[15] In my experience, making a decision usually involves being blasted, being led, or being ignored. Sometimes God simply *blasts* us, leaving little doubt about what he said in that moment or what the appropriate evaluation of a situation is. We just know. Sometimes we are *led*, and God's revelation comes to us in a more subtle form than a blast. This is a matter of our perception and of God's choice. We likely progress through a season of getting to know ourselves and our authenticity before various options, a season of inventorying our honest fears, wants, and so forth, and a season of being transformed in things. And then, when all that is done—when the words of advice have been heard, when feelings have been addressed, when counsel has been sought—there are times when, in our best moments, we can perceive an inclination toward this or that. We have, not a clear sense of the future, but enough of a sense to take the next step forward. However, we also go through times when we feel *ignored*. Though presented with options and having performed complicated spiritual gymnastics, we discover no indication of what seems to be from the Lord. There is simply no spiritual movement to one option or the other. And in some cases, we do not have the opportunity to wait around until greater confidence arises; circumstances demand action. In others, God himself may be pressing us to take greater personal responsibility, in which case we place ourselves before his presence and reaffirm our commitment to serve him above all. We weigh the pros and cons. We consider what others might do in our situation. We take the information collected and evaluate the situation, always attentive to feelings and reasons. And, when all is said and done, we simply make a rational choice, trusting ourselves to God. I always use examples from our own lives and others' to help people get a sense of how to navigate Ignatian election, because being able to recognize when we are blasted, led, or ignored can help us know when it is a good time to make a decision. Sometimes, however, we only perceive these after the fact.

Finally, we must form this group into discerning implementation. As with forming the group so that they are clear regarding their question, group members will need to have a sense of what they are going to do next. Discernment can flounder even after a quality decision due to poor implementation. Who must be contacted, and what is the wisest way to implement decisions? This can be discussed as a group, but if I am going to form this group into better discernment, I must also pay attention to helping the individuals and the group itself to learn quality implementation. Along with this, I would want to remind them of another myth—the myth that assumes the results will be "successful" because discernment has gone well. You might have an excellent process of selecting a pastor, yet that person does not work out. God's ways are bigger than our ways. Our responsibility is to be as faithful to our relationship with God as we can in the midst of the present discernment. The results are another matter entirely.

Through exercises, one-on-one conversations, group dialogues, and more, I would seek to form this group in greater discernment maturity. We often think that, with regard to discernment, "some people got it and some don't" or discernment is simply about God and we have little to do with it. I do not think either is true. Yes, the Holy Spirit is the primary agent in our discerning formation, but we ourselves play a part. I think that we can develop our ability to discern over time through active steps. This is what intentionally growing in wisdom is all about: experience, the Spirit, and our choices and formation. I have focused on the formation techniques involved, but of course this would all have to be done in the context of a careful discerning of the Spirit's work in this group. Some people might be ready for mutual story sharing; others might not. But that is the crux of discerning formation.

Discerning Formation

How do we wisely discern the appropriate formation strategy for a given community or individual? With this question, we have reached the apex of this text. This is where we have been headed all along. Christian spiritual formation cannot be reduced to a five-step formula, or a set of ten disciplines, or a phrase like "Let go and let God." Christian spiritual formation is a discerning art. Like other arts, it requires education, skills, procedures, and perspectives, but, also like other arts, it is much more than any of these. And for this reason, every artist and every art piece is unique. Wisdom can be noticed and it can be fostered; it can never be programmed. Authentic, well-discerned formation into increasing likeness to the person of Christ and the full, "all things new" gospel of Christ simply cannot be packaged. It is too rich, too subtle, too broad, too beautiful.

Over the centuries, we have packaged Christian spiritual formation within a number of ill-suited containers, many of which were designed to address penance. During the patristic period, Christians were expected to confess their sins openly and publicly and to welcome the severe penance that might be assigned. This approach rightly recognizes that holiness is not simply a matter of individual maturity and that the reputation of Christ is tied to the health of the church: *my* shortcomings are *our* business. It rightly acknowledges the wrongness of sin and motivates believers to change. And yet, divorced from sensitive pastoral care, public confession and extended penance—while clearly articulating the aims of formation—fail to supply appropriate means of formation for many ordinary Christians.[16]

The milieu of early monasticism fostered an approach to formation that combined sincere intention and mature wisdom. And yet the monastic culture was available (for the most part) only to those few who were willing to abandon the world.[17] Early Celtic Christianity pioneered the practice of private and frequent confession guided by a penitential manual that specified penances for specific sins. Some wise "soul friends" (known as *Anam Cara*) were able to see into the hearts of those who confessed and adapt the letter to meet the spirit/Spirit, nurturing authentic formation for many who flocked to them for pastoral care.[18] Ultimately—and unfortunately—however, the Roman medieval penitential system became overly tied to a theology of merit and to the practices of commutation and composition (leading to the use of indulgences). By the sixteenth century, many Western Christians either were trapped within an anxiety-driven salvation machine or were exploring their own formation on the edges—or outside the boundaries—of the church through various devotional practices and associations with various countermovements.

One significant component of the Protestant Reformation (or reformations) was the effort to reenvision the penitential system. Martin Luther saw formation as the freedom of a Christian to allow faith to work its way out through love in a life of unconditional acceptance and grateful response. John Calvin spoke of receiving the grace of Christ, duties, and self-denial. Thomas Cranmer desired that the newly independent Church of England maintain the practice of penance within a framework of Reformation theology.[19] Puritans, Pietists, Anglicans, Anabaptists, Socinians, and Methodists (along with post-Tridentine Roman Catholics) all struggled to express an approach to ongoing formation that honored the wisdom of the past without falling into the errors of previous frameworks of spiritual formation. Within this Reformation-era dialogue, I see worthy efforts toward formation as a discerning art. But since our aim in this text is not historical analysis but practical development, I will summarize the key features of this approach in terms of contemporary application.

An approach to formation that is not trapped in unsuitable packages involves a return to our discussion of salvation presented in chapter 5. There I presented two proposals regarding our understanding of salvation that were critical for our approach to formation: (1) initial conversion must be seen as only a part—not the whole—of salvation; and (2) salvation must be comprehended in its full breadth. Regarding the first proposal, it is important to see that salvation is simply incomplete as justification alone. But, on the other hand, if salvation is identified meritoriously with ongoing salvation (sanctification), then we have also misunderstood the mark. Christian relationship with God—one's spiritual/Spiritual life—is marked by ongoing transformation emerging from our unconditional acceptance by God. Consequently, formation is a discerning art. Some need to realize that they are unconditionally accepted and that they can rest free and forgiven. Others need to be reminded that their new association with the Christian church is meant to take them somewhere. Neither legalism nor antinomianism is authentic Christianity. Nevertheless, some will lean to one side—indeed, some will need to lean to one side—and some will lean to the other. The task of formation is to discern what is appropriate.

Likewise, regarding the second proposal, if we fail to honor the full breadth of the gospel and of the aims of formation, we end up identifying Christian formation with a small (and shallow) segment of the whole. Christian formation is distorted when it is reduced to "Don't drink, don't smoke, don't dance," or to "baptism in the Spirit," or to "social action," or to an interior and individualistic interpretation of "purgation, illumination, union." It is also true that if we honor the breadth of the gospel and yet make the full embodiment of the full gospel a mandate for all believers, we are demanding far more of most Christians than they can reasonably deliver. Rather than empowering them for a growing relationship with God, we end up oppressing them and harming that very relationship. The only reasonable option is to see Christian spiritual formation as a discerning art, wisely attending to the work of the Holy Spirit and nourishing growth where and when it is appropriate.

Those who are involved in formation—pastors, spiritual directors, congregational-care staff, helping professionals—will need to approach the very task of formation as a discerning art. As emphasized earlier, this means that our active cultivation of appropriate Christian transformation must be pursued as an effort to evaluate inner and outer stuff in light of our relationship with God with a view to a response (per our definition of *discernment*). Our very act of nurturing the maturity of a community or an individual involves a developing evaluation of situations, personalities, spiritual impressions, scriptural wisdom, and so on, with a view to identifying what is appropriate for this group or individual. Thus good formation directors must also strive to become good discerners: they are developing in discernment virtues, aware of their context and the context of the person or group they are helping to be formed, undistracted by the myths of discernment, and so on.

What might this actually look like in practice? Let's take a look at another example. Imagine yourself as a pastor of spiritual formation in a local congregation. Your job includes leading a few small groups dedicated to spiritual formation. This particular group has three members, Catherine, Manuel, and Frank, who meet on a twice-monthly basis. The curriculum you are using comes from what might be called an entry-level book on spiritual formation, one that includes practical suggestions at the end of each chapter. Two weeks ago, everybody read the chapter on using a rule of life, and each member was to come to the next meeting with a sketch of a personal rule of life that they were going to explore over the next few months. Last night, you all shared your rules. And while there have always been good relationships among these folk and no problems with the group dynamics, you are a bit unsettled. You sit in uncertainty the next day, wondering what to say to and how to advise these three congregants. How are you to lead these individuals, and how are you to lead the group as a whole?

Clearly Catherine was on board. You expected that. She was the first person to sign up for spiritual-formation groups—so excited that she even wanted to sign her three children up, though they each asked if it was OK that they not attend. She had already read a couple of books on the topic and was eager to put it all into practice. Her rule included a weekly day of fasting, service at the local homeless shelter, five chapters of Bible reading and lectio divina each day, removing the television from the home, and times of morning, noon, and evening prayer. Catherine was sure to be a leader in this group.

Perhaps Manuel just didn't understand the assignment. He put almost nothing down on paper aside from his desire to continue attending the group. English isn't his first language (he recently moved here from Venezuela), and some of this spiritual formation stuff seems a bit new to him. But he loves the group and is always eager to share and discuss the relevant issues each week. Indeed, Manuel is the person that you spend the most casual one-on-one time with outside the group.

Frank's rule was probably what you might have expected from a junior-year philosophy or theology student, which he is. Taking determined steps toward ecological responsibility (such as shopping for green products, wearing secondhand clothing, and writing monthly letters regarding environmental laws) and exploring centering prayer were the primary elements of his rule. He mentioned, though, that he did not want to share "how he was doing" in this rule with the group. You think that if he feels that you, the spiritual formation pastor, are pressuring him to "perform," he will simply leave the group.

Ideally, your discerning, formative leadership strategies would develop in relationship with each of these people—and with the group as a whole—over time and with a good deal of prayerful listening. But for the sake of brevity, let's skip ahead and summarize your reflections (some of which will draw on backgrounds not yet discussed). It appears that each person in the group wants to grow in relationship with God, but they are all expressing it differently. Catherine wants to do it all. Frank, who was hurt by the Pentecostal church he previously attended, is directing all his energy into new explorations of faith. But you can tell that, even though he is jaded, he really does want to follow Christ. Manuel is another story, however. You have always experienced him as a sincere believer, wanting to grow. But now with this assignment you wonder if you've misread him.

Obviously, they each come from different contexts: Catherine is a busy wife and mother; Frank is a single theology student; Manuel is also single but is not a scholar, despite being very intelligent (he works as an employee in the nearby oil refinery). Manuel is actually the oldest of the group, so whereas both Catherine and Frank were more than likely in their spiritual adolescence (climbing, dancing, journeying), you've assumed that Manuel was more settled—though it is hard to tell because of your language and cultural differences. After some prayer, you decide to meet with Manuel privately to see if everything is alright.

Good decision. In this meeting, Manuel clarifies himself openly. (It is not his style to hold back when he has something to say.) He explains to you that in

Venezuelan culture, relationship is everything. This is the motivation behind his involvement with you and this group, in fact. He was engaged in the relationships, and Catherine and Frank were showing him new aspects of spiritual life, which he was able to see and imitate in his own life. But to create some kind of rule, which appeared inflexible (just take a look at Catherine's!), seemed out of line. Didn't everyone know that extended family relationships required one to be frequently available elsewhere? One can never predict how long a birthday celebration might last and where one might be needed. You realize now that Manuel's periodic absences were for family reasons, and Manuel had family both here and in Venezuela. As Manuel explained further, he felt that turning a relationship into some kind of formal accountability structure was just wrong. True friends in Christ watched out for one another, but this rule thing was not the way it should be done. Manuel was glad to be sharing life together with you and to a lesser extent with the group. He truly was growing in Christ here. But he did not see how a formal rule could do anything but distort these beneficial relationships. And besides, the notion of a rule of life sounded too Roman Catholic and religious—and in Venezuelan Protestant culture, you just didn't do Catholic and religious things. By the time your meeting with Manuel was over, you understood: there really was a cultural issue here.

Both Manuel and Frank were having trouble with agency, at least in the way that it was presented in the rule of life assignment. For Frank, his relationship with God and his own self-agency were primary. The problematic situation at his old Pentecostal church involved an overly authoritative leader, and Frank was much more comfortable at present with the very hands-off sense of spiritual direction in the contemplative tradition he was exploring. Manuel had no trouble with authority; he experienced this at many churches back home. It was just that he did not see the agency of spiritual formation happening like this in the context of these relationships. It was just out of place. He would rather talk about his faith than write it up and analyze it.

For Catherine, it was all about the means. She had been on the church's governing board once, but it didn't work out. She had different interests. She loved the worship service but had little talent in anything relevant to serving in this capacity. On further reflection, you intuited that Catherine had perhaps found in this group, and in this particular assignment, an identity she could possess for herself. For some, it was important for a pastor to offer them permission to wholeheartedly "sell out" to Jesus. For instance, we want to bless those who sincerely want to sell everything and make a vow to remain single, just as we want to bless those who sincerely want simply to be faithful in a nourishing married relationship. But you began to wonder: Was this the best thing for Catherine or for Catherine's family? Catherine had difficulties with her children, and when they opted out of this group, she spoke ill of them to you. Perhaps this volume of spiritual disciplines would serve, in a strange kind of way, to distance Catherine from the loving relationships that were most important to her.

I wrote earlier of feeling blasted, led, or ignored as I worked toward discernment. God did not blast you as you reflected on this group, but increasingly—as you prayerfully considered each individual, the impressions gained through your reflection, and the aims of spiritual formation of both individuals and the group—you felt that it might be best if you just dropped the idea of keeping this rule for a few months and moved on to the next chapter in the group's book. This might be the most loving thing for everyone, and, indeed, at this stage it might be the action that would best form them in Christ. While you believe that rules of life have value, it simply might not be the best idea to dwell on it at this time and with these folks.

You would meet with Catherine and help her develop a more reasonable rule, thereby not entirely squelching her sense of positive direction in spirituality. You would let Frank develop on his own, making yourself available and open without creating any pressure on him. Let him play where he needs to play and heal with the time he needs to heal. Manuel would always be a friend. It was a rich joy to affirm this friendship in your recent one-on-one conversation. You still did not fully understand the culture of Venezuelan relationships, but you could appreciate them. So while you were not blasted by God, your prayer, love, wisdom, and listening all pointed to this sense of being led. It was surely a strange art, but you experienced, through this event, the combination of skill, training, procedures, and divine chance that is involved in discerning formation.

Going Deeper

1. We have talked about discernment virtues in this chapter: listening, obedience, shared concerns, and the like. When you look at your own character (or that of your community of faith), what virtues do you see? When you have discerned, what aspects of that journey have gone well and why? What virtues might need some improvement and why? Can you think of any other virtues to add to the list of those valuable for cultivating quality discernment? Identify these virtues and explain how they facilitate Christian discernment.

2. One aspect of discernment we did not cover thoroughly is the history of Christian discernment. This is a fascinating history and quite

informative. Look into some of the sources of history (you'll find a brief summary with key references in my *Brazos Introduction to Christian Spirituality*), or choose one figure or movement in history to study. Notice how certain criteria are emphasized in certain eras of history. How do different eras and circumstances shape the way discernment is seen? What shapes our way of looking at discernment today, and why?

3. Evaluate the preparation associated with a difficult group decision with which you are familiar. Identify the strengths and weaknesses of the discerners' preparation, including their awareness of the preparation process, their preparation regarding the particular situation, and the preparation undertaken by the facilitator and the participants. Were there any points at which problems in the preparation were evident? What might have been done in advance to address those problems? What might you remember from this review in your work as a leader of groups?

4. Doesn't all this talk about sources, evaluation, criteria, approval, implementation, and such make discernment just one more institutionally fabricated procedure? Isn't it too complicated? How do we—or even, *can* we—integrate all this with an understanding of Christianity as a simple relationship with God?

5. Perhaps the best practice for discernment is the uncomplicated God Hunt, during which you teach yourself to look for God's hand at work in everyday occurrences. Take a few minutes each day to review your day. Then ask one question: Where did I notice God today? (More instructions can be found earlier in this chapter.) Briefly record your findings in a journal. What do you learn from this exercise after doing it for one week? What do you learn after doing it for a year?

PART FOUR

THE MINISTRY

12

The Ministry of Christian Spiritual Formation

Overview

To explore the ministry of spiritual formation, we will return to the hypothetical novice mistress I described in chapter 1 and find out that her task is much like those found in all kinds of roles and ministries today. We will examine the role of a minister of spiritual formation as a way of teasing out what this ministry might look like today and learn about a few of the challenges and possibilities that we are likely to encounter as we develop a ministry of Christian spiritual formation. Having clarified the meaning of spiritual formation and how this ministry can be practiced, we will become aware of the church's current need for this ministry and how an intentional practice of this ministry, whether formal or informal, can contribute greatly to the renewal of the church.

We began the first chapter with a story of congregational formation (at Willow Creek Community Church), so it seems fitting to also open this final chapter with a story of congregational formation. For this story, however, we will step back to the 1940s.

Gordon Cosby was an eager evangelist. Winning souls was a daily commitment for him in his youth. He thought of entering missionary service, but a respected elder (who later became his mother-in-law) reminded him,

Some of you have got to stay home and make the same sacrifices as those who go to Indochina and take years to prepare, learning the language, the customs, and such things. You must learn a new language also, the language of the world, so that those who are worldly and sophisticated, but spiritually illiterate, can understand you. . . . If you do not do this, you will speak not only a foreign language in this pagan country, but one that repels.[1]

Gordon went to college and Baptist seminary with this vision in mind, and after graduating from seminary, he and his new wife, Mary Campbell Cosby, began to serve Ballston Baptist Church in Arlington, Virginia, just outside the nation's capital.

But World War II necessitated other plans. Gordon enlisted and served as a chaplain in the US Infantry. The experience of war demonstrated clearly to him the importance of character, for he saw that too many men who claimed to be Christians could not stand up under moral pressure. Membership in the church on paper did not always mean much in the heat of war. It was in the military that Gordon began to facilitate small groups to nurture the spiritual lives of men he oversaw and to select and invest in the most spiritually mature among them, who were then responsible for the others in their company. His experience with the ecumenical environment in the military convinced him that, upon reentry to the United States, he would start a congregation that welcomed people from every branch of Christianity.

When he returned, Gordon immediately set out to plant this new church. The congregation held services in a borrowed church building late Sunday afternoons, followed by an open conversation. As people expressed interest in joining the group, they were offered classes that came to be known as the School of Christian Living. In October 1947, members stood at the entry of their new office and together made the following commitments, among others:

- I come today to join a local expression of the Church, which is the body of those on whom the call of God rests to witness to the grace and truth of God.
- I recognize that the function of the Church is to glorify God . . . and to be God's missionary to the world. . . .
- I commit myself . . . to becoming an informed, mature Christian. . . .
- I will seek to bring every phase of my life under the Lordship of Christ.[2]

To make a long story short, Gordon's church, the Church of the Saviour in Washington, DC, became one of the most influential congregations in the United States, an honor it held for many decades. Missions, community, and integrity of character were part of its formational vision from the start. In 1953, when the church acquired two hundred acres, it started a ministry center to foster a rhythm of inward and outward journeys. Sensitive to local context, members invested themselves in race-related causes and pioneered the first coffeehouse in the capital. Intentional about agency and means, they developed a disciple-making program that reflected their understanding of membership. Conscious about the aims of formation, they held high standards for their members and spoke often about the need for every area of life to be submitted to Christ's lordship. They established small groups that nurtured both fellowship and mission—a model of group formation that has benefited many congregations over the decades. In 1974, the Church of the Saviour decentralized and became what it refers to as a "scattered church": a network of several local congregations committed to the original vision of the Church of the Saviour. The sermons preached by Gordon (who died in 2013) still inspire thousands.

People who remember the so-called golden days of the Church of the Saviour describe it as a movement of the Spirit of God, a time when the Lord brought them as individuals and as a congregation into "new land." Some have criticized the congregation for making the requirements for membership too high and for creating (formally or informally) a division of elites and others. This was a criticism that the leaders of the church were willing to risk as they experimented with congregational formation. Were they wise? Whether they were wise or not, the point is that they actively pursued the ministry of spiritual formation both with individuals and with an entire congregation. Cosby and his team intentionally facilitated the formation of the Church of the Saviour, pursuing a vision of the people of God increasingly formed into the life and mission of God.

The Great Commission (or co-mission) of Christ, the Spirit, and the church is full discipleship. "Go and make disciples of all nations, . . . teaching them to obey" (Matt. 28:18–20). The apostle Paul's vision is similar: "to call all the Gentiles to the obedience that comes from faith" (Rom. 1:5). Elsewhere, he exclaims, "My dear children, for whom I am again in the pains of childbirth until Christ is formed in you" (Gal. 4:19). Similarly, in 1 Peter we read, "Like newborn babies, crave pure spiritual milk, so that by it you may grow up in your salvation. . . . You also, like living stones, are being built into a spiritual house" (1 Pet. 2:2–5). "I am making everything new!" the One who is seated on the throne pronounces (Rev. 21:5). Formed stone by stone until at the end everything is new—this is our aim. This is what Christian spiritual formation is all about. I am not one to think that formation is everything. For example, I think that worship and evangelism are valuable whether they are formative or not. Nonetheless, I think we are in line with an important aspect of the Christian faith when we make the formation of congregations and individuals a priority.

Through the course of this text, we have come to understand Christian spiritual formation as a work of God and as a discerning art. As *Christian*, it is rooted in—and aims toward—the person and story of Jesus Christ. As *spiritual*, it attends to human depths, to the Holy Spirit, and thus to our relationship with God. As *formation*, it plans for change. As a *work of God*, it emerges from the creation, re-creation, and empowering invitation of the Trinity. As a *discerning art*, it seeks the appropriate step forward. We have seen how Christian spiritual formation involves all of who we are and all of our relationships. All things become new as we are formed in Christ. We foster relationship with God and we mature in prayer. We nurture relationships with one another and we mature together. We look deeply within our relationship with ourselves and we mature in mind, heart, and life. We open ourselves to the world and we mature in mission. All of this develops within the contexts of our history, our personality, our pain—a magnificent work of art in the making.

In part 2 of this book, I presented something of the *process* of Christian spiritual formation—how it all works. In part 3, we looked at the *task* of formation, examining what Christian spiritual formation involves from the perspective of those fostering that formation. In this final chapter, I want to narrow our focus even further. I want to explore the *ministry* of Christian spiritual formation. I believe that the ministry of Christian spiritual formation is one of the greatest needs of our time. It is a ministry that may accompany other roles and ministries even as it offers a distinct contribution to the church and the world.

What Is the Ministry of Christian Spiritual Formation?

Let us return to the image of the novice mistress. I know the world of cloistered nuns is unfamiliar to almost all of us, but bear with me as I describe this cultural and historical example and see how it illustrates something we do in many familiar roles and relationships. I persist in discussing this role because I am convinced that, with a few modifications, the ministry of novice mistress can—and should—be recovered today.

As I mentioned in chapter 1, the meaning of the phrase *spiritual formation* was significantly developed within the context of the training of monks and nuns. A nun, for example, might be placed in charge of the formation of a convent's young trainees (often called *novices*), guiding them into their new life as nuns. Her work involves education and character training, but, most importantly, her work is to facilitate the young novices in their development of a living relationship with God.

The most obvious features of the novice mistress's ministry are that it is both *vocationally oriented and spiritually centered*. In a community of the Sisters of Carmel, for example, she helps each woman entering to follow her vocation forward as a member of the community. The religious order and community are a place of wholehearted devotion to God, and a novice believes she will best give glory to God with her life here, in this place and with these people. For this reason, the novice mistress's work is really to nurture the novice's relationship with God with a view toward her transition from old contexts into new ones. The role is vocationally centered in that it attends particularly to one's calling; it is spiritually centered in that it is centrally aimed at nurturing relationship with God in the midst of life.

The next feature to observe—which follows from the first—is that the novice mistress *exercises leadership* in this relationship. The obvious reason an order assigns a novice to her mistress is that, although the novice has a relationship with God and can be guided by the Holy Spirit, she knows little about what it might mean to spend her life in a convent. Thus the novice mistress—well aware of the kinds of questions, fears, and troubles that a novice will likely experience at different stages of her life and of her relationship with the convent—makes sure to bring up the important issues at the appropriate times. A good novice mistress will give sensitive attention to each novice, listening to her story and watching for the movements of the Spirit. She will also assign responsibilities, offer resources, and suggest attitudes. The novice mistress leads, and the novice follows. The novice agrees to this submission from the moment she enters the convent. It is understood, a given. A good novice trusts the wisdom and love of the novice mistress. A good novice mistress spends herself in love for the novice. It is a discerning art of love.

We also see that the novice mistress employs a combination of *formal and informal means* to accomplish her spiritual aims. A novice mistress might use a defined curriculum as part of the novice's training. In our present example, a novice would find herself going through a "Welcome to the Carmelite Order" workbook, complete with readings, discussion questions, and so on meant to help her learn the way things are in the order and in the local community. The culture of monastic life is learned in part by reading, in part by simply living at the convent, and in part by an ongoing relationship with the novice mistress. The novice has freedom to ask her mistress, "Why is it we eat meals in silence?" and the resulting question-and-answer exchange is part of her formation process. Furthermore, a good novice mistress will assign the novice different responsibilities, enable her to experience new things, and introduce discussions that will, step by step, facilitate the novice's acquaintance with and competence in the life of a nun in this order and in this community.

Of course, any and *every area of life* is part of this formation. How the novice eats, how she dresses, how she reads and reflects on the Scriptures, how she sings in choir, how she speaks to others both within and outside the convent—all of these matters are fair game for the ministry of formation. The novice's relationship with possessions, with her own sexuality, and with the abbess are all important matters for a novice mistress to explore, for the novice will be taking vows of poverty, chastity, and obedience. When she signed up for this, she knew (as much as one can know hypothetically) that it was a matter of all things new. And again, that is the point, for a nun's is a life wholly devoted to God, and the novice and the order have agreed that, by offering to God every aspect of life within the context of this order and this local community, the novice may be able to give God the greatest possible glory and, consequently, find the greatest happiness in life.

Finally, all of this nurturing care depends on the novice mistress's *loving, sensitive perception* of the steps of formation most appropriate for this novice. This is a work of discernment. The assumption in the very structure of this arrangement is that the novice mistress invests a great deal of prayerful listening on behalf of her novices. The novice mistress is doing more than fulfilling job requirements. She is, more profoundly, exercising the *ministry* of Christian spiritual formation.

I hope you see where I am going with this illustration. Vocationally and spiritually centered, an exercising of leadership, formal and informal means, every area of life, loving and sensitive perception—the task of a novice mistress may seem quite foreign to those of us who have never been in a Carmelite monastery. Yet it is actually the very task of formation defined in this book: an active cultivation of appropriate Christian transformation in all areas of life. The novice mistress accomplishes this within a very particular setting and toward the novice's formation into a very particular vocation. But while this is a ministry that can be illustrated well in a monastic setting, it is also a ministry that can be (and already is) exercised in many settings today.

We all have *vocations*. God invites us all into life. We are members of families. We are nurses and carpenters. We are participants in local congregations and networks of fellow Christians. We are citizens and tenders of the earth. We discern our roles vaguely and embody our roles uniquely. Are we really so different than a nun who discovers her place in the convent over time and with an eye to her own distinctive blend of charisms? Like her, we too can enlist others to assist us in discovering our life's vocation and forming us into our own constellation of roles, whatever our spheres may be. True, my own minister of spiritual formation might not be as familiar with the culture of carpenters, for example, as a traditional novice mistress is with the culture of monastic liturgy. But just as the novice mistress may help a young nun by facilitating relationships with someone who can help her (perhaps with her Latin lessons), so people exercising the ministry of formation today can delegate elements of the formation process as appropriate. This is simply part of what it means to discern what is appropriate. Some of us find that just having someone with whom we can share spiritual stories is not always enough (though it is certainly valuable). It is not always enough to have a spirituality professor who introduces me to various practices of the Christian life. It is not always enough to attend a Bible study and apply the text over the next week. There are seasons when what we need is a real minister of spiritual formation—someone to guide us as we tie together story and Spirit and practice into a co-discerned vocation or set of roles toward which we feel God's invitation. We need help if we are to enter into the obedience of faith, assistance from someone who will also feel a little labor pain until we are formed in Christ.

We have companions who *take the lead* in our lives. We have pastors, counselors, spiritual directors, mentors, and so on. Those who help and those who seek help can negotiate their relationship so it best supports the ministry of Christian spiritual formation. This relationship might arise within a structure of formal authority—perhaps as part of a relationship between an assistant pastor and a senior pastor. The assistant might request that the senior provide guidance toward Christian spiritual formation. They would discern in tandem the elements of the assistant's vocation. The assistant would yield a measure of responsibility for his or her growth to this leader, and the senior would prayerfully suggest steps (means of grace, agents, viewpoints, and such) that are designed to facilitate the assistant's maturity in Christ in the particular context of this co-discerned vocation. This relationship will need to be close enough that the one exercising the ministry of formation can watch the other's life carefully and invest where needed; but it will need also to be not so close that it might involve unhealthy enmeshments. This kind of relationship could also be initiated through a recognition of spiritual authority. On the one hand, the one offering the ministry of spiritual formation receives an anointing from the Spirit of God (with the blessing of others to whom he or she remains accountable) for work with another and then initiates the relationship. On the other hand, the one desiring to receive from this ministry perceives the spiritual authority and trustworthiness of another and initiates the relationship. I can imagine a variety of scenarios involving those who need to learn the ministry of Christian spiritual formation and others who desire to submit to someone practicing this ministry—none of which necessitate a convent or a monastery.

We have *spiritual aims*. We might not all understand the concept of Christian perfection as thoroughly as a Carmelite nun might. Yet we share a vision for "all things new." We step toward the hope that our hearts and minds will grow in greater likeness to the heart and mind of Christ. We desire to grow in union with God in prayer, in authenticity with ourselves in integrity, and in harmony with others in love. We desire to increase—in whatever measure is appropriate for us here and now—in likeness to the person and gospel of Jesus Christ, following the lead of the Holy Spirit. Just as a novice mistress might, within the context of a convent, introduce practices and assign responsibilities to cleverly stimulate a novice's encounter with a certain aspect of the person or gospel of Christ, so too a mature friend might do the same for us in our own circumstances of life. The ministry of Christian spiritual formation depends not on the structure of a monastic institution but rather (and more profoundly) on the commitment of our hearts to permit another to lead us into holiness.

We employ *means*. The means of formation outside the convent may be different from the means within. Yet a carpenter can learn from an appropriate practice of silence just as a nun can. A mother of preschoolers can develop solitude in her moments in the bathtub, as can a novice. The trials of an executive are just as much a means of grace as those of a novice. A good pastor, mentor, or spiritual friend will learn which are the best formal means to use when nourishing spiritual maturity for people of different backgrounds. I have taught refugees from Laotian tribes that barely have a written language, and I have taught doctoral students, and I have learned that they each need some formal means of spiritual development, something they can follow and count on. But I have also learned that they all—and each in their own way—need me to use appropriate informal means to foster growth in their relationship with God in the context of their own vocation. I give suggestions to one. I give assignments to another. And, most of all, I listen.

Which brings us to the final point. We all need and desire those who exercise *sensitive perception* over our lives. Oh, for people of wisdom surrounding us to nurture us into Christ through endurance, encouragement, and prayerful, sensitive observation! The ministry of spiritual formation, whether exercised by a small-group leader or a parent, will require wisdom. The one exercising formation outside the convent—just like the novice mistress within the convent—will need to be sensitive to the contexts and the charisms that shape the person being formed. Good formation directors need not only a familiarity with the means of formation but also (and perhaps even more) wisdom about how means are experienced by different people. This is a work of discernment.

You probably understood my point long ago. As I was talking about the novice mistress and her characteristics, you were saying to yourself, "But I already know this. I experience this ministry regularly from my spiritual director, my mentor, my discipler, my pastor, my coach." Bingo! This is exactly what I want you to see. Christian spiritual formation is something many people do all the time under different names, sometimes without knowing it. Pastors, friends, counselors, and others exercise the ministry of spiritual formation within the context of their own life. Each relationship will exhibit its own blend of gift and rule, its own blend of mutual responsibility for the progress of the relationship and growth in Christian maturity. What is the ministry of Christian spiritual formation? *It is the offering of one's self and a prayerful willingness to take responsibility for the sake of cultivating appropriate transformation in others who themselves consent to the same offering.* Christian spiritual formation is the performance of a discerning art. It is oriented toward forming people into their Christian vocation in view of their own contexts and charisms by employing appropriate means and agents. A worthy ministry indeed! Figure 12.1 illustrates the elements of this ministry as it is exercised within a variety of contexts.

Figure 12.1
The Ministry of Spiritual Formation

WHO
- Close friends
- Small group
- Spiritual directors, mentors, pastors, and more

HOW
- Vocationally and spiritually centered
- Exercising leadership
- Using formal and informal means
- Implicating all of life
- Rooted in prayerful and sensitive discernment

WHAT
- Offering oneself in a prayerful sense of responsibility for the sake of cultivating appropriate transformation in others

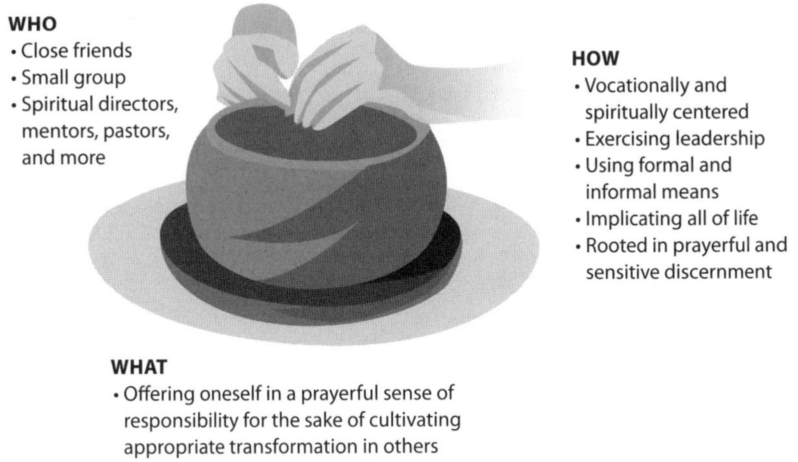

The Challenges of Exercising the Ministry of Christian Spiritual Formation

Of course, recovering the ministry of spiritual formation today will have its own set of challenges. When considering the perspective of the person offering this ministry, we might think first of *training*. How does one learn this ministry? You might find it interesting that often novice mistresses receive little formal training. It often works like this. A nun lives a full life in the convent. She is devoted to God, and over time others note that she has a care for others. She discerns well. The abbess (the head of the convent) can see that when given small leadership roles, this woman is able to lovingly assign tasks to others, watch them work, and give feedback such that their discussion is not merely a conversation about work but is also a step of spiritual formation. There is an element of divine anointing about her ministry. This nun attends well to her experience and that of others, recognizing the subtle movements of the Holy Spirit. When the time is right, the abbess assigns this woman to the role of novice mistress. The abbess makes available reading material and programs in spiritual direction, mentoring, coaching, and such to the novice mistress. But both the abbess and the developing nun know this: the ministry of spiritual formation is more than the development of a skill. It is as much a way of being present to the Spirit of God as anything. I see the development of ministers of spiritual formation today in a similar light. It is good that we immerse ourselves in Scripture, that we acquaint ourselves with models in history, that we are able to recognize psychological and sociological patterns. But our challenge is to provide training without reducing Christian spiritual formation to a program.

Another challenge we face in offering this type of ministry is bearing the sense of *responsibility*. It is one thing to make ourselves available for spiritual direction or advice when someone calls. It is quite another to feel the pains of childbirth as we carry someone toward formation into Christ. We wonder, "When I suspect that the 'novice' is flaking out, should I text him and say something?" Or we ask, "I think that she might benefit from one of those situations where she discovers her own weakness, but do I intentionally assign something that will put her into a situation like that?" Should we ministers of spiritual formation think of ourselves as Christian Zen masters or desert elders who stretch others to their edge just because we think we know what is best for them? Who are we to think we can direct someone else?

My response to this challenge is threefold. First, many others bear this same kind of weight all the time. Parents are the most obvious formation directors.

Spiritual direction in the Eastern Orthodox context assumes both a high level of self-revelation on the part of the one coming for direction and a high level of authority on the part of the one offering direction. We must simply learn to be "prayed up" for such a ministry. Second, while this ministry is not for everybody—and part of the wisdom of Christian spiritual formation is knowing when it is not appropriate to exercise it—there are times when we are selling ourselves and others short by not offering this type of ministry. We may need to carry on and take on the risks of leadership for the sake of Christ. Third, if we are afraid of exercising authority, we can make ourselves accountable to others by employing a system of supervision—a mechanism for talking in a safe and supportive environment about our ministry and these relationships.[3] In this way, we can step into the risks of having authority in ministry with the knowledge that we are not exposing ourselves and others without submitting to appropriate checks and balances.

And then there are the challenges seen from the perspective of the one receiving this ministry, the first being a different question of *authority*. How can we trust this kind of ministry in light of Christianity's history of abuses? This is a good and important question that should not be brushed aside. Sisters and brothers have been hurt by abuses of leadership in all traditions. As I mentioned above, the ministry of spiritual formation is not for everybody, and both parties must be ready to participate: the leader to lead and the follower to follow. Just as the leader can establish supervision relationships to ensure quality care, so also the follower can initiate appeal mechanisms so that there is a place to go with questions or concerns. It does not eliminate the possibility of abuse, but it helps create an atmosphere of trust that is crucial in today's society.

And then there is the question of our own *motives* as followers. We acknowledge a danger that leaders will use the excuses available in a society (rightly) fearful of abuse to abdicate from appropriate authority, and we acknowledge that followers can exploit the same cultural distrust in order to avoid appropriate surrender and obedience. It is often said among nuns and monks that the vow of poverty is the easiest, for we are only giving up a few things; that the vow of chastity is the next difficult, for we are facing our desires; and that the vow of obedience is hardest of all, for in obedience we are giving up our own wills. The real question is why this is so. What must we face within ourselves as we exercise the ministry of spiritual formation?

The fact is, we are all embedded in community anyway. We are already being shaped by relationships of one kind or another. So what kind of community do you want to foster your growth in Christ? What would that look like if it didn't involve receiving the ministry of Christian spiritual formation?

The real questions are ones of agency and of the means of grace. Where is the Spirit leading? Once again it is a matter of discerning the appropriate.

The Need for Spiritual Formation

Sure, there are challenges in recovering this ministry. But I think the challenges are worth facing. I believe the ministry of Christian spiritual formation is one of the greatest needs of our time. We are today overstimulated with words and images, overconnected with acquaintances, overloaded with resources, and overburdened with the needs around us. What we need is not another menu of practices. We need people who will guide us through the appropriate practices into an authentic spiritual life. I am learning this in my own occupation as a professor. Once upon a time, I stood in front of the class and gave lectures, providing information as the expert. But those days are over. My students have more than enough information instantly available on their phones. Increasingly, I let them access the information on their own and then help them see how to use it to serve their life. My role has changed from the sage on the stage to the guide on the side. I am a novice at this, but I'm learning.

Over the course of my own spiritual life, I have come to value a few means of grace—at least those I have much control over—with special regard. I would identify these four as a kind of "holy nexus" of formation: consecration, self-examination, rule of life, and nurturing relationships. The first of these is consecration. We consecrate ourselves to God through "praying the prayer," through confirmation or baptism, through some form of open, well-considered, and wholehearted belief in Jesus Christ. A marriage begins with a simple "I do," but that "I do," if true, means everything in the years that follow. We are formed through the trials of marriage and faith because we have already said "I do" and are prepared to be formed through them.

Self-examination, the second means of grace, is the act of setting aside moments to attend to our experience and, through this, to notice the presence and work of the Spirit. It can involve a moral inventory, but it might also be an uncomplicated noticing of life itself. Our consecration is assumed in self-examination, for we are noticing our experience in light of our intention to follow the Spirit's lead and in light of the person and gospel of Christ. We pay attention to thoughts and feelings that arise or that have already been revealed. We attend to their character. We receive one and reject another. We learn to know the voice of God and to dream of how to follow it. This is the beauty of self-examination.

The third means of grace is a rule of life. I do not necessarily mean a fully developed contract like the Benedictine rule. No, I mean some concrete sense of what I am doing in life here and now. What Scriptures are front and center for me? What virtues or vices are in need of attention? Are there themes that seem to return again and again in my self-examination? Your rule may be something written—and I often encourage people to write from a sense of their own area of growth in their relationship with God—but it could be just a simple awareness of what it takes to stay sober.

But often these three means are not enough. I can commit, I can notice, and I can even have a sense of where I am going. But I don't go there without a little help from my friends. We need that fourth means of grace: nurturing relationships and safe people with whom we can share. Going a step further, I'll say that for some of us, some of the time, we need more than just safe relationships. We need relationships that are not always too safe—relationships that will hold us to account, that will push us where we want to go even when we say we don't want to go there. We are too burned, hurt, and shy to open ourselves or to commit. And yet we are also lost and in need of a guide, a wise and slightly dangerous friend who will take risks with us (and perhaps even for us) so that we can grow in Christ. The ministry of Christian spiritual formation is the link that ties together consecration, self-examination, rule of life, and nurturing relationships—the nexus that provides a workable framework for practical nurture and for an increase in our desire and commitment to obey all that God has commanded, an increase in likeness to Christ and the gospel.

Thus far, I've addressed the need for the ministry of Christian spiritual formation with a view to the formation of individuals. But as we have learned, formation is also a matter of community change. Take families, for example. I believe we desperately need those who would take active (servant) leadership in families and households; we need those who will nurture not only the faith of the individual members but also the life and character of the household as a unit. We need more than individuals growing in faith. We need models—the world needs models—of community at the most basic level: in the home. God desires the formation of an expression of life together toward which the world can be attracted, as to an icon. This will not happen by accident. Parents and elders must take up the responsibility and lead households intentionally into Christ. I did mention earlier the dangers of stepping into the ministry of spiritual formation in an environment that might involve an unhealthy enmeshment of relationships, but I do not think that this is necessarily problematic in a household. Indeed, the Scriptures seem to indicate that leadership over a congregation and leadership within a household have some points of connection (1 Tim. 3:4).

Likewise, the church is in need of pastors, denominational officials, and lay leaders who have the courage to form congregations into a fuller expression of "all things new." The world is longing for the hospitality of Christ, for the healing of Christ, and for the truth of Christ. We the church often find it easy to proclaim these with our mouths but hard to demonstrate in the culture of our congregational life. We need those who would risk leading us beyond our words and who will form us through a school of Christian living like the one established by the Church of the Saviour. The image of sensitive leaders meeting with individuals and asking them how it is going with their soul is an incomplete picture. I am more than happy to make and receive such inquiries, but they are not enough. The novice mistress of the congregation must discern the appropriate step forward and assign the steps necessary to take us there as a community. Imagine instead prayerful leaders who are in pains that Christ be formed in us such that people will observe us and exclaim, "See how they love one another!"

The need is especially keen among groups of new religious monastic or missional experiments. Countermovements and communities on the fringes have chosen a measure of disorientation from the onset. It is hard to stay the course, to persevere through experimentation, and to attend to the Spirit in the midst of unexpected conflicts, failures, and repeated revisions. The combination of individual personalities, community dramas, and larger structural and cultural matters makes it especially difficult to discern the appropriate while maintaining creative experimentation. Oh, for willing elders who will come to the side of such groups with a commitment to nurture! Oh, for the denominational or organizational leaders who would permit such experiments within their structures and offer their appropriate—but not smothering—support!

Finally, I am seeing a few elders raised up by God to lead networks here and there. They are leading small networks of semi-connected individuals or exercising the ministry of Christian spiritual formation in the context of large networks of congregations and movements. Men and women with an apostolic anointing are, by God's hand, becoming the parents of networks of believers, and these networks are growing in Christ. All I can say is, "More, Lord!"

What is Christian spiritual formation? It is a Spirit- and human-led process by which individuals and communities mature in relationship with the Christian God (Father, Son, and Spirit) and are changed into ever-greater likeness to the life and gospel of this God. We have learned in this book that in order to understand and to wisely practice Christian spiritual formation, we must pay attention to a number of crucial elements: aims, contexts, agents, process, and means. These combine to create unique environments in which we engage the task of formation. The task of Christian spiritual formation is our active cultivation of appropriate Christian transformation. We take initiative, in response to the Spirit's own initiative and the gospel message, to discover and act on the appropriate next step of growth. As we engage in the task of formation, we find ourselves actually being formed: in our relationship with God through prayer; in our life together; in our thinking, feeling, and choices and actions; and in our relationship with the world through a life of mission. Because the gospel story is a rich and magnificent "all things new" story, and because we as communities and individuals are distinct in context and much more, the task of Christian spiritual formation is a task of discernment, requiring a prayerful sensitivity to God's Spirit and other people. But as we engage in this task on an ongoing basis, we begin to exercise the ministry of Christian spiritual formation: the offering of one's self and a prayerful willingness to take responsibility for the sake of cultivating appropriate transformation in others.

"The harvest is plentiful but the workers are few" (Matt. 9:37). May God raise up many workers eager to offer the ministry of Christian spiritual formation, and may we respond to the invitation, for the sake of the church, the world, and the glory of God.

Going Deeper

1. One way of going deeper with regard to the ministry of spiritual formation might be to explore your own personal history of the ministry of spiritual formation (a reflection exercise suggested in previous chapters too). You might first want to examine your own experience as someone receiving the ministry of spiritual formation. Though you may not have received this ministry in a formal way, have you in your past experienced something like what I have presented in this chapter? If so, who exercised leadership over your spiritual growth? What formal or informal means were used? How was sensitive discernment expressed to you? Now examine your history of offering something like the ministry of Christian spiritual formation presented in this chapter. For whom and in what contexts did you offer it? What formal or informal means did you employ? In what way was your ministry vocationally or spiritually centered? What areas of life were addressed in your ministry?

2. It also might be interesting to tease out some of the nuances of this ministry as it might be exercised within different roles and contexts. How might the ministry look when exercised by a pastor? What would be different if this ministry were exercised by a close friend, a counselor,

a life coach, or a spiritual director? What kinds of agreements or understandings would be necessary or important in different situations? How might the task of spiritual formation be adjusted to fit different roles and situations? If you initiated it, how would it be different than if it were initiated by the one receiving this ministry? How might you, as the minister of spiritual formation, feel about exercising this ministry in different settings?

3. A few challenges might come with an attempt to revitalize a ministry of Christian spiritual formation for today—challenges regarding leadership and authority, motive, and training. Are there others? Are there challenges unique to the ministry of Christian spiritual formation due to the different context within which it might be used today?

4. I emphasized the need for this ministry. But is there really a need for this ministry? Perhaps I am just so interested in my own field of study that I can't see other matters that are really of much greater need. What do you think? If there is a need for this ministry, why does that need exist? On what is this need based? If this need is really not all that widespread, then what is driving the interest in spiritual formation these days?

5. I can conclude this book by suggesting one obvious practice: that of the ministry of Christian spiritual formation. One good way to begin is by exercising prayerful, sensitive discernment in the relationships in which you are involved daily. Ponder (though do not offer your advice unless asked) what might be the most appropriate step of growth for this person or for that congregation. Spend some time thinking about context, means, and agents. Consider what it might look like if that person were to employ these means with those agents. Then perhaps you could go a step further and start meeting with a peer to share your insights with each other. There is nothing like learning to think like a minister of spiritual formation to help you grow into one.

Epilogue

My Personal History of Spiritual Formation

I have been a Christian for forty-five years now, and in those years I have observed my own experience of Christian spiritual formation change. I feel that in some ways I have been transformed by the Spirit and formed through the influence of various agents in my life. But I have also seen my own perspectives about spiritual formation change in dialogue with trends, research, and my own encounters with God. Perhaps it might help if I briefly tell something of that story.

Not long after I was converted to Christ at age fifteen in Spokane, Washington—it was one of those night-and-day experiences—I somehow knew I needed to change a few things. For example, I felt convicted about my swearing, but it was hard to quit. The habit was ingrained. In the end, I made little marks on my arm when I cursed, and for every mark I would put a certain amount of money in the offering plate at church. It worked. Nothing like a little penance to stimulate the means of grace! I remember being discipled in a small group by a leader of a parachurch high-school ministry. I woke up early in the morning and did my homework for the group. I did extra Bible study and prayer. I remember claiming promises, confessing sins, looking in Scripture for examples to follow, doing lots of witnessing, and talking with my leader about it all. I consider high school to have been a golden season of growth.

When I got to college, I was challenged in new ways. I no longer had the high-school group or the leader to guide me. There were intellectual challenges as well. But I kept up with Bible studies, often with Cheri, a good friend from high school who went to the same college as me (and whom I would marry). I became frustrated at the way some Christians approached spiritual growth, for it seemed like the Christian life was often promoted as a matter of simple actions: receive Christ; study the Bible, resist temptation, and witness; and wait for the second coming. I remember that one day I made an outline of what I called "The Doctrine of the Changed Life, with Emphasis on the Word *Life*." In that outline, I compared what I thought was a shallow approach to the changed life—predominantly a transformation of the will—with what I thought God was teaching me in Scripture and elsewhere. In my own model, I saw God desire to change my philosophy, my creativity, my relationship with social structures, and so on. It was my first real glimpse into the "all things new" vision of formation. I began to make serious commitments and to take significant steps to see change in each of these areas of my life. I did not give up Bible study or witnessing. It was just that I felt that God wanted more of me, and I saw more in God and in the gospel.

About two years after finishing college, Cheri and I (now married) moved to Chicago so I could attend seminary. My seminary years developed as a combination of three influences, symbolized by three different locations. There was the seminary itself, a bastion of solid, conservative biblical train-ing. I loved school and grew both intellectually and spiritually through my studies. Then there was our church in inner-city Chicago, where we became acquainted with racial issues, poverty (and poor people), and many exciting and creative ways of living and sharing the gospel with others. And it was largely through this church that we were introduced to the third location: the monastery or retreat center. This retreat center, administered by the Sisters of the Cenacle, was where Cheri and I went once a month during our seminary years for a day of silence and prayer. It was there (and in church) that I became acquainted with a host of new practices and a uni-verse of new literature known as the classics of Christian spirituality. The discovery of new spiritual practices like lectio divina, contemplative prayer, self-examination, and spiritual direction was a delight to my spirit, and for some reason I devoured these practices like a starving man at a smorgasbord. Through the classics of Christian spirituality, I became acquainted with a new set of mentors and models. But my formation—and my approach to formation—in these years was really developed through the mix of all three: school, inner-city church, and retreat center. I processed all three together in regular meetings with one of my professors from school, who listened graciously and helped me through my identity questions. I remember, at the end of my seminary career, reading through the New Testament with colored pens and highlighting in three colors the passages that addressed the transformation of what I identified as doctrine, devotion, and conduct. I knew I needed to grow in all three.

We returned to Spokane after seminary, and I struggled with learning how to be a father, a business owner, and a pastor. The last one was particularly hard. It is one thing to apply your approach to spiritual formation in your own life. It is quite another to do this for others. By that time, I had a wide view of the aims of formation and a long list of practices that were necessary in order to reach those aims. And I expected near perfection of everyone within my reach, for I had not yet learned that the intention of formation must be accompanied with the wisdom of formation. I had not learned the simple aim of increase. The church I copastored began to fall apart, but God met me when I needed him most and revealed to me my own pharisaism. That trial was one of the best things that ever happened to me.

Another piece of my growth in formation during those years in Spokane was a fresh discovery of the role of the Holy Spirit in formation. Needless to say, by the end of those years, I was learning that programs and practices might not be enough for a congregation or for my own life. I needed the Holy Spirit, and through Bible study and paying attention to my experience, I began to sense the Holy Spirit's leading in my life. In time I learned something of how to notice the Spirit's touch in others as well. We moved to the San Francisco Bay Area so I could work on a PhD in Christian spirituality. While in school, I worked as a house painter for a few years, and eventually I accepted an offer to serve as an associate pastor in a Vineyard church. By then, through the formation of my studies in the wisdom of Christian spirituality, the trials of the previous years, a few practices, and the ministry of the Spirit, I was better prepared for professional ministry. I grew personally in my relationship with God and was able, through exploring formation as a discerning art, to help others grow as well.

When I was nearly finished with my doctoral work, we moved to a small town in Colorado to be closer to Cheri's family. We joined a church that was both charismatic and liturgical. I started meeting with an older man for accountability meetings—and we are still meeting nearly eighteen years later. I think that my formation—and my approach to formation—here in Colorado has been a time of "the ordinary": learning to hold a vision, to examine myself regularly in light of that vision, to articulate how I think I can step forward in the midst of my own crazy mix of ranching and teaching and ordinary church life, and to talk about that with someone else who knows when to encourage me to rest and when to encourage me to press in.

Looking back at the whole of it, I see that various agents (Spirit, self, others) served as my primary guides in different seasons. There have been seasons where particular means of grace (practices, trials, community) were very important to my formation. Struggles with prayer, with people, with my own emotions, and with mission have all had their place in my formation. As I grew older, my ability to cultivate others' formation became part of my own formation. The contexts of my own formation—and with this my own sense of what my spiritual formation was about—shifted as we moved from one tradition to another. Over time, my sense of the "all things new" aim of formation has only grown stronger and deeper—and hopefully a bit wiser.

And as I sit here right now, imagining people who think that the church is unchristian, and as I picture the beautiful "all things new" vision of Christian spiritual formation that through the Holy Spirit we can live into, I can only say this: Christian spiritual formation matters. It matters to me personally. It matters to the church of Christ. It matters to the world.

Notes

Preface

1. Evan B. Howard, *The Brazos Introduction to Christian Spirituality* (Grand Rapids: Brazos, 2008).
2. Evan B. Howard, "Evangelical Spirituality," in *Four Views on Christian Spirituality*, ed. Bruce Demarest (Grand Rapids: Zondervan, 2012).

Chapter 1 Christian Spiritual Formation

1. For this story, see Greg L. Hawkins and Cally Parkinson, *Move: What 1,000 Churches Reveal about Spiritual Growth* (Grand Rapids: Zondervan/Willow Creek Association, 2011), 15–18.
2. My account of the Vineyard here is based on emails and conversation with the individuals involved.
3. Stephen D. Summerell, "Overcoming Obstacles to Spiritual Formation in the Lives of Vineyard Pastors" (PhD diss., Azusa Pacific University, 2007).
4. For what follows, see Todd D. Hunter, *The Accidental Anglican: The Surprising Appeal of the Liturgical Church* (Downers Grove, IL: InterVarsity, 2010), 19–82.
5. Hunter, *Accidental Anglican*, 29.
6. Hunter, *Accidental Anglican*, 113.
7. Hunter, *Accidental Anglican*, 58. For more on the Anglican Church in North America, see http://www.anglicanchurch.net/.
8. Todd D. Hunter, *Giving Church Another Chance: Finding New Meaning in Spiritual Practices* (Downers Grove, IL: InterVarsity, 2010).
9. See, e.g., Lester Ruth and Robert Webber, *Evangelicals on the Canterbury Trail: Why Evangelicals Are Attracted to the Liturgical Church*, rev. ed. (New York: Morehouse, 2013).
10. David Kinnaman and Gabe Lyons, *UnChristian: What a New Generation Thinks about Christianity . . . and Why It Matters* (Grand Rapids: Baker Books, 2007), 79–80.
11. David Kinnaman, *You Lost Me: Why Young Christians Are Leaving the Church . . . and Rethinking Faith* (Grand Rapids: Baker Books, 2011), 21, 28 (italics in the original).
12. Irenaeus, *Against Heresies* 4.11.
13. Augustine, *On Christian Doctrine* 1.22, in *Saint Augustine: On Christian Teaching*, trans. R. P. H. Green (Oxford: Oxford University Press, 1997), 12–13.

14. See especially Bernard-Marie Chevignard, "Formation, Spirituelle," in *Dictionnaire de Spiritualité et Mystique*, ed. M. Viller, F. Cavallera, and J. de Guibert (Paris: Beuchesne, 1964), vol. 5, cols. 699–716.

15. "Decree on Priestly Formation," chap. 4, in *The Documents of Vatican II*, ed. Walter M. Abbott (New York: Guild Press, 1966), 444–45.

16. It was originally named the Department of Prayer and Spiritual Life, but director Steven Harper renamed it in 1984 in light of what he saw developing in the study and practice of spirituality.

17. Richard Foster, *Celebration of Discipline* (New York: HarperCollins, 1978).

18. See also Steven L. Porter, "Is the Spiritual Formation Movement Dead?," *Journal of Spiritual Formation and Soul Care* 8, no. 1 (Spring 2015): 2–7.

19. See, e.g., Paul Bramer, "Christian Formation: Tweaking the Paradigm," *Christian Education Journal*, 3rd ser., 4, no. 2 (Fall 2007): 352–63; Bramer, "Spiritual Formation and Christian Education," *Christian Education Journal*, 3rd ser., 7, no. 2 (Fall 2010): 334–39; and Commission on Accrediting, *Degree Program Standards* (Pittsburgh: Association of Theological Schools: 2015), 2–3 (secs. A.2.1, A.2.4). One might also note similar shifts in the practice of Christian counseling, which has in some circles demonstrated a distinct shift in the direction of spiritual formation (e.g., the works of Larry Crabb and David Benner). As I write this book, I am teaching a curriculum that incorporates the concept of practice-based education at a large seminary (Fuller Theological Seminary).

20. In spiritual formation literature, the word *conform* has a positive connotation, as in "conformed to the image of Christ" (Rom. 8:29).

21. See, e.g., Charles Van Engen, *Mission on the Way: Issues in Mission Theology* (Grand Rapids: Baker, 1996), 240–52; Dwight J. Zscheile, ed., *Cultivating Sent Communities: Missional Spiritual Formation* (Grand Rapids: Eerdmans, 2012); and *Journal of Spiritual Formation and Soul Care* 6, no. 1 (Spring 2013), a special issue on Christian spirituality and Christian mission. The 2014 Apprentice Institute conference on "Formation for Mission: Becoming the Change Our World Needs" addressed this interaction of mission and formation. For more on the Apprentice Institute, see https://www.friends.edu/about/apprentice-institute/. Organizations like the Link Care Center in Fresno, CA, are also interested in moving beyond therapy toward an approach that includes both spiritual formation and missions interest. More recently, some Christians have questioned the use of the term *mission*, considering it to be too heavily freighted with notions of conquest and colonial baggage. See, e.g., Scott Bessenecker, "Abandoning Our Colonizing Mission," *Overturning Tables* (blog), posted April 30, 2016, http://www.overturningtables.net/abandoning-colonizing-mission/. I address this question and others related to the formation of mission further in chap. 10.

22. See, e.g., James C. Wilhoit, *Spiritual Formation as if the Church Mattered* (Grand Rapids: Baker Academic, 2008); David A. deSilva, *Sacramental Life: Spiritual Formation through the Book of Common Prayer* (Downers Grove, IL: InterVarsity, 2008); Paul Pettit, ed., *Foundations of Spiritual Formation: A Community Approach to Becoming Like Christ* (Grand Rapids: Kregel, 2008); and James K. A. Smith, *Imagining the Kingdom: How Worship Works* (Grand Rapids: Baker Academic, 2013). I will address the church-formation dialogue further in chaps. 6 and 8.

23. The next few paragraphs are a summary of reflections contained in my essay "The Metaphysics of Power: Reflections on the Basic Framework of Psychology, Community, Politics, and Spiritual Formation," http://spiritualityshoppe.org/the-metaphysics-of-power-reflections-on-the-basic-framework-of-psychology-community-politics-and-spiritual-formation/.

24. Richella Parham, *A Spiritual Formation Primer* (Englewood, CO: Renovaré, 2013), 6.

25. Gordon Fee, "On Getting the Spirit Back into Spirituality," in *Life in the Spirit: Spiritual Formation in Theological Perspective* (Downers Grove, IL: InterVarsity, 2010), 44. Note how throughout this paragraph Fee uses both *spirit* and *Spirit*. There is no such distinction between these in the original biblical languages.

26. "But if Christ is in you, then even though your body is subject to death because of sin, the Spirit gives life because of righteousness" (Rom. 8:10). Translations of this passage vary. As I mentioned above, translation of spirit passages is notoriously difficult.

27. I will be introducing other perspectives in the chapters ahead.

28. Jonathan Morrow, "Introducing Spiritual Formation," in *Foundations of Spiritual Formation: A Community Approach to Becoming Like Christ*, ed. Paul Pettit (Grand Rapids: Kregel, 2008), 33–34.

29. Peter Damian, "The Book of the Lord Be with You," chap. 8, in *St. Peter Damian: Selected Writings on the Spiritual Life*, trans. Patricia McNulty (London: Faber & Faber, 1959), 62.

30. M. Robert Mulholland Jr., *Invitation to a Journey: A Road Map for Spiritual Formation* (Downers Grove, IL: InterVarsity, 1993), 12.

31. Dallas Willard, *Renovation of the Heart: Putting on the Character of Christ* (Colorado Springs: NavPress, 2002), 22 (italics in the original).

32. Pettit, introduction to *Foundations of Spiritual Formation*, 24 (italics in the original).

33. Howard, *Brazos Introduction*, 268.

34. Jeffrey P. Greenman, "Spiritual Formation in Theological Perspective: Classic Issues, Contemporary Challenges," in *Life in the Spirit: Spiritual Formation in Theological Perspective*, ed. Jeffrey P. Greenman and George Kalantzis (Downers Grove, IL: InterVarsity, 2010), 24.

35. Quoted in Parham, *Spiritual Formation Primer*, 6.

36. Though, of course, my concepts of formation and change are to be understood in light of my comments on formation above.

37. Furthermore, simply from an academic perspective, if we do not recognize and explore the practical agency of humans in Christian spiritual formation, I see little difference between articulating an account of Christian spiritual formation and a treatment of a doctrine of sanctification.

Chapter 2 The Story of Christian Spiritual Formation

1. This is a summary of the story often understood as the Origenist understanding of creation and salvation (following Origen, an early Christian ascetic). For a review of current research on this story, see Elizabeth A. Clark, *The Origenist Controversy: The Cultural Construction of an Early Christian Debate* (Princeton: Princeton University Press, 1992); Paul A. Patterson, *Visions of Christ: The Anthropomorphite Controversy of 399 CE* (Tübingen: Mohr Siebeck, 2012); and Augustine Casiday, *Reconstructing the Theology of Evagrius Ponticus: Beyond Heresy* (Cambridge: Cambridge University Press, 2013).

2. For a similar outline see, e.g., N. T. Wright, *The New Testament and the People of God* (Minneapolis: Fortress, 1992), 140–43.

3. I have discussed the God of Christian spirituality in greater detail in Howard, *Brazos Introduction*, 113–44.

4. See, e.g., Tom Nelson, "A Helper for What?," chapel talk given at Talbot School of Theology, posted March 3, 2015, http://open.biola.edu/resources/a-helper-for-what.

5. Soon after this (Lev. 26:12), we find the reciprocal side of this covenant identity: "And you will be my people." Either together or apart, these phrases—*I will be your God* and *you will be my people*—are repeated again and again in Scripture.

6. I address this key dynamic in our relationship with God (God's initiation, our response, and God's response to our response) in Howard, *Brazos Introduction*, 204–23.

7. How we identify ourselves in relation to our stories is one of the matters discussed in the field of discourse analysis. See, e.g., J. P. Gee, *An Introduction to Discourse Analysis: Theory and Method*, rev. ed. (New York: Routledge, 2014).

8. Samples of this kind of approach to "true religion" or "real Christianity" or the like can be found in Menno Simons, *The Complete Writings of Menno Simons: c. 1496–1561*, ed. J. C. Wenger, trans. Leonard Verduin (1956; repr., Scottdale, PA: Herald, 1984), 53–62; Johann

Arndt, *True Christianity*, ed. Peter C. Erb, Classics of Western Spirituality (New York: Paulist Press, 1979), 69; Jonathan Edwards, *Religious Affections*, ed. John E. Smith, vol. 2 of The Works of Jonathan Edwards (New Haven: Yale University Press, 1959), 89; Kenneth J. Collins, *The Scripture Way of Salvation: The Heart of John Wesley's Theology* (Nashville: Abingdon, 1997), 148–52; William Wilberforce, *A Practical View of the Prevailing Religious System in the Higher and Middle Classes in This Country Contrasted with Real Christianity*, 9th ed. (1797; repr., London: T. Cadell & W. Davis, 1811); and John R. W. Stott, *Basic Christianity*, 2nd ed. (Downers Grove, IL: InterVarsity, 1971), 7–9. See also D. Bruce Hindmarsh, "Contours of Evangelical Spirituality," in *Dictionary of Christian Spirituality*, ed. Glen G. Scorgie (Grand Rapids: Zondervan Academic, 2010), 146–52; and Howard, "Evangelical Spirituality," 166–67.

Chapter 3 The Fullness and Aims of Christian Spiritual Formation

1. See, e.g., Mulholland, *Invitation to a Journey*, 64–73; Willard, *Renovation of the Heart*, 95–216; and Diane J. Chandler, *Christian Spiritual Formation: An Integrated Approach for Personal and Relational Wholeness* (Downers Grove, IL: InterVarsity, 2014).

2. In this chapter, I will draw from and summarize what I have written elsewhere on these topics. For my treatment of human experience, see Howard, *Brazos Introduction*, 77–112; for the nature of relationship, see pp. 195–227; for my treatment of some of the terms regarding the aims of Christian spiritual formation, see pp. 274–79.

3. Terms used to identify the core immaterial character of human experience have varied through Christian history. While some distinguish between *soul* and *spirit*, others see them as somewhat synonymous. Still others use the word *heart* to speak of the center of human life and being (with a nod to the Christian faith's Hebrew background). My aim is not to argue for one or another of these models; rather, I want simply to summarize the basic character of human experience as both embodied and more. For another exploration of these terms, see, e.g., Willard, *Renovation of the Heart*, 27–44. And, of course, we cannot properly consider the human spirit apart from an understanding of the Holy Spirit, so I will speak of the Holy Spirit and the relationship of the Spirit and spirituality throughout this book. For another integration of pneumatology and spirituality, see, e.g., F. LeRon Shults, "Reforming Pneumatology," chap. 2 in *Transforming Spirituality: Integrating Theology and Psychology*, by F. LeRon Shults and Steven Sandage (Grand Rapids: Baker Academic, 2006).

4. Various passages of Scripture divide parts of human experience differently, and I will make no attempt here to reconcile these variations. I am simply using a common paradigm as a means of illustrating the various operations of human experience and, ultimately, how God addresses the fullness of who we are.

5. See chap. 9 for a fuller treatment of the formation of thinking, feeling, and acting.

6. See Howard, *Brazos Introduction*, 87–92. In my earlier writings, I used the technical philosophical term *judging* to identify this stage. But people now understand *judging* not in light of its philosophical background, but more often in the context of a negative valuation (e.g., judging people is bad). Consequently, I have chosen to adopt the term *evaluating* to describe this stage.

7. See Richard Foster, *Streams of Living Water: Celebrating the Great Traditions of Christian Faith* (San Francisco: HarperSanFrancisco, 1998). I have replaced Foster's term *incarnational* with *sacramental*. I have also added a category that I call the *progressive* tradition. See Howard, *Brazos Introduction*, 350–54.

8. Once again, we see the complexities of giving an adequate account of formation that is both Christian and spiritual. On the one hand, formation is about relationship with God, who is Spirit, the source, object, means, and end of our life. And yet it is also about Christians, ordinary persons with a wide range of thoughts and feelings and relationships, all of which are changed (and ought to be made new) in the midst of their formation in Christ. I will be exploring the dynamics of our relationship with God further in the chapters ahead.

9. I will touch on the healing of the soul more directly in chap. 9.

10. Jonathan Edwards speaks of "the glory of God" as the ultimate aim of human existence and the ground beneath true virtue. See Jonathan Edwards, *Ethical Writings*, ed. Paul Ramsey, vol. 8 of The Works of Jonathan Edwards (New Haven: Yale University Press, 1989), 399–629. We might also use the term *union* to name the aim of spiritual formation. On *union*, see Thomas D. McGonigle, "Union, Unitive Way," in *The New Dictionary of Catholic Spirituality*, ed. Michael Downey (Collegeville, MN: Liturgical Press, 1993), 987–88.

11. Jonathan Edwards, *The "Miscellanies," a–500*, ed. Thomas A. Schafer, vol. 13 of The Works of Jonathan Edwards (New Haven: Yale University Press, 1994), 163–64.

12. For a good survey of the doctrine of deification, see Norman Russell, *The Doctrine of Deification in the Greek Patristic Tradition*, Oxford Early Christian Studies (Oxford: Oxford University Press, 2004).

13. John Meyendorff, *Byzantine Theology: Historical Trends and Doctrinal Themes* (New York: Fordham University Press, 1979), 165.

14. Kallistos Ware, *How Are We Saved? The Understanding of Salvation in the Orthodox Tradition* (Minneapolis: Light & Life, 1996), 64.

15. Vladimir Lossky, *The Mystical Theology of the Eastern Church* (Crestwood, NY: St. Vladimir's Seminary Press, 1998), 196.

16. The precise meaning of the Greek here is debated. It has been rendered as "obedience which comes from faith," the "obedience to the faith," and "faith and obedience." I simply want to point out the importance, for Paul, of obedience, which is sustained in many of the translations.

17. John Calvin, *Institutes of the Christian Religion*, ed. John T. McNeill, trans. Ford Lewis Battles (Louisville: Westminster, 1960), 3.3.14 (p. 607). Calvin uses the terms *obedience* and *obedient* 255 times in this work.

18. J. Heinrich Arnold, *Discipleship* (Farmington, PA: Plough Publishing House, 1994), 272–73.

19. See Howard A. Snyder, *The Community of the King*, rev. ed. (Downers Grove, IL: InterVarsity, 2010).

20. This aspect of the realm of God as realized through corporate spiritual formation is discussed in Susanne Johnson, *Christian Spiritual Formation in the Church and Classroom* (Nashville: Abingdon, 1989), 43–54.

21. F. LeRon Shults and Steven Sandage similarly talk about a "differentiated form of spiritual attachment to God, self, and others" that facilitates intimacy with God and others and at the same time promotes an orientation to justice. See Shults and Sandage, *Transforming Spirituality*.

22. George A. Maloney, introduction to *Nil Sorsky: The Complete Writings*, ed. and trans. George A. Maloney, Classics of Western Spirituality (New York: Paulist Press, 2003), 19.

Chapter 4 The Contexts and Agents of Christian Spiritual Formation

1. After introducing these contexts in this chapter, I will explore them more fully as we consider formation together in chap. 8.

2. See, e.g., Elizabeth Conde-Frazier, S. Steve Kang, and Gary A. Parrett, *A Many Colored Kingdom: Multicultural Dynamics for Spiritual Formation* (Grand Rapids: Baker Academic, 2004).

3. See Kees Waaijman, *Spirituality: Forms, Foundations, Methods* (Leuven: Peeters, 2002), 9–304.

4. Waaijman, *Spirituality*, 117–18. For more on the schools of Christian spirituality, see Evan B. Howard, "Schools of Spirituality," in *Reading the Spiritual Classics: A Guide for Evangelicals*, ed. Jamin Goggin and Kyle Strobel (Downers Grove, IL: InterVarsity, 2013), 63–78.

5. It is interesting to note that the term *congregation* is used for a particular expression of religious life within the Roman Catholic tradition. Different congregations adopt rules and

constitutions, forming unique congregations of religious (i.e., members of a religious order). *Parish* would be another word to describe the concrete embodiments of schools within some traditions.

6. I am not arguing that formation is the only or the primary function of a local congregation. Doxology and mission, for example, are vital functions of a local expression of the body of Christ. Indeed, the simple task of being a community of Christ is itself a worthy function apart from the value of the community for personal or corporate growth. My point is simply that formation is a necessary function of congregational life and that we ought to plan for this. I will address this further in chap. 8.

7. I will address the issue of networking spirituality more fully in chap. 8.

8. See Edward Maletesta, "Charism," in *The New Dictionary of Catholic Spirituality*, ed. Michael Downey (Collegeville, MN: Liturgical Press, 1993), 140–43; and Michael Downey, "Charism," in *The New Westminster Dictionary of Christian Spirituality*, ed. Philip Sheldrake (Louisville: Westminster John Knox, 2005), 184–85.

9. Waaijman, *Spirituality*, 212.

10. The phrase *religious life* is the proper Roman Catholic language for general reference to monks, nuns, friars, and the like. The vocabulary regarding such groups is notoriously complicated. See Evan B. Howard, "What Do We Call It? New Monasticism and the Vocabulary of Religious Life," http://spiritualityshoppe.org/what-do-we-call-it-new-monasticism-and-the-vocabulary-of-religious-life/.

11. I use the term *spiritual director* here simply because it is the most commonly used term in the context of Christian spiritual formation. I could also speak of—and make finer nuances between—"coach," "discipler," "mentor," and so on, but my aim here is not to develop these finer distinctions but rather to introduce more generally one-on-one relationships within which we are formed. For more, see, e.g., Paul D. Stanley and J. Robert Clinton, *Connecting: The Mentoring Relationships You Need to Succeed in Life* (Colorado Springs: NavPress, 1992); Gary W. Moon and David G. Benner, *Spiritual Direction and the Care of Souls: A Guide to Christian Approaches and Practices* (Downers Grove, IL: InterVarsity, 2004); and John T. McNeill, *A History of the Cure of Souls* (New York: Harper & Row, 1951).

12. As I mentioned earlier, different versions of the Bible differ in their translations of the Hebrew and Greek language for spirit and Holy Spirit. Some translations use *wind* where another will use *spirit*. You must read multiple translations (or study the concept in the original languages) in order to catch the nuances.

13. I can only begin to summarize the vast literature on spirit and the Holy Spirit. For a representative sample of approaches, see Anthony C. Thiselton, *The Holy Spirit—in Biblical Teaching, through the Centuries, and Today* (Grand Rapids: Eerdmans, 2013); Gordon Fee, *God's Empowering Presence: The Holy Spirit in the Letters of Paul* (Grand Rapids: Baker, 1994); John R. Levison, *Filled with the Spirit* (Grand Rapids: Eerdmans, 2009); Yves Congar, *I Believe in the Holy Spirit*, trans. David Smith (New York: Crossroad, 1997); Amos Yong, *Who Is the Holy Spirit?* (Brewster, MA: Paraclete, 2011); Jürgen Moltmann, *The Spirit of Life: A Universal Affirmation*, trans. Margaret Kohl (Minneapolis: Fortress, 1992); Clark H. Pinnock, *Living Flame of Love: A Theology of the Holy Spirit* (Downers Grove, IL: InterVarsity, 1996); and Max Turner, *The Holy Spirit and Spiritual Gifts* (Grand Rapids: Baker, 1996).

14. Turner, *Holy Spirit*, 4–5 (italics in the original). See also George T. Montague, *The Holy Spirit: Growth of a Biblical Tradition* (New York: Paulist Press, 1976), 41, 72–73.

15. Note here the parallel with Gen. 1–2 and the theme of new creation present in this passage.

16. See Klaus Issler, "Jesus' Example Prototype of the Dependent, Spirit-Filled Life," in *Jesus in Trinitarian Perspective*, ed. Fred Sanders and Klaus Issler (Nashville: B&H Academic, 2007), 189–225.

17. Basil of Caesarea's *On the Holy Spirit*, Augustine of Hippo's *On the Trinity*, and Athanasius's *Letter to Serapion on the Holy Spirit* are classic discussions of the divinity and personhood of the Holy Spirit as a legitimate member of the divine Trinity.

18. See, e.g., W. Maxwell Cohen, Thomas C. Südhof, and Charles F. Stevens, *Synapses* (Baltimore: Johns Hopkins University Press, 2001).

19. For this, see Howard, "Metaphysics of Power," 27–39.

20. On the indicative and the imperative, see, e.g., George Eldon Ladd, *A Theology of the New Testament*, rev. ed. (Grand Rapids: Eerdmans, 1993), 536–37, 563, 565, 568–69.

21. See Richard Lovelace, *Dynamics of Spiritual Life: An Evangelical Theology of Renewal* (Downers Grove, IL: InterVarsity, 1979); and Lovelace, *Renewal as a Way of Life* (Downers Grove, IL: InterVarsity, 1985).

22. Maloney, introduction to *Nil Sorsky*, 19.

23. See Moon and Benner, *Spiritual Direction*.

24. William A. Barry and William J. Connolly, *The Practice of Spiritual Direction* (New York: Seabury, 1982), 8.

Chapter 5 The Process of Transformation and the Task of Formation

1. On testimony, see Gordon T. Smith, *Beginning Well: Christian Conversion and Authentic Transformation* (Downers Grove, IL: InterVarsity, 2001), 221–27; Thomas Long, *Testimony: Talking Ourselves into Being Christian* (San Francisco: Jossey-Bass, 2004); D. Bruce Hindmarsh, *The Evangelical Conversion Narrative: Spiritual Autobiography in Early Modern England* (New York: Oxford University Press, 2005); and Thomas Hoyt Jr., "Testimony," in *Practicing Our Faith*, ed. Dorothy C. Bass, 2nd ed. (San Francisco: Jossey-Bass, 2010), 89–101.

2. Classic portraits of Christian spirituality using the image of a journey can be found in such works as Gregory of Nyssa's *Life of Moses*, John Comenius's *The Labyrinth of the World and the Paradise of the Heart*, and John Bunyan's *Pilgrim's Progress*.

3. For my summary of Christian views of salvation—speaking of the greatness, the tragedy, and the restoration of human experience—see Howard, *Brazos Introduction*, 145–94.

4. For a framework of historical, initial, ongoing, and final salvation, see Howard, *Brazos Introduction*, 236–54.

5. For a few representative samples of reflection on salvation, see Bruce Demarest, *The Cross and Salvation: The Doctrine of Salvation*, Foundations of Evangelical Theology (Wheaton: Crossway, 1997); Joel Green, *Why Salvation?* Reframing New Testament Theology (Nashville: Abingdon, 2013); and Michael J. Gorman, *Inhabiting the Cruciform God: Kenosis, Justification, and Theosis in Paul's Narrative Soteriology* (Grand Rapids: Eerdmans, 2009).

6. See, e.g., Ware, *How Are We Saved?* For a historical perspective, see Russell, *Doctrine of Deification*.

7. See, e.g., John Theodore Mueller, *Christian Dogmatics: A Handbook on Doctrinal Theology* (St. Louis: Concordia, 1955); and Louis Berkhof, *Systematic Theology*, 4th ed. (Grand Rapids: Eerdmans, 1941).

8. For Maximus, see, e.g., Lars Thunberg, *Microcosm and Mediator: The Theological Anthropology of Maximus the Confessor* (Chicago: Open Court, 1995). For Augustine, see Rebecca Harden Weaver, *Divine Grace and Human Agency: A Study of the Semi-Pelagian Controversy* (Macon, GA: Mercer University Press, 1996), and other discussions of Augustine's later writings.

9. See, e.g., the discussions in Berkhof, *Systematic Theology*, 415–22; Peter Erb, introduction to *Johann Arndt: True Christianity* (New York: Paulist Press, 1979), 7–9; and Gordon R. Lewis and Bruce A. Demarest, *Integrative Theology* (Grand Rapids: Zondervan, 1994), 3:56–58. See also Thomas C. Oden's brief introduction to the order of the terms of salvation in and the sections of his volume that follow this order in his *Life in the Spirit: Systematic Theology* (Peabody, MA: Prince Press, 1992), 3:79, 80–204.

10. Cf. Howard, *Brazos Introduction*, 154–73.

11. Martin Bucer, *Instruction in Christian Love*, trans. Paul Traugott Fuhrmann (1523; repr., Eugene, OR: Wipf & Stock, 2008), 27.

12. Bucer, *Instruction in Christian Love*, 28.

13. Bucer, *Instruction in Christian Love*, 28.

14. Thomas Merton, letter published in *Information Catholiques Internationales*, April 1973, back cover, quoted in Emilie Griffin, *Turning: Reflections on the Experience of Conversion* (Garden City, NY: Image, 1982), 196.

15. Donald L. Gelpi has discussed the forms of conversion in a number of works. See especially his *Committed Worship*, vol. 1, *Adult Conversion and Initiation* (Collegeville, MN: Liturgical Press, 1993), 3–55; and Gelpi, *The Conversion Experience: A Reflective Process for RCIA Participants and Others* (Mahwah, NJ: Paulist Press, 1998). For similar accounts of forms of conversion, see Bernard Lonergan, *Method in Theology* (Minneapolis: Seabury, 1972), 237–44; Robert Doran, *Subject and Psyche: Ricoeur, Jung, and the Search for Foundations* (Washington, DC: University Press of America, 1977); and Bernard J. Tyrrell, *Christotherapy II: The Fasting and the Feasting Heart* (New York: Paulist Press, 1982). In what follows, I am drawing a great deal from Gelpi's work, although unlike Gelpi I am considering conversion strictly within the context of Christian life. For my own treatment of plural, multifaceted conversion, see Evan B. Howard, *Affirming the Touch of God: A Psychological and Philosophical Exploration of Christian Discernment* (Lanham, MD: University Press of America, 2000), 235–90; and Howard, *Brazos Introduction*, 254–59.

16. For more on the fundamental pattern of Christian spirituality—God's initiation, our response, and God's response to our response—see Howard, *Brazos Introduction*, 204–23.

17. For consideration of a variety of these factors, see, e.g., Chester P. Michael and Marie C. Norrisey, *Prayer and Temperament: Different Prayer Forms for Different Personality Types* (Charlottesville, VA: Open Door, 1984); Elizabeth Liebert, *Changing Life Patterns: Adult Development in Spiritual Direction* (New York: Paulist Press, 1992); Gary Thomas, *Sacred Pathways: Discover Your Soul's Path to God* (Nashville: Nelson, 1996); Joann Wolski Conn, ed., *Women's Spirituality: Resources for Christian Development*, 2nd ed. (New York: Paulist Press, 1996); John Eldredge, *Wild at Heart: Discovering the Secret of a Man's Soul* (Nashville: Nelson, 2001); and Conde-Frazier, Kang, and Parrett, *Many Colored Kingdom*.

18. For other samples of the threefold way, see Adolphe Tanquerey, *The Spiritual Life: A Treatise on Ascetical and Mystical Theology*, 2nd rev. ed., ed. Herman Branderis (Tournai, Belgium: Desclée, 1930); and Joseph de Guibert, *The Theology of the Spiritual Life*, trans. Paul Barrett (New York: Sheed & Ward, 1953). A more contemporary expression of this may be found in Jordan Aumann, *Spiritual Theology* (London: Sheed & Ward, 1980). For Aquinas, see Simon Tugwell, "A Dominican Theology of Prayer," *Dominican Ashram* 1, no. 3 (September 1982): 128–44; and *Albert and Thomas: Selected Writings*, ed. and trans. Simon Tugwell, Classics of Western Spirituality (New York: Paulist Press, 1988).

19. For a brief introduction to Carmelite spirituality, see Keith J. Egan, "Carmelite Spirituality," in *Exploring Christian Spirituality*, ed. Kenneth J. Collins (Grand Rapids: Baker Books, 2000), 97–107. On Holiness, Pentecostal, and Keswick models of spiritual growth, see George M. Marsden, *Fundamentalism and American Culture: The Shaping of Twentieth-Century Evangelicalism, 1870–1925* (Oxford: Oxford University Press, 1980), 77–101; and Vinson Synan, *The Holiness-Pentecostal Tradition: Charismatic Movements in the Twentieth Century*, 2nd ed. (Grand Rapids: Eerdmans, 1997).

20. See, e.g., James W. Fowler, *Stages of Faith: The Psychology of Human Development and the Quest for Meaning* (San Francisco: Harper & Row, 1981); Francis Kelly Nemek and Marie Theresa Coombs, *The Spiritual Journey: Critical Thresholds and Stages of Adult Spiritual Genesis* (Wilmington, DE: Michael Glazier, 1987); Liebert, *Changing Life Patterns*; Friedrich L. Schweitzer, *The Postmodern Life Cycle: Challenges for Church and Theology* (St. Louis: Chalice,

Notes to Pages 92–107

2004); and Janet Hagberg and Robert Guelich, *The Critical Journey: Stages in the Life of Faith*, 2nd ed. (Salem, WI: Sheffield, 2005).

21. Again, I think there is a difference between normative and descriptive schemas. For example, Jonathan Edwards's tensions with the preparationist models were based not only on reflection on Scripture but also on his firsthand observations of the transformations taking place during the First Great Awakening. He saw development of authentic conversions that did not go through the prescribed stages.

22. The classic expression of this is Bruce W. Tuckman, "Developmental Sequence in Small Groups," *Psychological Bulletin* 63, no. 6 (June 1965): 384–99.

23. Some of this is treated in Israel Galindo, *The Hidden Lives of Congregations: Understanding Church Dynamics* (Lanham, MD: Rowman & Littlefield, 2014). See also James P. Wind and James W. Lewis, eds., *American Congregations*, 2 vols. (Chicago: University of Chicago Press, 1998); and Ed Stetzer, *Comeback Churches: How 300 Churches Turned Around and Yours Can Too* (Nashville: B&H, 2010). See also the musings on church growth and church planting by such authors as Warren Bird, Nelson Searcy, and Kerrick Thomas.

24. Howard, *Brazos Introduction*, 279–82.

25. Fostering stability and tending stillness where these are needed are also ways of cultivating change where those aspects have not been present. Change is not just a whirlwind of difference.

Chapter 6 The Means of Christian Spiritual Formation

1. John Wesley, "Sermon XVI: The Means of Grace," in *The Works of John Wesley* (1777; repr., Peabody, MA: Hendrickson, 1984), 5:187.

2. John Wesley, "Minutes of Several Conversations between the Rev. Mr. John Wesley and Others," *The Works of John Wesley* (1757; repr., Peabody, MA: Hendrickson, 1984), 8:322–24. Compare Wesley's list with the summary of American Puritan devotional practices in Charles Hambrick-Stowe, *The Practice of Piety: Puritan Devotional Disciplines in Seventeenth-Century New England* (Chapel Hill: University of North Carolina Press, 1982).

3. See also Dallas Willard, who speaks of a "golden triangle" of spiritual growth—the action of the Holy Spirit, ordinary events of life, and planned disciplines—in *The Divine Conspiracy: Rediscovering Our Hidden Life in God* (San Francisco: HarperSanFrancisco, 1998), 347–64.

4. Max Turner, "Spirit Endowment in Luke-Acts: Some Linguistic Considerations," *Vox Evangelica* 12 (1981): 45–63.

5. Paul does not use the word *Spirit* in Rom. 12 to describe God's distribution of gifts, but this passage is so similar to 1 Cor. 12 and so consistent with Paul's general theology that I think it is fair to see this passage as another Pauline understanding of the way that the Spirit provides or enhances ordinary abilities to serve the body of Christ.

6. See Steve L. Porter and Brandon Rickabaugh, "The Activity of the Spirit in Sanctification: Fiat, Interpersonal, or Life-Sharing?" (paper, Evangelical Theological Society Meeting, San Diego, November 2014).

7. Sam Hamilton-Poore, *Earth Gospel: A Guide to Prayer for God's Creation* (Nashville: Upper Room, 2008), 7.

8. Anthony of Egypt (also known as Antony), quoted in Thomas Merton, *Wisdom of the Desert: Sayings from the Desert Fathers* (New York: New Directions, 1960), 62; and Martin Luther, *Weimarer Ausgabe*, 48.201.5, cited in Heinrich Bornkamm, *Luther's World of Thought*, trans. Martin H. Bertram (St. Louis: Concordia, 1958), 179.

9. On nature-deficit disorder, see Richard Louv, *Last Child in the Woods: Saving Our Children from Nature-Deficit Disorder* (Chapel Hill: Algonquin, 2008).

10. See, e.g., Steven Chase and Belden C. Lane, *Nature as Spiritual Practice* (Grand Rapids: Eerdmans, 2011); and Belden C. Lane, *Backpacking with the Saints: Wilderness Hiking as Spiritual Practice* (Oxford: Oxford University Press, 2014).

11. For the 75 percent, see Paula Spencer Scott, "Feeling Awe May Be the Secret to Health and Happiness," October 7, 2016, http://parade.com/513786/paulaspencer/feeling-awe-may-be-the-secret-to-health-and-happiness/. For the research on awe more generally, see Dacher Keltner, "Awe: For Altruism and Health?" *Slate*, http://www.slate.com/bigideas/why-do-we-feel-awe/essays-and-opinions/dacher-keltner-opinion.

12. See Wendell Berry, *What Are People For?* (New York: North Point, 1990).

13. I am drawing, in what follows, from parts 1 and 2 of my essay "Dying to Live: Reflections on Asceticism, Spiritual Disciplines, and Everyday Life," posted February 8, 2014, http://spiritualityshoppe.org/dying-live-asceticism-summarized/, and February 20, 2014, http://spiritualityshoppe.org/dying-live-ii-asceticism-applied/.

14. See, e.g., the list of sixty-two different spiritual disciplines summarized in Adele Ahlberg Calhoun, *Spiritual Disciplines Handbook* (Downers Grove, IL: InterVarsity, 2005).

15. In 590, Gregory the Great identified seven deadly sins (pride, greed, lust, envy, gluttony, wrath, sloth), which he developed from earlier lists of vices. The work of discerning and then confronting those vices toward which one was predisposed has been considered a vital practice throughout the history of Christianity. I discuss the expansion of our view of this list of sins to include social as well as personal sins in chap. 8, and changing habits in chap. 9. See also, e.g., Dennis Okholm, "Sins, Seven Deadly," in *Zondervan Dictionary of Christian Spirituality*, ed. Glen G. Scorgie (Grand Rapids: Zondervan, 2011), 755–56.

16. For this approach to spiritual warfare, see Evagrius of Pontus, *Talking Back (Antirrhêtikos): A Monastic Handbook for Combating Demons*, trans. David Brakke (Kalamazoo, MI: Cistercian Publications, 2009).

17. See David Peterson, *Engaging with God: A Biblical Theology of Worship* (Downers Grove, IL: InterVarsity, 1992).

18. *The Book of Common Prayer* (New York: Church Hymnal Corporation, 1979), 79.

19. *Book of Common Prayer*, 79.

20. For the structure of worship as a reflection of relationship with God, see Maximus the Confessor, "The Church's Mystagogy," in *Maximus the Confessor: Selected Writings*, ed. and trans. George C. Berthold, Classics of Western Spirituality (New York: Paulist Press, 1985), 181–225; Dan Albrecht, *Rites in the Spirit: A Ritual Approach to Pentecostal/Charismatic Spirituality*, Journal of Pentecostal Theology Supplement Series (Sheffield, UK: Sheffield Academic, 1999); and Hunter, *Giving Church Another Chance*. See also Smith, *Imagining the Kingdom*. I have treated the spirituality of Christian worship more thoroughly in the "Spirituality of Christian Worship" video lecture series available at https://vimeo.com/evanbhoward.

21. John Calvin, *Institutes* 3.8.1 (Battles, 702). See also 3.8.1–6.

22. Elizabeth Lewis Hall, "Hard Road to Glory: The Role of Suffering in Personal and Relational Formation" (paper, Annual Conference in Renewal Theology, Regent University, Virginia Beach, VA, March 20, 2015).

23. Diadochus of Photiki, "On Spiritual Knowledge and Discrimination: One Hundred Texts," n. 94, in *The Philokalia: The Complete Text*, ed. and trans. G. E. H. Palmer, Philip Sherrard, and Kallistos Ware (London: Faber & Faber, 1979), 1:291.

24. See Catherine of Siena, *The Dialogue*, dialogue 12, trans. Suzanne Noffke, Classics of Western Spirituality (New York: Paulist Press, 1980), 46.

25. See, e.g., Matt. 13:21–22; Mark 13:13; Luke 9:62; 21:19, 36; Acts 20:24; 1 Cor. 1:8; 11:2; 15:2; 1 Thess. 3:2; 2 Thess. 1:4; 2:15; 3:4; Heb. 10:35–39; James 1:12; Rev. 2:2, 10, 13, 19, 26. On grit, see, e.g., Angela L. Duckworth, *Grit: The Power of Passion and Perseverance* (New York: Scribner, 2016).

26. Cited in Laura Swan, *The Forgotten Desert Mothers: Sayings, Lives, and Stories of Early Christian Women* (Mahwah, NJ: Paulist Press, 2001), 49. See also Elizabeth A. Castelli, "Pseudo-Athanasius: The Life and Activity of the Holy and Blessed Teacher Syncletica," in *Ascetic Behavior in Greco-Roman Antiquity: A Sourcebook*, ed. Vincent Wimbush (Minneapolis:

Fortress, 1990), 265–311, especially 280, 304–5. Castelli describes Amma Syncletica as suffering from illness herself, such that the endurance of illness became for her a special form of ascetical practice.

27. Stephen A. Macchia, *Crafting a Rule of Life: An Invitation to the Well-Ordered Way* (Downers Grove, IL: InterVarsity, 2012), 14.

28. For more on rules of life, see my video lectures at http://spiritualityshoppe.org/.

Chapter 7 Formed into Prayer

1. For Athanasius's treatment of praying the Psalms, see "Letter to Marcellinus" 15, in *Athanasius: The Life of Antony and the Letter to Marcellinus*, trans. Robert C. Gregg, Classics of Western Spirituality (New York: Paulist Press, 1980), 114. For Origen's classic treatment of the Lord's Prayer, see *On Prayer* 22.1–30.3, in *Origen: An Exhortation to Martyrdom, Prayer, and Selected Works*, trans. Rowan A. Greer, Classics of Western Spirituality (New York: Paulist Press, 1979), 123–63.

2. See Origen, *On Prayer* 14.2; John Cassian, *Conferences* 9.9; and Tertullian, *On Prayer* 2–8. For a review of this history, see Tugwell, "Thomas Aquinas: Introduction," in *Albert and Thomas*, 273–78.

3. Theophan the Recluse in *The Art of Prayer: An Orthodox Anthology*, comp. Igumen Chariton, trans. E. Kadloubavsky and E. M. Palmer (London: Faber & Faber, 1966), 23.

4. For a brief history of Christian prayer, see Howard, *Brazos Introduction*, 302–6. For a more thorough history of Christian prayer to the fifteenth century, see Roy Hammerling, ed., *A History of Prayer: The First to the Fifteenth Century* (Leiden: Brill, 2008).

5. See, e.g., Hans Urs von Balthasar, *Prayer*, trans. Graham Harrison (San Francisco: Ignatius, 1955); Chariton, *Art of Prayer*; Richard Foster, *Prayer: Finding the Heart's True Home* (San Francisco: HarperSanFrancisco, 1992); and Andrew Murray, *With Christ in the School of Prayer* (New Kensington, PA: Whitaker House, 1981).

6. See Evan B. Howard, *Praying the Scriptures: A Field Guide for Your Spiritual Journey* (Downers Grove, IL: InterVarsity, 1999), 26–32, 111–12.

7. Simon Tugwell, *Prayer: Living with God* (Springfield, IL: Templegate, 1975), 14.

8. On prayer meetings, see, e.g., Jonathan Edwards, "An Humble Attempt to Promote Explicit Agreement and Visible Union of God's People in Extraordinary Prayer," in *Apocalyptic Writings*, ed. Stephen Stein, vol. 5 of The Works of Jonathan Edwards (New Haven: Yale University Press, 1977), 307–436; Samuel Backus, *The Prayer Meeting Assistant* (New York: A. S. Barnes, 1852); J. B. Johnston, *The Prayer Meeting and Its History as Identified with the Life and Power of Godliness and the Revival of Religion* (Pittsburgh: United Presbyterian Board of Publication, 1870); and Lewis Thompson, *The Prayer Meeting and Its Improvement* (Chicago: W. G. Holmes, Skeen and Stuart Printers, 1878).

9. See entries on "meditation" and "contemplation" in the standard dictionaries of Christian spirituality, such as Downey, *New Dictionary of Catholic Spirituality*; Sheldrake, *New Westminster Dictionary of Christian Spirituality*; and Scorgie, *Dictionary of Christian Spirituality*.

10. I have treated this topic in more depth in *Praying the Scriptures*. Jim Wilhoit and I have also explored this in our *Discovering Lectio Divina: Bringing Scripture into Ordinary Life* (Downers Grove, IL: InterVarsity, 2012).

11. On the use of our bodies in prayer, see, e.g., Simon Tugwell, ed. and trans., *The Nine Ways of Prayer of Saint Dominic* (Dublin: Dominican Publications, 1978); Stephanie Paulsell, *Honoring the Body: Meditations on a Christian Practice* (San Francisco: Jossey-Bass, 2002); and Roy DeLeon, *Praying with the Body: Bringing the Psalms to Life* (Brewster, MA: Paraclete, 2009).

12. Simon Tugwell, *Prayer in Practice* (Springfield, IL: Templegate, 1974), 18–19.

13. Does *pneuma* in John 19:30 refer to the core of Jesus's person, his life, or simply his breath? On life breath, see Job 27:3; Ps. 146:4.

14. I have adapted the next few paragraphs from Wilhoit and Howard, *Discovering Lectio Divina*, 109–11.

15. C. F. D. Moule, *The Holy Spirit* (Grand Rapids: Eerdmans, 1978), 81. Note that Moule's comments here are made within a chapter titled "Spirit, Church, and Liturgy." The form of our prayer (whether spontaneous or liturgical) does not determine the presence or absence of the Spirit within our praying. The Spirit can give birth to authentic prayer expressed in any number of forms.

16. Abraham Kuyper, *The Work of the Holy Spirit*, trans. Henri DeVries (1900; repr., Grand Rapids: Eerdmans, 1979), 639 (italics in the original).

17. See, e.g., Evan B. Howard, "Mysticism," in Scorgie, *Dictionary of Christian Spirituality*, 179–84; and Howard, *Brazos Introduction*, 324–25. For a full review of the history of Christian mysticism up to the Reformation, see Bernard McGinn's comprehensive, multivolume series *The Presence of God: A History of Western Christian Mysticism* (New York: Crossroad, 1991–) (6 of 7 planned vols. in print). On the theme of union, see, e.g., Reginald Garrigou-Lagrange, *The Three Ages of the Interior Life*, trans. M. T. Doyle, 2 vols. (1947; repr., Charlotte: TAN Books, 1991); Lewis Smedes, *All Things Made New: A Theology of Man's Union with Christ* (Grand Rapids: Eerdmans, 1970), republished in a much-condensed form as *Union with Christ: A Biblical View of the New Life in Jesus Christ* (Grand Rapids: Eerdmans, 1983); and J. Todd Billings, *Union with Christ: Reframing Theology and Ministry for the Church* (Grand Rapids: Baker Academic, 2011).

18. See Dennis E. Tamburello, *Union with Christ: John Calvin and the Mysticism of St. Bernard* (Louisville: Westminster John Knox, 1994).

Chapter 8 Formed Together

1. When I refer to small-scale dwelling communities, I am thinking of household-sized groups that are not necessarily composed of family members but that are also not simply accidental collections of roommates.

2. Christopher J. H. Wright, *The Mission of God: Unlocking the Bible's Grand Narrative* (Downers Grove, IL: InterVarsity, 2006), 369. For another example of this connection, see Paul Hiebert's foreword to Van Engen's *Mission on the Way*, where he states what is becoming a common affirmation: "Mission is not one of the many tasks the church is called upon to do. It is of the very essence of the church itself" (11). As we have seen and as we will see further, mission and community (and integrity) cannot be neatly separated.

3. I might also note here that the term *mission* is used in theology particularly with regard to the Father's sending the Son and the Spirit. Mission is essentially an expression of the trinitarian character of God. Once again, community and mission cannot be separated.

4. On family spirituality, see, e.g., Ernest Boyer Jr., *Finding God at Home: Family Life as Spiritual Discipline* (San Francisco: Harper & Row, 1988); Marcia J. Bunge, ed., *The Child in Christian Thought* (Grand Rapids: Eerdmans, 2001); Rodney Clapp, *Families at the Crossroads: Beyond Traditional and Modern Options* (Downers Grove, IL: InterVarsity, 1993); and Edmund S. Morgan, *The Puritan Family: Religion and Domestic Relations in Seventeenth-Century New England* (1944; repr., New York: Harper & Row, 1966).

5. For resources on family liturgies (which can be adapted for small-scale dwelling communities), see, e.g., Lacy Finn Borgo and Ben Barczi, *Good Dirt: Kingdomtide* (CreateSpace Independent Publishing, 2014); David Robinson, *The Christian Family Toolbox: 52 Benedictine Activities for the Home* (New York: Crossroad, 2001); and Wendy Wright, *Sacred Dwelling: A Spirituality of Family Life* (Leavenworth, KS: Forest of Peace Publishing, 1994), 40–46.

6. See also Bunge, *Child in Christian Thought*, particularly discussions of John Chrysostom, 61–77; Anabaptists, 209; August Hermann Francke, 270; and Susanna Wesley, 282–84.

7. Edith Schaeffer, *What Is a Family?* (Old Tappan, NJ: Revell, 1975), 67–92.

8. For a refreshing view of home life, see Wendell Berry, *Home Economics* (New York: North Point, 1987); and Berry, *What Are People For?*

9. See David G. Hunter, *Marriage, Celibacy, and Heresy in Ancient Christianity: The Jovinianist Controversy* (Oxford: Oxford University Press, 2007). See also Bunge, *Child in Christian Thought*, for a full survey.

10. See, e.g., Wright, *Sacred Dwelling*, 123–35; Paul Evdokimov, *The Sacrament of Love*, trans. Anthony P. Gythiel and Victoria Steadman (1980; repr., Crestwood, NY: St. Vladimir's Seminary Press, 2001), 65–84; and Boyer, *Finding God at Home*, on the "two ways."

11. See, e.g., Clapp, *Families at the Crossroads*, 89–113; Evdokimov, *Sacrament of Love*, 65–180; The Rutba House, *School(s) for Conversion: 12 Marks of a New Monasticism* (Eugene, OR: Cascade, 2005), 112–23; and Wesley Hill, "Celibacy for the Common Good: How Celibate People Strengthen and Enrich Their Communities," *First Things*, March 6, 2015, http://www.firstthings.com/blogs/firstthoughts/2015/03/celibacy-for-the-common-good/.

12. Thus Clapp speaks of the church as the "first family." See *Families at the Crossroads*, 67–88.

13. See chap. 6. It is impossible to give a full treatment of the relationship of ecclesiology and spirituality. My own understanding of church has been informed generally by reading Hans Kung, *The Church* (New York: Doubleday Image, 1976); Veli-Matti Kärkkäinen, *An Introduction to Ecclesiology: Ecumenical, Historical, and Global Perspectives* (Downers Grove, IL: InterVarsity, 2002); Miroslav Volf, *After Our Likeness: The Church as the Image of the Trinity* (Grand Rapids: Eerdmans, 1998); and others. On the spirituality of Christian worship, see my video lectures on this topic, the first of which is at https://vimeo.com/129649903.

14. Margaret Guenther, *Holy Listening: The Art of Spiritual Direction* (Cambridge, MA: Cowley, 1992).

15. See Darrell L. Guder et al., *Missional Church: A Vision for the Sending of the Church in North America* (Grand Rapids: Eerdmans, 1998), 179.

16. Jualynne Dodson and Cheryl Townsend Gilkes, "There's Nothing like Church Food," *Journal of the American Academy of Religion* 63, no. 3 (Fall 1995): 535.

17. See my video lecture titled "The Interpersonal Encounter of Worship" at https://vimeo.com/133122547.

18. Clifford Geertz, *The Interpretation of Cultures: Selected Essays* (New York: Basic Books, 1973).

19. Richard Valantasis, *Dazzling Bodies: Rethinking Spirituality and Community Formation* (Eugene, OR: Cascade, 2014), 86.

20. See the examples presented in Ana María Pineda, "Hospitality," in *Practicing Our Faith: A Way of Life for a Searching People*, ed. Dorothy C. Bass, 2nd ed. (San Francisco: Jossey-Bass, 2010), 29–42.

21. On this, see, e.g., Lesslie Newbigin, *The Gospel in a Pluralist Society* (Grand Rapids: Eerdmans, 1989), 10–12, where he discusses four points that he feels are important for us as faithful bearers of our message. I am impressed that Newbigin's points can be easily presented as four essential characteristics of good hospitality—missions, community, integrity, formation—that cannot be separated.

22. See Basil of Caesarea, *Long Rules* 7. See St. Basil, *Ascetical Works*, Fathers of the Church 9, trans. M. Monica Wagner, CSC (Washington, DC: Catholic University of America Press, 1962), 247–52.

23. See, e.g., Graham Gould, *The Desert Fathers on Monastic Community* (Oxford: Clarendon, 1993).

24. One who has emphasized the significance of these social sins is René Girard. See, e.g., *The Girard Reader*, ed. James G. Williams (New York: Crossroad, 1996); and, from a similar perspective, Gil Bailie, *Violence Unveiled: Humanity at the Crossroads* (New York: Crossroad, 1995).

25. Tertullian, *Apology* 39.

26. Galindo, *Hidden Lives of Congregations.*

27. I am indebted to Diane Zemke for this list of best practices. Some of these are woven into her book *Being Smart about Congregational Change* (CreateSpace Independent Publishing, 2014).

28. Monk Cosmas Shartz quoted in "Conversations by E-Mail," *In Communion: Journal of the Orthodox Peace Fellowship of the Protection of the Mother of God* 59 (February 2011): 35, http://incommunion.org/2011/02/20/conversations-by-e-mail-winter-2011-ic-59/; quoted by Macrina Walker, "A Little Monastic Realism," *A Vow of Conversation* (blog), February 27, 2011, http://avowofconversation.wordpress.com/2011/02/27/a-little-monastic-realism/.

29. I am drawing here from Ken Sande, *The Peacemaker: A Biblical Guide to Resolving Personal Conflict,* 3rd ed. (Grand Rapids: Baker Books, 2004).

30. On crucial conversations, see Kerry Patterson, Joseph Grenny, Ron McMillan, and Al Switzler, *Crucial Conversations: Tools for Talking When Stakes Are High* (New York: McGraw Hill, 2002).

31. A nice outline of steps of forgiveness can be found in Miroslav Volf, *Exclusion and Embrace: A Theological Exploration of Identity, Otherness, and Reconciliation* (Nashville: Abingdon, 1996), 140–47.

32. I coined this phrase in Howard, *Brazos Introduction,* 349 and 431, drawing from the insights of Robert Wuthnow, *After Heaven: Spirituality in America since the 1950s* (Berkeley: University of California Press, 1998).

33. For more on our emerging network society and social networks more generally, see, e.g., Yochai Benkler, *The Wealth of Networks: How Social Production Transforms Markets and Freedom* (New Haven: Yale University Press, 2006); Manuel Castells, *The Rise of the Network Society,* 2nd ed. (New York: Wiley-Blackwell, 2009); Nicholas A. Christakis and James H. Fowler, *Connected: The Surprising Power of Our Social Networks and How They Shape Our Lives* (New York: Back Bay, 2009); and Albert-László Barabási, *Linked: How Everything Is Connected to Everything Else and What It Means for Business, Science, and Everyday Life* (New York: Basic Books, 2014). For a treatment of networking with particular attention to Christianity and technology, see Heidi A. Campbell and Stephen Garner, *Networked Theology: Negotiating Faith in Digital Culture* (Grand Rapids: Baker Academic, 2016).

34. From reading studies of the emerging generations, my sense is that their openness to change, style of connecting, dependencies on technology, concerns about hierarchy, and other factors make emerging generations even more prepared for a network society. See, e.g., Pew Research Center, *Millennials: A Portrait of Generation Next* (February 2010), http://www.pewsocialtrends.org/files/2010/10/millennials-confident-connected-open-to-change.pdf; Kinnaman and Lyons, *UnChristian;* and Kinnaman, *You Lost Me.*

35. Howard, *Brazos Introduction,* 51–54.

36. See The Barna Group, "New Research on the State of Discipleship," December 1, 2015, https://www.barna.com/research/new-research-on-the-state-of-discipleship/.

37. See, e.g., Josh Packard and Ashleigh Hope, *Church Refugees: Sociologists Reveal Why People Are Done with Church but Not Their Faith* (Loveland, CO: Group, 2015); and Wayne Jacobsen, *Finding Church: What If There Is Really Something More?* (Newbury Park, CA: Trailview Media, 2014).

38. See http://www.innerchange.org/ and http://www.innerchange.org/about.html.

39. For surveys of these groups, see, e.g., Rutba House, *School(s) for Conversion;* Scott Bessenecker, *The New Friars: The Emerging Movement Serving the World's Poor* (Downers Grove, IL: InterVarsity, 2006); Graham Cray, Ian Mobsby, and Aaron Kennedy, *New Monasticism as Fresh Expression of Church* (Norwich, UK: Canterbury, 2010); Bernadette Flanagan, *Embracing Solitude: Women and New Monasticism* (Eugene, OR: Cascade, 2014); and Elaine A. Heath and Larry Duggins, *Missional, Monastic, Mainline* (Eugene, OR: Cascade, 2014). For

an academic reflection on (primarily) one expression, see Wes Markofski, *New Monasticism and the Transformation of Evangelicalism* (Oxford: Oxford University Press, 2015).

40. See, e.g., Evan B. Howard, "Spiritual Formation and Elitism: Reflections on Early Councils and Contemporary Practice," http://spiritualityshoppe.org/spiritual-formation-elitism-reflect ions-early-councils-contemporary-practice/.

41. For a sample of reflections on the history of monasticism with a view toward what can be learned, see, e.g., Dennis Okholm, *Monk Habits for Everyday People: Benedictine Spirituality for Protestants* (Grand Rapids: Brazos, 2007); Karen Sloan, *Flirting with Monasticism: Finding God on Ancient Paths* (Downers Grove, IL: InterVarsity, 2006); Jon Stock, Tim Otto, and Jonathan Wilson-Hartgrove, *Inhabiting the Church: Biblical Wisdom for a New Monasticism* (Eugene, OR: Cascade, 2007); Ivan J. Kauffman, *"Follow Me": A History of Christian Intentionality* (Eugene, OR: Cascade, 2009); and Greg Peters, *The Story of Monasticism: Retrieving an Ancient Tradition for Contemporary Spirituality* (Grand Rapids: Baker Academic, 2015).

42. I have compiled the tables of contents found in a number of these foundational documents in a PDF found at http://spiritualityshoppe.org/a-collection-of-rules-constitutions-covenants -and-such/. For a collection of more general reflections that I've titled "Old Monastic Wisdom for New Monastic People," see http://spiritualityshoppe.org/old-monastic-wisdom-for-new -monastic-people/.

43. See n. 39 above.

44. Newbigin, *Gospel in a Pluralist Society*, 221.

Chapter 9 Formed in Thinking, Feeling, and Acting

1. See, e.g., Chandler, *Christian Spiritual Formation*; Mulholland, *Invitation to a Journey*; Parham, *Spiritual Formation Primer*; and Willard, *Renovation of the Heart*. See also Howard, *Brazos Introduction*, 84–87, and throughout the book.

2. Ineda P. Adesanya, "Becoming a Contemplative Sistah: Finding Weird Joy in Spiritual Freedom," in *Embodied Spirits: Stories of Spiritual Directors of Color*, ed. Sherry Bryant-Johnson, Rosalie Norman-McNaney, and Therese Taylor-Stinson (New York: Morehouse, 2014), 67.

3. Adesanya, "Becoming a Contemplative Sistah," 67.

4. Adesanya, "Becoming a Contemplative Sistah," 72.

5. Adesanya cites Robert W. Kellemen and Karole A. Edwards, *Beyond the Suffering: Embracing the Legacy of African American Soul Care and Spiritual Direction* (Grand Rapids: Baker Books, 2007).

6. On Christian catechesis, see, e.g., William Harmless, *Augustine and the Catechumenate* (Collegeville, MN: Liturgical Press, 1995); and J. I. Packer and Gary A. Parrett, *Grounded in the Gospel: Building Believers the Old-Fashioned Way* (Grand Rapids: Baker Books, 2010).

7. See Howard, *Affirming the Touch of God*, 235–309.

8. For more on the revealing work of the Spirit, see, e.g., Turner, *Holy Spirit and Spiritual Gifts*, 166–78; and Amos Yong, *Spirit-Word-Community: Theological Hermeneutics in Trinitarian Perspective* (Eugene, OR: Wipf & Stock, 2002), 119–244.

9. On this, see James K. A. Smith, *Desiring the Kingdom: Worship, Worldview, and Cultural Formation* (Grand Rapids: Baker Academic, 2009); and Esther Lightcap Meek, *Longing to Know: The Philosophy of Knowledge for Ordinary People* (Grand Rapids: Brazos, 2003).

10. See especially Ellen T. Charry, *By the Renewing of Your Minds: The Pastoral Function of Christian Doctrine* (New York: Oxford University Press, 1997).

11. Consider, e.g., Robert K. Johnston, *God's Wider Presence: Reconsidering General Revelation* (Grand Rapids: Baker Academic, 2014).

12. See Jean Leclercq, *The Love of Learning and the Desire for God: A Study of Monastic Culture*, trans. Catherine Misrahi, 3rd ed. (New York: Fordham University Press, 1982).

13. Jonathan Edwards, *Religious Affections*, ed. John E. Smith, vol. 2 of The Works of Jonathan Edwards (New Haven: Yale University Press, 1959), 95. See pp. 96–124 for Edwards's defense, which I briefly summarize here.

14. For a historical survey of philosophical views concerning emotions, see H. M. Gardiner, Ruth Clark Metcalf, and John Beebe-Center, *Feeling and Emotion: A History of Theories* (New York: American Book Company, 1937). For a survey of empirical theories of emotion, see Randolph R. Cornelius, *The Science of Emotion: Research and Tradition in the Psychology of Emotion* (Upper Saddle River, NJ: Prentice Hall, 1996). I specifically review research on emotions and apply the insights from the scientific study of emotion to our understanding of Christian discernment in Howard, *Affirming the Touch of God*. My summary, which follows, is drawn largely from that work.

15. Social scientists are confirming the value of these kinds of choices. On forgiveness, see, e.g., Gary Thomas, "The Forgiveness Factor," *Christianity Today*, January 10, 2010, http:// www.christianitytoday.com/ct/2000/january10/1.38.html. On community support, see, e.g., Alan Deuschman, *Change or Die: Three Keys to Change at Work and in Life* (New York: HarperBusiness, 2007), who speaks of the importance of relationships that provide hope. The importance of community support has also been demonstrated through research using the data of the massive Framingham heart study; see, e.g., https://en.wikipedia.org/wiki/Framing ham_Heart_Study. For a sample study regarding weight loss, see Beth C. Marcoux, Leslie L. Trenkner, and Irwin M. Rosenstock, "Social Networks and Social Support in Weight Loss," *Patient Education and Counseling* 15 (1990): 229–38.

16. For the research and practice of tiny habits, such as my habit of writing down things for which I'm grateful, see the website of B. J. Fogg at https://bjfogg.com/.

17. For examples of the Christian practice of the healing of emotions, see Francis MacNutt, *Healing* (1974; repr., Notre Dame, IN: Ave Maria, 1999); Leanne Payne, *The Healing Presence: Curing the Soul through Union with Christ* (Grand Rapids: Hamewith, 1995); and John Sandford and Paul Sandford, *The Transformation of the Inner Man* (South Plainfield, NJ: Bridge Publishing, 1982). See also resources developed by Christian psychiatrist Dr. Karl Lehman, available at http://www.immanuelapproach.com/.

18. Wright, *Mission of God*, 385.

19. For a few examples of literature on spiritual warfare, see, e.g., Neil T. Anderson, *The Bondage Breaker* (Eugene, OR: Harvest House, 2000); Richard Beck, *Reviving Old Scratch: Demons and the Devil for Doubters and the Disenchanted* (Minneapolis: Fortress, 2016); Gregory Boyd, *God at War: The Bible and Spiritual Conflict* (Downers Grove, IL: InterVarsity, 1997); and C. Peter Wagner and F. Douglas Pennoyer, eds., *Wrestling with Dark Angels: Toward a Deeper Understanding of the Supernatural Forces in Spiritual Warfare* (Ventura, CA: Regal, 1990).

20. For more on the influence of evil forces over sociopolitical powers, see Walter Wink, *Naming the Powers: The Language of Power in the New Testament* (Philadelphia: Fortress, 1984); Wink, *Unmasking the Powers: The Invisible Forces That Determine Human Existence* (Philadelphia: Fortress, 1986); and Wink, *Engaging the Powers: Discernment and Resistance in a World of Domination* (Philadelphia: Fortress, 1992).

21. Henry Scougal, *The Life of God in the Soul of Man* (Boston: Nichols and Noyes, 1868), 4–7 (italics in the original).

Chapter 10 Formed into Mission

1. See, e.g., Bessenecker, "Abandoning Our Colonizing Mission."

2. Newbigin, *Gospel in a Pluralist Society*, 1.

3. David Bosch, *Transforming Mission: Paradigm Shifts in the Theology of Mission* (1991; repr., Maryknoll, NY: Orbis, 2011), 5.

4. Darrell L. Guder et al., *Missional Church: A Vision for the Sending of the Church in North America* (Grand Rapids: Eerdmans, 1998), 77.

5. Newbigin, *Gospel in a Pluralist Society*, 134–35.

6. Guder et al., *Missional Church*, 82.

7. Wright, *Mission of God*, 62 (italics in the original).

8. Allen Hilton, "Living into the Big Story: The Missional Trajectory of Scripture in Congregational Life," in Zscheile, *Cultivating Sent Communities*.

9. J. D. Douglas, ed., *Let the Earth Hear His Voice*, official reference volume, papers and responses, International Congress on World Evangelization (Minneapolis: World Wide Publications, 1975), 4–5.

10. Wright, *Mission of God*, 275; for a broader view, see chap. 8, "God's Model of Redemption," pp. 265–323.

11. On the Salvation Army, see, e.g., Shaw Clifton, *Who Are These Salvationists? An Analysis for the 21st Century* (Alexandria, VA: Crest, 1999); Frederick L. Coutts, *No Discharge in This War: A One-Volume History of the Salvation Army* (London: Hodder & Stoughton, 1975); and John D. Waldron, ed., *Creed and Deed: Toward a Theology of Social Services in the Salvation Army* (Toronto: The Salvation Army, 1986).

12. This is where I would disagree with comments such as those presented in Mike Breen, "Why the Missional Movement Will Fail," http://www.vergenetwork.org/2011/09/14/mike-breen-why-the-missional-movement-will-fail/.

13. See, e.g., Guder et al., *Missional Church*, 18–45, 52–55; and Van Engen, *Mission on the Way*, 159–90.

14. This, of course, does not mean that there is no place for good old-fashioned "foreign missions." There is. It is rather a matter of rediscovering our identity "at home" as fundamentally missional—in addition to whatever role foreign missions may have.

15. Some of these issues are discussed in, e.g., Conde-Frazier, Kang, and Parrett, *Many Colored Kingdom*; Michelle A. Gonzalez, *Embracing Latina Spirituality: A Woman's Perspective* (Cincinnati: St. Anthony Messenger Press, 2009); Alex Tang, *Till We Are Fully Formed: Christian Spiritual Formation Paradigms in the English-Speaking Presbyterian Churches in Malaysia* (Selangor Darul Ehsan, Malaysia: Malaysia Bible Seminary, 2014); and Gerrie ter Haar, *How God Became African: African Spirituality and Western Secular Thought* (Philadelphia: University of Pennsylvania Press, 2009).

16. On contextualization, see, e.g., Bosch, *Transforming Mission*, 297–305, 435–42, 458–68; and Van Engen, *Mission on the Way*, 71–89. See also Wright, *Mission of God*, 441–53, on wisdom and mission. For inspiration toward missional living, see, e.g., Michael Frost and Alan Hirsch, *The Faith of Leap: Embracing a Theology of Risk, Adventure, and Courage* (Grand Rapids: Baker Books, 2011); and Charles Van Engen, *God's Missionary People: Rethinking the Purpose of the Local Church* (Grand Rapids: Baker, 1991).

17. Newbigin, *Gospel in a Pluralist Society*, 124.

18. On communities of the Spirit, see, e.g., Guder et al., *Missional Church*, 142–82.

19. I have not addressed here the role of the spirit/Spirit's wider presence and movement in nature, arts, community life, and elsewhere. A fuller treatment of mission and spirit/Spirit would require such a discussion. On aesthetics and formation, see Evan B. Howard, "Formed into the Beauty of God: Reflections on Aesthetics and Christian Spirituality," originally published in *Ogbomosho Journal of Theology* 16 (2011), a journal sponsored by the Nigerian Baptist Theological Seminary in Ogbomosho, Nigeria. This article is also available at http://spiritualityshoppe.org/formed-into-the-beauty-of-christ/.

20. On reconsidering the gospel, see Guder et al., *Missional Church*, 86–87.

21. For a range of examples, see Bruce Demarest, *Soul Guide: Following Jesus as Spiritual Director* (Colorado Springs: NavPress, 2003); Guenther, *Holy Listening*; Thomas N. Hart, *The Art of Christian Listening* (New York: Paulist Press, 1980); and Francis Kelly Nemek and Marie Theresa Coombs, *The Way of Spiritual Direction* (Wilmington, DE: Michael Glazier, 1985), 51–94.

22. Bosch, *Transforming Mission*, 424 (italics in the original).

23. Wright, *Mission of God*, 337 (italics in the original).

24. Guder et al. state, "The community, in its corporate life, is called to embody an alternative social order that stands as a sign of God's redemptive purposes in the world: this is the concrete social manifestation of the righteousness of God" (*Missional Church*, 149). See also the valuable questions to ponder on pp. 238–46.

25. See, e.g., Henri J. M. Nouwen, *Life of the Beloved: Spiritual Living in a Secular World* (New York: Crossroad, 1992); and Christian Scharen, "Practices of Dispossession: The Shape of Discipleship in a Church Taken, Blessed, Broken, and Given," in Zscheile, *Cultivating Sent Communities*, 102–23.

26. See, e.g., Clayton Schmidt, *Sent and Gathered: A Worship Manual for the Missional Church* (Grand Rapids: Baker Academic, 2009).

27. See, e.g., Bosch, *Transforming Mission*, 89, 327, 510.

Chapter 11 Discerning Formation

1. The sections in this chapter on the definition of and formation into discernment are covered in Howard, *Brazos Introduction*, 371–401. See also Howard, *Affirming the Touch of God*; Howard, "Discerning Experience and Experiencing Discernment," *Epiphany International* 7, no. 2 (Autumn 2001): 45–55; and Howard, "Beneath the Plan, Beyond the Call: The Practice of Discernment and the Mission of God," *Catalyst: Contemporary Evangelical Perspectives for United Methodist Seminarians* (March 2014), http://www.catalystresources.org/beneath-the-plan-beyond-the-call-the-practice-of-discernment-and-the-mission-of-god-2/.

2. John Cassian, *The Conferences*, trans. Boniface Ramsey, Ancient Christian Writers 57 (New York: Newman, 1997), 88–89.

3. Gordon T. Smith, *The Voice of Jesus* (Downers Grove, IL: InterVarsity, 2003).

4. Luke Timothy Johnson, *Scripture and Discernment: Decision Making in the Early Church* (Nashville: Abingdon, 1996).

5. Clare Copeland and Jan Machielsen, eds., *Angels of Light? Sanctity and the Discernment of Spirits in the Early Modern Period* (Leiden: Brill, 2013); see also Moshe Sluhovsky, *Believe Not Every Spirit: Possession, Mysticism, and Discernment in Early Modern Catholicism* (Chicago: University of Chicago Press, 2007).

6. James L. Jaquette, *Discerning What Counts: The Function of the* Adiophera Topos *in Paul's Letters*, SBL Dissertation Series 146 (Atlanta: Scholars Press, 1995).

7. See Kirsteen Kim, "Case Study: How Will We Know When the Holy Spirit Comes?," *Evangelical Review of Theology* 33, no. 1 (2009): 93–96; and Kevin Orlin Johnson, *Apparitions: Mystic Phenomena and What They Mean* (Dallas: Pangaeus, 1995).

8. This was precisely the question behind Jonathan Edwards's essays on revival published between 1741 and 1746. See Edwards, *The Great Awakening*, ed. C. C. Goen, vol. 4 of The Works of Jonathan Edwards (New Haven: Yale University Press, 1972). On discerning trends further, see Howard, *Affirming the Touch of God*, 349–71.

9. The Greek word *dokimazō*, used in these two passages, is a significant guide to the Pauline understanding of discerning prudence in the Christian walk. See Gérard Therrien, *Le discernement dans les écrits Pauliniens*, Études Bibliques (Paris: Librairie Lecoffre, 1973).

10. Howard, *Brazos Introduction*, 375.

11. See Katherine Dykman, Mary Garvin, and Elizabeth Liebert, *The Spiritual Exercises Reclaimed: Uncovering Liberating Possibilities for Women* (New York: Paulist Press, 2001); and Susan W. Rakoczy, "Transforming the Tradition of Discernment," *Journal of Theology for Southern Africa* 139 (March 2011): 91–109.

12. Dallas Willard addresses many misconceptions regarding discernment in his wise book *Hearing God: Developing a Conversational Relationship with God* (Downers Grove, IL: InterVarsity, 1999).

13. Karen Mains, *The God Hunt: The Delightful Chase and the Wonder of Being Found* (Downers Grove, IL: InterVarsity, 2003). See also http://kmains.blogspot.com/ and http://blog.karenmains.com/tag/the-god-hunt/.

14. See Elizabeth Liebert, *The Way of Discernment: Spiritual Practices for Decision Making* (Louisville: Westminster John Knox, 2008); and James Ryle, *Hippo in the Garden: A Non-Religious Approach to Having a Conversation with God* (Orlando, FL: Creation House, 1993).

15. Ignatius of Loyola, "Spiritual Exercises," secs. 169–88, in *The Spiritual Exercises and Selected Works*, ed. George Ganss, Classics of Western Spirituality (New York: Paulist Press, 1991), 161–65. See also Jules Toner, *Discerning God's Will: Ignatius of Loyola's Teaching on Christian Decision Making* (St. Louis: Institute of Jesuit Sources, 1995).

16. See, e.g., McNeill, *History of the Cure of Souls*, for a survey of the development of the rite of penance.

17. For a survey of the culture (and the literature) of early monastic formation, see, e.g., William Harkness, *Desert Christians: An Introduction to the Literature of Early Christian Monasticism* (Oxford: Oxford University Press, 2004). See also Evan B. Howard, "Desert Spiritual Formation: Then and Now" (paper, Evangelical Theological Society Meeting, San Diego, November 2016).

18. On the Celtic approach to penance and the development of the penitentials, see Ian Bradley, *Colonies of Heaven: Celtic Models for Today's Church* (London: Darton, Longman & Todd, 2000); Westley Follett, *Céli Dé in Ireland: Monastic Writing and Identity in the Early Middle Ages* (Woodbridge, UK: Boydell, 2006); and Catherine Thom, *Early Irish Monasticism: An Understanding of Its Cultural Roots* (London: T&T Clark, 2006).

19. See Calvin, *Institutes of the Christian Religion* 3.3–8. On Cranmer, see Ashley Null, *Thomas Cranmer's Doctrine of Repentance: Renewing the Power to Love* (Oxford: Oxford University Press, 2007).

Chapter 12 The Ministry of Christian Spiritual Formation

1. Elizabeth O'Connor, *Call to Commitment: The Story of the Church of the Saviour, Washington, D.C.* (New York: Harper & Row, 1963), 7–8. The following paragraphs are based on the story presented in this book and on the Church of the Saviour website, "The Church of the Saviour Story," http://inwardoutward.org/the-church-of-the-saviour/our-story/. I thank Vicki Walker for reminding me of this congregation.

2. O'Connor, *Call to Commitment*, 20–21.

3. See, e.g., Mary Rose Bumpus and Rebecca Bradburn Langer, *Supervision of Spiritual Directors: Engaging in Holy Mystery* (Harrisburg, PA: Morehouse, 2005). See also the excellent discussion and links to resources on supervision at the Spiritual Directors International website, "Spiritual Direction Supervision," http://www.sdiworld.org/resources/spiritual-direction-supervision.

Scripture Index

Subject Index

acting. *See* will
Adesanya, Ineda, 176
aesthetics. *See* beauty
affections. *See* emotions
agents of Christian spiritual
  formation, 11, 17, 36,
  70–81
aims of Christian spiritual
  formation, 11, 16–17, 35,
  54–61, 223, 233, 238
"all things new," 14, 28, 30–
  35, 44, 167, 176–77, 198,
  200, 222, 250
  in conversion, 84
  in households, 154
  in the ministry of spiritual
    formation, 236
  in salvation, 87–89
  in spiritual direction, 79
antinomianism, 110
Antony of Egypt, 106
Aquinas, Thomas, 91
Arnold, J. Heinrich, 57
ascetical practice (asceticism).
  See disciplines, spiritual
Augustine of Hippo, 7, 87
authority, 80–81, 179, 237
  over the enemy, 88–89
  God's, 57
  in the ministry of spiritual
    formation, 237

Barna Research Group, 5–6
Barry, William, 77

Basil of Caesarea, 161
Bayly, Lewis, 180
beauty, 177, 242
  and formation, 267n19
  of God, 48, 56, 121, 137
  of the gospel story, 25, 90
  of holiness, 55
belief. *See* faith
Bible. *See* Scripture
Bloom, Benjamin, 8
Bonaventure, 91, 92
Booth, William and Cath-
  erine, 199
Bosch, David, 196, 204
*Brazos Introduction to Chris-
  tian Spirituality, The,*
  (Howard), vii
breadth of formation. *See*
  fullness of Christian spiritual formation
Bucer, Martin, 87–88

Calhoun, Adele, 106
calling. *See* vocation (calling)
Calvin, John, 57, 117, 143, 223
Celebration of Discipline
  (Foster), 8
charism, 68
Charry, Ellen, 180
Christian education, 8–9
church, 9–10, 15, 37, 67–68,
  157–63
Church of the Saviour (Wash-
  ington, DC), 231–33

community, viii, 14–15, 37,
  151–73, 241
  as agent of spiritual forma-
    tion, 76–77
  community support, 97,
    145, 163, 186
  formation, nature of, 152
  getting along in, 161–63
  maturity, stages of, 92–94
  as means of spiritual forma-
    tion, 114–17
  and the Spirit, 152–53
conflict, 28, 39, 162–63, 188–
  89, 264, 266
congregation. *See* church
Connolly, William, 77
contemplation, 132
context of Christian spiritual
  formation, 11, 18, 28, 35,
  64–70, 201, 225
conversion, 84, 89
Cosby, Gordon, 231–33
counteragents. *See* spiritual
  warfare
countermovements, 68–70,
  222
covenant, 27, 28–29, 32–33
Cranmer, Thomas, 223
creation and recreation, 28–30
culture, 65–66, 102
  missional, 206

Damian, Peter, 15
darkness (dark night), 93, 147